Your Forever Friend

Jo Catherine Sullivan

Your Forever Friend

IN MEMORY: A TRIBUTE
TO PRESTON HIPP

● ● ●

*May our tour together be your launch
into Jesus Calling accompanied by
Your forever friend,
MB Preston Hipp
Laura - 843-708-2228*

Pringle Franklin

Created by Jesus Street Press
Charleston, S.C., USA
Copyright 2017 Pringle Franklin
All rights reserved.

ISBN: 1545466343
ISBN 13: 9781545466346

Also by the author

Hope & Healing in Marriage: True Stories of Renewed Love

Dedication

This book is dedicated to the memory of Preston Hipp, who died at home on Tradd Street in Charleston on Sept. 8, 2016, after an eight-year battle against aggressive and inoperable prostate cancer. Preston was only 57 years old when he died, leaving behind a loving wife, Laura Wichmann Hipp, and three devoted daughters-- Olivia, Delia, and Victoria-- as well as Chester, his faithful shadow with wagging tail and curly ears.

In addition, Preston's departure left a crater-sized hole in our Lowcountry community. As many testified after his death, Preston served as a spiritual mentor to countless souls, embodying the ideals of walking in faith.

Preston had a gentle way of looking people in the eye and listening with sincerity and presence. His quiet compassion and wisdom inspired others to trust him with their most personal thoughts and secrets. Preston knew how to pack meaning into a 10-minute conversation, leaving each person with the sense that he or she had authentically been heard.

Somehow, he had a knack for showing up at just the right moment. I will be ever grateful for his phone call a fews hours before I was to give a keynote speech to the women of St. Philip's Church during Advent 2013. Preston knew that I might be feeling nervous, and he wanted to encourage me. His calm prayer for the Lord's hand on the event and his kind words, "I am proud of you," left me feeling 100 percent ready to step up and offer my testimony about the power of prayer.

Likewise, the morning after our friend John P. Zervos died unexpectedly on March 3, 2010, Preston drove his truck over to Johnny's office building on Calhoun Street and sat parked nearby, silently praying. His presence was like that of a guardian angel. Just seeing Preston sitting there was enough to give courage to Michael Zervos as he faced the grief-filled task of going through his brother's office.

The Rev. Marc Boutan of St. Philip's Church recalls the uncanny timing of Preston's visit to his home to see his grown daughter, Renée, who was languishing from advanced cancer. "Preston brought her flowers and sat with her for several minutes," Marc said. "Little did we know she would die the next day." Marc and his wife Trish were very moved by Preston's visit.

Longtime friend Barre Butler has a similar story following a lightning strike that destroyed the Butler's residence. A few days after the blaze, Barre was alone in his yard, looking at his burned up home, feeling lower than low. Who should show up to offer companionship and encouragement when needed most? You guessed it: Preston. (Barre tells his full story here in the section "Remembrances Delivered at the Service".)

It must have been the Holy Spirit. Preston paid attention to the inner voice. Rarely did a soul seem more useful in daily service to God's people, and yet, the Lord must have needed him for higher purposes in the Great Beyond.

Despite the loss of her husband's physical person, Laura senses his continued love and presence in her waking and in her sleeping moments. She waits for him. She knows; it will not be long before she sees her beloved Preston again and feels his arms enfold her in a gigantic embrace.

● ● ●

"Preston, there are SO, SO many people who look up to you and believe that THEY are your best friend, because that is the way you make everyone feel --- like your best friend."

----------F. C. "Bunky" Wichmann, Jr., in a
letter to Preston, August 2016

Bunky and Preston were more like brothers than brother-in-laws. "I want you to stay, not to leave me alone to finish my days without you," Bunky would write to Preston in a letter, shortly before Preston's death.

Preston, in September 2015, with his close friends David Gross and Clark Hanger. The trio, nicknamed *the three amigos,* was known for a variety of boyish stunts, including burning a gigantic pile of dried Christmas trees after the holidays.

A Reader's Guide

Why a tribute book? Because so many people love and admire Preston Hipp. <u>Your Forever Friend</u> does not attempt to tell Preston's life story from beginning to end. It is a treasury of memories. The book's title reflects the sentiment, dear reader, that Preston is still *your* friend, despite his departure from his body.

In addition, the turn of phrase was used by Preston in a letter that he wrote to that bewitching Laura Wichmann back in their on-again, off-again dating days; he wrote the letter during one of their break-ups and promised that even if they did not ultimately wind up together, he would always love her; he signed his note: *your forever friend.*

Toward the end of this book, you will find Christmas letters that Laura and Preston wrote for their friends and family during their first year of marriage. In closing her letter that December 1988, Laura said:

"We presently have the challenge of meshing our lives and possessions together in this small house, but even the boxes of his things that surround us serve as a joyful reminder of the reality that my forever friend is now my forever husband."

My hope was to include everyone in these pages who wanted to share how Preston had touched their heart. Laura and I attempted to spread the word far and wide. If anyone did not hear about the project and feels left out, please know that no one was purposely excluded.

Likewise, many dear friends of Preston found it too difficult to put down in words what he had meant to them. Their voices are not included here by their own choice. Laura has shared many of the beautiful letters that friends and family wrote to her after Preston's passing. I am sorry that we could not include all of the letters here, as there was only room for a sampling.

Each and every letter received was most appreciated by Laura and the girls. As were the many gifts, ranging from lovely flowers and deliciously prepared food to a brand new refrigerator! Also worth mentioning are the many hours of service that Laura and Preston's friends poured out on behalf of the Hipp Family, from mounting a glorious post-funeral reception to mopping floors to providing tedious clerical duties to organizing boat trips out to Preston's harbor crosses to guiding Laura through the new and confusing territory of managing her family's affairs.

Each act of service was a tribute to the remarkable life of this remarkable man. To all who love and miss Preston, I pray this book will give you the feeling of being able to draw close to him again for a moment, even as you gaze at his friendly face on the book's cover. The portrait artist Johanna Spinks has certainly captured Preston's likeness (for more details, see A Note About the Cover Art).

For the curious: the production costs were provided by Jesus Street Press, as Preston Hipp was an honorary writer on the blog *Living on Jesus Street*. The sales of the book do not make a profit; each person simply pays the printing cost per book upon ordering.

In organizing the collection, it seemed most sensible to work by categories and in chronological order. However, the reader is encouraged to jump around from section to section and land wherever his or heart leads him. There is no right or wrong way of entering herein.

Preston was widely admired as a family man; he adored his wife, Laura, and their three girls, pictured here at home for Laura's 50th birthday on Nov. 6, 2006, from left to right: Victoria, Delia, and Olivia.

About the Cover Art

The oil portrait on *Your Forever Friend's* cover was painted by award-winning portrait artist Johanna Spinks from Malibu, California who has graciously allowed us to reprint the image. Preston had the honor of being the inaugural person painted in Charleston for a series of portraits Johanna has been working on for over six years, capturing different cities and towns through their people. The other locales are both in California: Ventura and Malibu. So far, more than 130 people have been painted for this series.

In the fall of 2015, Johanna painted Preston on a beautiful sunny day in his living room with his lovely wife Laura watching near by, along with Katherine Mengedoht, series co-creator in Charleston; Katherine coordinated the portrait sitting details before Johanna flew in from California. In December 2015, *The Charleston Mercury's Carolina Compass* featured both the portrait and an article about Preston. A copy of the article is included in this collection (See the section "Stories Published About Preston").

Preston was the first person to sit for The Face Of Charleston; the creation of the portrait was poignant, considering the advanced stage of Preston's battle against prostate cancer. Following her artistic intuition, Johanna decided to use a water scene of the Ashely River and James Island as seen through the Hipp's living room window for the sketch's background.

"This seemed entirely right when I later found out Preston's nickname was the Prince of Tides," Johanna said. To show his appreciation for Johanna's work, Preston threw an oyster roast a few days later in his backyard for her and Katherine, along with family, friends and a few local dogs.

"It seemed Preston really liked his sketch," Johanna said. "I felt we had a connection. And I will never forget The Prince of Tides working tirelessly and graciously for everyone on that oyster roast in his backyard that afternoon as the sun was setting on the sparkling water nearby."

It would be the last time Johanna would see Preston. More of Johanna's work may be seen at her website: https://www.johannaspinks.com/

Acknowledgements

Your Forever Friend would not have been possible without contributions from the scores of people who loved Preston and took the time to write down their memories. Most especially, I wish to thank Laura Wichmann Hipp for sharing her heart, for proof-reading, for searching out letters and photos and the answers to detailed questions. Also I am grateful to Susan Maguire for typing out countless handwritten items, including letters, and for accomplishing other tedious tasks.

Many of the photos in the book came from a digital album put together by Madeleine McGee, while additional photos came from Monti Hanger. Joe Nicholson captured the image of the large group of friends under the Harbor Cross. The oil painting on the front cover was donated by the portrait artist Johanna Spinks, and LaVonne Marshall created the marvelous book cover. Here I do offer my heartfelt gratitude.

Table of Contents

Preston Gives His Testimony

Men's Luncheon, St. Philip's Church

Charleston, S.C.

January 5, 2011

Preston as "Mongo", during his days on the Porter-Gaud football team.

Introduction

BY MAYBANK HAGOOD

(Editor's note: This is a transcription of a speech.)

I was asked to introduce Preston, but I think most of you in the room know Preston somehow, some way. Some of us have known Preston, you know, really, going back to childhood, and some have known Preston here at St. Phillip's and around the community in the last two decades, and some have probably met him recently.

I want to tell you just a very brief thing on Preston, and it had a major impact on me. For those of us that have known Preston since the early days, I can tell you he was the meanest, baddest, S.O.B. on the football field you've ever met in your life. As a matter of fact, back in the days of *Blazing Saddles*, his nickname was Mongo. And, I can truthfully say, and I mean this with all respect:

> Preston, you are the only older guy in Charleston that I was really scared of, and it's true. I was.

And so, then I go off to boarding school, and I go off to work, and I go back to business school, and I move back about 15 years later. And, it's the late 80s at St. Phillips, and George Mims was our music director.

And, George had a flare for the extravagant, and literally it was the first Christmas I was back. And, I'd seen Preston around the church some, and I noticed a major difference in Preston from the Mongo days.

But, what really caught my attention was the Christmas pageant when Present showed up in a full-length, silver, sequined—I can't call it anything other than a gown, with wings on. And he was the Angel Gabriel. And, I literally—it made me stop, because I figured if Preston Hipp could do that and do it with all of the humility that he did it in, then something's changed in his life. And, it really had a major impact on me, Preston, in helping me start down a path of introspection and looking at where I was in my life.

And for those of you who have known Preston for the last 20 or 30 years, there's really no one that I know of in our community that's been more quietly effective in bringing more men, whether it is in a prison ministry or here on Friday mornings at our Men's Bible Study—there's nobody that's had more of an effect in his own quiet way of bringing people together to start their journey of figuring out their walk with Christ.

And with that, I'm going to turn it over to Preston Hipp.

Preston Hipp

Well, man, I have to say, it's a very humbling thing to see this many people turn out on a nasty, rainy, Wednesday lunchtime. And I appreciate you making the effort to come out and hear what God has to say through me. As the body of Christ, we underestimate how powerful it is.

Happy New Year to each one of you. It's a pleasure and a privilege to be here with you today, 2011 years after the birth of our Lord Jesus Christ.

So, raise your hand if you've made a New Year's Resolution. Good for you. Good for you. A new year is a great time to assess your life and to set goals for things that you want to do or maybe some things that you want to *stop* doing.

I noticed that some of you didn't raise your hands. Maybe you realize that a simple proclamation is not going to change your behavior because the problem with each new year is that our sin nature tags along with us, and we find it very hard to change some old habits.

Well, I hope everybody had a wonderful Christmas. Christmas is indeed a magical time of year. God coming to Earth in the form of a man as a little baby in a manger is beautiful. The only problem with Christmas is all the other things that we add to it. Sometimes, it can be pretty overwhelming. It can be exhausting, and I know I had a bit of a hard Christmas because my Aunt Gertrude died.

She had a heart attack on Thanksgiving afternoon of all things. And it was a severe heart attack, and she actually had an out of body experience, which was pretty cool because she got to meet God. And when she saw God, she said, "Oh, God I'm so disappointed to be here. I guess this is my time. I had so many things on Earth I wanted to do." And God said, "Well actually, Gertrude, there are a lot of things that I want you to do. And I'm going to give you another 30 years down on Earth to do them."

And when she awoke in the hospital, she was so excited. *I've got 30 more years of life to do all these things.* So, she felt, well shoot, as long as I have 30 years I might as well go ahead and get "some work done", as the ladies like to say. So, she got a facelift. She got some liposuction. She got a boob job. She even had her beautician come in and give her a new haircut and a new color. And the only problem is that when she left the hospital right before Christmas, an ambulance ran her over and killed her.

Well, now she's back up in Heaven, and she's pretty angry with God. And when she sees him, she goes, "Hey God, I thought I had another 30 years on Earth. I thought you had all these things for me to do." And God kind of looked her up and looked her down and He cocked his head back, and He said, "Sorry about that, Gertrude. I didn't recognize you."

We know Christians are kind of like my Aunt Gertrude. We don't like for people to see our flaws. We don't like for people to see our weaknesses. We don't like for people to see our sin nature. We don't want people to know that there's a spiritual war of good and evil going on in our heads and in our hearts. So, in every way and, at least in some way, each one of us in this room is a hypocrite or an impostor.

Did you know that there's at least one man in this room that probably feels uncomfortable being in a room with this many Christians? Somehow, he doesn't feel like he belongs here. He doesn't feel like he's good enough to be here. And, I've got a word for that man. Don't worry about it. You're going to fit in with the rest of the hypocrites just fine.

Because you know the good news is that God wants to win this battle with good and evil with our sin nature, and He has his hand out to us every day all day long to draw us closer to Him. And, if we are willing to turn to God, He will give us the victory. So, today, I just want to tell you a few stories in my life about how God has given me gifts in my spiritual journey, and I hope it will be an encouragement to you.

Now, the first gift that God gave me in my spiritual journey were Christian parents that brought me up in church. But you know there was only one problem. I didn't get it. Oh, I got the concepts well enough, but there's this saying in Christianity. The longest distance in Christianity is the 18 inches from your head to your heart. So, what I didn't get is that you could have a personal relationship with God.

And, unfortunately, when I was 14 years old, there was a tragedy in our family that had a negative spiritual impact on my life. On Friday, October 25, 1973, I woke up to the sound of loud crying. It was the kind of wailing that when you hear it, you know something bad has happened. The night before, my sister, Bonney, who was 20 years old, had driven her car off the edge of Highway 61 and hit a tree and was killed immediately. A tragedy will do one of two things in your life. It's going to draw you closer to God or it's going to draw you further away from God. And at 14 years old, I said if God is truly a God of love, if God is truly a God of power, then this would not have happened to my sister. And for the next five years, I really closed God out of my life.

But, God had a gift for me. When I was 19 years old, my girlfriend and I drove down to Orlando to go to Disney World for New Year's Eve. And, we stayed with her former college roommate and her husband, and this couple were strong Christians.

And through the night, they managed to get the subject of the conversation onto God and having a relationship with God, which I found pretty annoying.

But, at the end of the conversation, the man asked if he could pray for me, and I said that was fine. And, he prayed. But, when he was done praying, he suddenly started speaking in tongues, which if you're not familiar with that, speaking in tongues is a spiritual prayer language that's very unusual. And, brothers, he might as well have dropped a piano on my heart because that fast, the casing that I put around my heart to keep God out was suddenly broken, and God came into me like a flood. And, I knew one thing and one thing only: that God existed.

Now, that might not sound too profound right here or right now, but to a 19-year old who had just spent the last five years blocking God out of his heart, it opened my eyes. Just as I know for a fact that this floor is right here, I knew that God existed. He revealed Himself to me.

Well, the next morning we had to go back to Charleston, and the man gave me a Christian book to read, and when I got home, I started to read it. And, a funny thing happened as I read that Christian book. The Holy Spirit started moving in my heart so dramatically that I had to put the book down and just walk around the room because I felt like I was in a science fiction movie and some alien being was going to come bursting out of my chest. It was that dramatic.

But, if you're familiar with the parable of the sower, I was the second seed that fell on shallow soil that sprang up dramatically but, because it had no roots, it withered away just as dramatically because I was not established in a Christian church. My spirituality that flared up disappeared just as quickly.

Years later, whenever I'd look back on that period of my life, I'd always go, *what if.* What if that man had followed up with me and made sure that I was established in a church? What if God had established me in a church at the age of 19? Trust me. My life would of been so much better. But, that's just one of those questions we're going to have to leave 'til we get to Heaven.

Young Preston with his father, Charles Rucker Hipp, Sr., and his siblings Charley, Bonney (L), and Dee (R).

Those next four years from the age of 19 to 23 were the darkest years of my life spiritually, and I just shudder to think about how much better my life could have been.

But, God had a gift for me. I became a real estate appraiser at the Charleston County Assessor Office, with our own John McMurphy and Joanna Drake McMurphy. And, one of the other appraisers was the pastor of a small church, and his son-in-law worked in that office as well. They were nice enough people, but they were very religious, so I always made sure to keep my distance from them.

Until, one day I was looking at the office bulletin board, and in the top right corner of that bulletin board, there was a little three-by-five index card that described a Bible study at the son-in-law's house. And as I was staring at it, the son-in-law walked up, and I turned and looked at him. And I said, "How do I get to your house to go to this Bible study?"

He told me, and he walked off. At which point, I said to myself, *what the hell was that about? I'm not going to that Bible study.*

Well, that Thursday night as I'm driving my car down Ashley Avenue, I am still having this conversation with myself. *Preston, what are you doing, going to this Bible study? This is insane.* Well, let me tell you, I was plenty intimidated when I walked through the door of that room and into that Bible study.

But, God had a gift for me because the real estate appraiser, that pastor of that small church, was one of the greatest expository Bible teachers I've ever met in my life. And the Bible, which I had always considered just another book that I never was inclined to read, suddenly exploded and became the Living Word of God.

Preston in 1984, the year he met his bride, Laura Wichmann. He is seen here on *Mobjack*, the Wichmann family yacht.

And if you remember, five years earlier when I was 19, I'd experienced that upwelling of the Holy Spirit in my heart. Now God just fell upon me like a flood. I could not get enough of the Bible. It was like drinking water from a fire hydrant. The whole experience was just amazing, and I had this incredible joy.

> I felt like a heavy burden had been lifted off my shoulders, and I knew that my life would never be the same from that point on.

Well, God had another gift for me. That August at the Rockville Regatta of all places, I met a woman who loved God and changed my life forever named Laura Wichmann. We dated for four years and were married on April 9, 1988, and I joined St. Phillip's Church.

And God had a gift for me. Jay Fowler, who is the assistant minister right here at St. Phillip's, started a small group that was specifically for couples that had been recently married. Now, we all know how hard it is adjusting to being married. It's hard enough staying married, but the adjustment to being married is very difficult. Well, with nine other couples and the books that we studied, going through that experience together really blessed our marriage and benefited us so much.

And Jay also started the Friday Morning Men's Bible Study that Maybank mentioned and that I've gone to for over 20 years. And men, I can't tell you how much it blesses me every Friday to walk into that room and hear what God is doing with my friends in the Bible. It's just exciting every time I go on Fridays.

Well, what God was doing was placing me in a Christian environment. He was giving me spiritual roots because he did not want me to fall away like I did in 1978. He wanted to make sure that I was firmly planted in his church.

Well, I need to fast forward to the summer of 2008. I was 49 years old and in excellent health when suddenly the rate of my urination declined dramatically. To make a long story short, I had an aggressive form of prostate cancer, and they weren't sure if it had jumped into my lymph node system and possibly into my bones.

So, the first step was to get a CAT scan and find out where the cancer was. If you've never seen a CAT scan machine before, it's basically a small pipe and you lie down on this trolley and they slide you into this pipe. And with a little imagination, it looks eerily familiar to the same kind of drawer they have at the morgue when they slide you into the wall. And, let me tell you, when they shoot that contrasting dye into your body and they shove you down that pipe and the technicians leave the room and cut all that equipment on, and all those magnets start banging around with all that noise, gentlemen, that is a lonely experience.

And I call tell you, you can have all the people you know in the waiting room, but it's just you and God in that pipe when that thing starts off. And, you will find out what kind of faith you have right then and there.

But, you know that God had a gift for me. He gave me two verses from the Gospel of John: 21:9 and 12. And I don't have time to go through the significance of those two verses. They're in your handout.

● ● ●

John 21:9-12 New International Version (NIV)

9 When they landed, they saw a fire of burning coals there with fish on it, and some bread.

10 Jesus said to them, "Bring some of the fish you have just caught." 11 So Simon Peter climbed back into the boat and dragged the net ashore. It was full of large fish, 153, but even with so many the net was not torn. 12 Jesus said to them, "Come and have breakfast." None of the disciples dared ask him, "Who are you?" They knew it was the Lord.

• • •

And they (the verses) may not mean anything to you, but they meant everything to me because it reminded me of the 23rd Psalm, where God said, "I will prepare a table for you in the presence of your enemies." And I knew that God's provision was going to be sufficient for me, and He gave me tremendous spirit of peace in that experience. And so, every time that I had a CAT scan or a radiation treatment, I would meditate on those verses, and God gave me a spirit of peace that everything was going to be all right.

Well, you know the thing about our flesh is it wants to avoid pain. It's like my Aunt Gertrude. We want to have a procedure and just fix it or at least cover it up. But, brothers, we can learn to press into God in our hardships; and I don't care if they're physical hardships or relational hardships or financial hardships or whatever your hardships are, Jesus Christ suffered more than any man, not just because He was crucified, but because He became a literal sin offering for the sins of the whole world throughout history.

And Jesus Christ will meet you at your point of pain.

So, no matter how deep you're suffering or how deep your pain is, if you will turn to God, if you'll turn to Jesus, He'll meet you there. He won't necessarily heal you,

but He will teach you things, and it'll be the greatest spiritual experience of your life.

Now, nobody wishes hardships on themselves, but if hardships come your way, I promise you that Jesus is there to help you through it.

It's not always easy. We know that. And, I don't have time to talk about the last two years, where my brother and business partner, Charley, came down with leukemia and died; or my brother-in-law, Bill Pridgen, contracted a brain tumor and died; or my sister-in-law, Lisa, contracted lung cancer and died; that her husband got cancer and died; that my two first cousins contracted cancer and died; all within the course of two years.

It doesn't always turn out like we want it. Or when the economy collapsed, and the banking system collapsed, and the real estate development business that I had with my brother went from flying so high to grinding to a halt overnight.

But, you know, gentlemen, I'm determined to not let tragedy drive me away from God. When tragedy strikes in my life, I go running towards God, and I will never again react like the situation in 1973 when my sister died—it wasn't God's fault that I ran away. It was my fault, but God made sure through his love that He drew me back into Himself.

In closing, gentlemen, I would say there's nothing exceptional about Preston Hipp. But, what is exceptional is that we have the opportunity to have a personal relationship with an awesome God, an awesome God that can change things in the twinkling of an eye. And, for that reason we should always have hope, no matter what our trial is, that God can not only change it but He can change it very quickly.

And gentlemen — each man in this room — you are unique unto God, and God has a gift for you. And God has things for you to do that only you can do. So, I just pray that you would reach out to God and seek these gifts so that as you journey through life, you'll be blessed with all the gifts that God has to give you. And, if you make one New Year's Resolution, make it to draw closer to God, and I can promise you, you will not be disappointed. Thank you.

Stories Published about Preston

Living Through Years of Plenty, Years of Lack

BY PRESTON HIPP

In Genesis 41, Pharaoh has a dream about seven sleek and fat cows grazing among the reeds. Then seven ugly and gaunt cows came out of the Nile River and ate the seven sleek and fat cows. God gave the interpretation of Pharaoh's dream to a young Hebrew prisoner named Joseph. The seven sleek and fat cows represented seven years of bumper crops. The seven ugly and gaunt cows represented seven years of drought and failed crops.

My life has been a variation of Pharaoh's dream. As a real estate developer, 2000 to 2007 were "sleek and fat" years for me. I enjoyed great health and financial success. I was in my forties during this period. I loved to work out, was in fantastic condition, and rarely got sick. I never went to a doctor but planned on getting a physical when I turned 50 on May 23, 2009. The development business I ran with my brother, Charley Hipp, was doing exceptionally well. I was happily married to Laura Wichmann Hipp and really enjoying life with our three daughters, Olivia, Delia, and Victoria.

THE GAUNT COWS GOBBLE UP THE FAT COWS

In the third quarter of 2008, the real estate bubble popped, taking the banking industry with it. My vocation was thrown upside down in the explosion. On September 8, 2008, I found out I had an aggressive prostate cancer. Several body scans showed the cancer had already migrated out of my prostate gland — or was close enough to the edge — to rule out surgery.

I went through radiation in the winter of 2009. During this period, my brother came down with leukemia. In the 1990s, Charley had survived large T-cell lymphoma, so he was familiar with the challenges of cancer. Once again, Charley went through the chemotherapy process fighting like a tiger but with a loving spirit that was an inspiration to everyone around him. Initially, we were hopeful: Charley won a hard-fought victory over the leukemia using own his bone marrow harvested and frozen since 1993. Sadly, the victory was short lived. The leukemia came back at the end of 2009. Charley's determination to conquer his cancer was legionary. Unfortunately, he died of a heart aneurism on February 10, 2010 at age 63.

Shortly after that, my PSA numbers started going up again, indicating my prostate cancer was still active. Prostate cancer needs testosterone to grow like a fire needs oxygen to burn. Removing the testosterone does not kill the cancer but slows its growth dramatically. In the summer of 2012, I received my first hormone shot. Hot flashes were a side effect. I laugh that I have great empathy for all my female friends going through menopause as well as for pregnant women with compressed bladders. One of the creeds of prostate cancer patients is never pass a bathroom. Perhaps worst of all, because the shot blocks my body's ability to produce testosterone, I have lost a great deal of muscle mass. I feel withered, as if I have aged 12 years in the last two.

THE LONELIEST PLACE IN THE WORLD

Despite my devotion to Christ, I have been wrestling with the "ugly and gaunt" years. Why me? Had I offended God in some unknown way? Was there some hidden lesson to learn before God would remove the curses? Would I ever return to the land of plenty?

Loneliness stalks me. While I am extremely blessed with a loving wife, extended family, life-long friends, and a wonderful church community, there are some roads you are forced to walk alone. Sometimes a crowded room is the loneliest place in the world.

My best therapist is my Springer Spaniel, Chester. He is my constant companion and never says a word. His ministry is one of presence and not advice. Advice usually sounds hollow in a solitary valley anyway.

Trials and hardships are exceptionally good at getting you closer to God. You think you are close to God in times of plenty, but there is always an element of independence and self-satisfaction. This affliction of pride is so subtle you usually miss it, but it can really obstruct your relationship with God. Ironically, it takes a severe trial to grasp in your gut what the Bible means by finding joy in hardship.

Blessed is the man who endures trial, for when he has stood the test he will receive the crown of life which God has promised to those who love him.
James 1:12

Faith is clinging to the belief in God's unshakable goodness while walking the dark and difficult path. Trust me: there is still plenty of frustration, anxiety and panic in my life. My fears are like the Old Faithful geyser in Yellowstone. They are not constant, but they are predictable. I have an uncanny ability to wake up at 3 in the morning.

This drove me crazy until I realized God was waking me up to spend some uncluttered time with him. Now I wake up and say, "Oh, hi God, anyone you want me to pray for tonight?" Or I spend time thanking God for my life's blessings. You never conquer your fears but with God's help, you can weaken their grip on you tremendously.

But when the kindness and love of God our Savior appeared, He saved us, not because of righteous things we had done, but because of His mercy. He saved us through the washing of the rebirth and renewal by the Holy Spirit.
Titus 3:4-5

The "washing" often feels like God is using a hammer and chisel to carve off the unwanted parts of me. God is carving me out of a block of wood that has been imprisoning me. Viewed from this lens, suffering becomes less of an enemy and almost a friend. The process is very scary and hurts, but you start to lose your fear because you understand the trial has a purpose in your life from a loving God. The more you see of God, the more of him you want to see. "Stuff" loses its appeal compared to knowing God. Surrendering your will and fully turning to God creates a depth to the relationship that is far more satisfying than anything this world can offer.

GOD WHISPERS
You become more open to hearing God.

For example: recently I was on my way to an early morning Bible study led by my nephew Matt Pridgen. I am typically very observant of the road in front of me, but halfway up the Cooper River Bridge, a blob appeared out of nowhere thirty feet ahead in the predawn darkness. There was no way to avoid it, so under the car it went. Clunk. The object had more heft than I had hoped. It hit hard and got stuck under my Ford Escape. When I looked out my window, I saw sparks coming from under the SUV.

Apparently I had run over a piece of scrap sheet metal going 60 miles per hour. No one wants to stop and block traffic on that congested bridge, but clearly I could not drag this crushed metal thing any farther. I was really in a jam when blue lights pierced the darkness; the car immediately behind me was a City of Charleston Police cruiser. We both made for the far right lane and stopped.

After getting out, I lay down on the concrete bridge deck to assess the damage. The sheet metal was jammed under my suspension, and it wouldn't budge when I pushed, pulled, and vigorously worked to free it. The policeman and I finally wrestled the object out after 15 minutes of exhaustive effort under my car. He wanted to leave it on side in the hiker/biker lane and be done with it. "No," I said, surprising him. "I want to take it to Bible study to show them why I am late."

I thanked the officer profusely for his help and went to get in my car. As my hand grabbed the door handle, out of the corner of my eye I caught the bright orange full moon setting over the western horizon. God spoke to me, saying, "Preston, I placed the piece of sheet metal on the bridge in front of your car. The policeman represents the help I will send you. You will have to struggle intensely but I will give you the victory. Do not lose hope."

I did not hear the voice with my ears but it was very clear in my head.

PRAYING WITH THE WAITRESS
The Bible study was wonderfully uplifting and afterwards, Matt and I went to breakfast. Matt is the most on-fire Christian I know, and he always asks the server if there is something we can pray about for her.

Often this exchange is awkward because the server is not expecting this question and he or she is focused on the task of bringing our food. This time was different. The waitress, who appeared to be about 25 years old, had lost a teaching job. She was waitressing to make ends meet until another job was available. She shared this story freely, and Matt started praying for her. She immediately started joyfully weeping; a burden was lifted from her life and replaced with the peace that passes all understanding.

Later that night, I was crossing the Cooper River Bridge again when I saw the alluring full moon rising in the east. I chuckled to myself, remembering my earlier struggle and God's reassuring promise. The full moon was like God winking at me and saying: "It is going to be a long scrape, but I am going to be with you until the end."

The next morning I still had that mangled sheet metal in the rear of my car. Impulsively, I decided to nail the unsightly scrap to one of the trees in the yard at my office. Another one of my nephews, Charles Hipp, and I work in a converted ranch house, so we have plenty of space and autonomy over the grounds. I usually keep a box of 16-penny nails in my storage building, but this time I could only find one ridiculously large nail about the size of a pencil. As I pierced the sheet metal with the thick nail, the symbolism hit me like a ton of bricks. Jesus loved me enough to be nailed to a cross and to die for my sins.

Every day I make a point of saying a prayer with my hand on that sheet metal. One of my prayers is for this season of "ugly and gaunt cows" to end, but if it does not, at least I know God is with me. Unlike many cases of prostate cancer, mine is expected to shorten my life. Eventually, the effectiveness of the shots will wane, allowing the cancer to wake up and spread. I try not to think about it, but when I report for my scheduled check ups, I am forced to consider this menace lurking within me.

Despite this, if I died today, I would not feel cheated. I have enjoyed more blessings in 54 years than many people receive in 80 years.

Looking again at Pharaoh's dream, we see God using the prophecy of famine to deliver Joseph from prison and exalt him to the second-highest position in Egypt. As the story ends, Joseph stands in splendor before his long-lost Hebrew brothers, the same guys who had betrayed him and sold him into slavery when he was young. Here the former slave and prisoner forgives his brothers, famously declaring that God produced good out of their evil intentions. Romans 8:28 offers this same profound hope, promising that God works all things together for good for those who love him.

I pray some part of my rambling is an encouragement to you. Don't give up if you feel like you are not getting it. Just keep asking God to reveal Himself to you in a fresh way. That is what He wants, so He won't let you down. Enjoy the journey.

A FEW OF THE READER COMMENTS
Alexa Wilde:
Dear Preston, it's late on a Saturday night, or rather early Sunday morning, and somehow I was lead to your website. I am distressed to hear of your challenges. When I lived in Charleston I always thought of you and Laura as the most loving and charming of people.

Let's go back a good many years, shall we? I remember you portraying Gabriel in the Christmas celebration at St Philips. Do you remember? You looked quite the part, I can tell you! I've always remembered it. At first there were some giggles from your friends, but I found it both appropriate and inspiring. My prayer is that the bearer of good news will be with you.

I remain in faith offering prayers for your good health and that of your family.

In reply to Alexa Wilde.
Alexa, I am glad my story blessed you.
God has seen me through many ups and downs since then. He is good and faithful.

I remember being the Angel Gabriel very well, including the good-natured ribbing I took for it. I pray God's blessings in your life. Preston

Susan Keller:
Dear Preston, every time I see you at Hollings, I shout out a prayer, " O God, not this sweet and holy man!" But He alone knows the number of our days and His purposes are higher and more wondrous than anyone can imagine. May He continue to enfold you in the deep recesses of His heart reserved only for those faithful ones given a cup of such suffering. Bless you, dear brother. This revealing of your soul's journey has strengthened my own resolve to love and serve Jesus no matter what.

Terry McBee:
Thank you, Preston. I copied down your last paragraph and taped it to the mirror on my desk. *(Don't give up if you feel like you are not getting it. Just keep asking God to reveal Himself to you in a fresh way. That is what He wants, so He won't let you down. Enjoy the journey.)*

I needed the encouragement. Have been in a "hole" lately. We pray for you every night.

LIVING ON JESUS STREET

I Went From Having Cancer to Cancer Having Me

YET JESUS APPEARED WHEN I WAS TRAPPED IN THE BELLY OF THE BEAST

BY PRESTON HIPP

CHARLESTON, S.C. — On May 24, 2014, I had an emergency surgery to create a colostomy. It's easy for me to remember the date because it was the day after my 55th birthday. Also, the event was a tremendous game-changer mentally.

I went from having cancer to cancer having me.

Perhaps I should take a moment to explain in layman's terms. The surgery team cut my colon in two and rerouted my digestive tract away from the rectum. The new route now delivers all solid food waste to a surgically-created hole in my abdomen. The waste empties into an ostomy bag. This is a heavy-duty plastic bag that has openings at both ends. One end of the bag is attached to my skin and the other end is sealed by a clamp. Several times per day, I must unclamp the ostomy bag and empty its contents into the commode.

Lovely right? Trust me, I could go on but I will spare you. I really wish I could have a more noble ailment like a heart issue.

Even though I knew the purpose of the surgery, it was still a shock the first time I looked down and saw the ostomy bag attached to my abdomen. It was even more shocking when the nurse removed the bag to show me how the system works and how to avoid trouble. Again, I will spare you the details.

In summary, it was a very humbling and somewhat humiliating experience. But something unexpected happened during my recovery from the surgery that I have shared with very few people, something that has given me the courage to continue to hope.

• • •

The hardest part of any day in a hospital is the middle of the night.

The hours tend to blur together. Sleep is elusive. You are in a strange bed, in a strange room filled with strange, noisy equipment. Even though Laura, my wife, was faithfully by my side trying to get some sleep on a foldout chair, I felt very alone with my thoughts. There seems to be an endless supply of time to wrestle with fear and entertain dire scenarios over and over again. If you finally do manage to sink into sleep, inevitably, you will be awakened in the deepest part of your sleep cycle by a nurse wanting to check your vital signs.

What can you do? It's a hospital.

This particular night the vital signs had an added twist. The male nurse was dragging a mobile scale behind him. He wanted my weight. Apparently some genius had figured out the best time to obtain your most consistent weight is at three o'clock in the morning. I wish I was making this up, but it is totally true.

I tend to be too accommodating in life, plus he caught me off guard as I had been sound asleep. So I wrangled myself out of bed — tubes, wires and all — to mount the scale. Accurate weight achieved, I re-wrangled myself back into the bed. Eventually the nurse exited, but now I was in no condition to ease back to sleep.

I was officially agitated.

Low points are emotional creatures. Your physical conditions might not change, but they can seem to take on different characteristics. The same hospital room, same beeping machines, and same bee hive of busy staff that had been my miracle workers just yesterday were now transformed into a hellish prison.

My cancer tormented me.

I felt trapped like Jonah in the belly of the whale — with no way out. I felt like I was going to die a slow death by digestive juices in the oozing darkness of the beast. I curled up into a fetal position and felt hopeless.

Then I saw him.

I opened my eyes and looked right into the face of Jesus. He was not looking down from Heaven or floating in the room. He was right there, lying in the narrow bed with me. There was no flaw in His features, no crown of thorns on His head. He was regally perfect. He looked directly into my eyes and beamed. His Presence radiated love that vaporized my fears and loneliness. He assured me of his plans for me. He was going to make sure I got out that hospital to fulfill them.

By this point I was too giddy to process the details. I only wanted to bask in the presence of his love. It was like being in a warm Jacuzzi filled with champagne. The bubbles tickled and made me laugh with pure joy.

I have no idea how long that experience lasted. Time did not exist. The saying that "Jesus will meet you at your point of need" sounds cliché, but I can testify that Jesus met me at my point of need that night. He took my fear and gave me peace. He took my despair and gave me hope. He gave me a glimpse of his eternal Kingdom that changed my perspective on the importance of things in our temporary world.

I like to remember Romans 8:38-39, which says, "For I am convinced that neither death nor life, neither angels nor demons, neither the present not the future, nor any powers, neither height nor depth nor anything else in all of creation, will be able to separate us from the love of God that is in Christ Jesus our Lord."

P.S.: After this, I refused to step on that scale again. The nurse was okay with it.

A FEW OF THE READER COMMENTS
Jack Owens:
Preston, thank you for your encouraging words that reinforce God's assurance that He will never leave our sides, that His love and grace is sufficient in even the worst of times if we will only turn to Him. Preston, your friendship has helped to strengthen my faith and make me a better person and pastor.

Tracy Graudin:
I confess to envy when I first read this account, Preston. (Jesus has never appeared to me in my suffering.) However, I read it again yesterday and am rejoicing with you! You've been so faithful to give glory to the Lord. I know you have suffered a great deal and seeing Jesus face to face has given you strength to continue walking in the good works He still has planned for you. Love and continued prayers for you, Preston!

Adelaide Herring

Just minutes before reading the powerful blog, I had been studying from Wendy Blight's book, *I Know His Name*. One of the names of God from the Bible is El Roi, the One who sees you. In Chapter 2, I was taken to David's Psalm 23, painting the Lord as the shepherd who leads, provides for, protects his flock, the one who is with us in the darkest moments with comfort and guidance; when death's darkness casts his shadows, not just literal death but that lonely place we some-times find ourselves, we are not to be overcome with fear. He is faithful to tend to us, just as he manifested himself to David who was preyed upon by Saul like an animal, just as he manifested himself in Preston's hospital room and brought joy and reassurance to his heart and soul; he bestowed a spiritual refreshing to Preston's "nephesh" or entire being. ....Paul, too, knew the pain of suffering.

One has only to read 2 Corinthians 11: 21 – 33 to see that he endured relentless adversity. However, and here lies the affirmation I received, Preston ended his latest entry with Romans 8:35 – 38 and this was the very passage I had just been reflecting upon in Wendy's book in which Paul pens that nothing can separate us from God's love...

In reply to Adelaide:

Adelaide, Thank you for your heartfelt, beautiful response to my story. I think we will be amazed how many of our earthly difficulties origi-nated from God's hand of mercy to draw us closer to Him. As much as I hate the suffering, I love the resulting intimacy with God. I do wish there was a way to bottle it for people who are physically prosper-ing but spiritually withering. God is good. He always has His hand extended to help us. Love in Christ, Preston

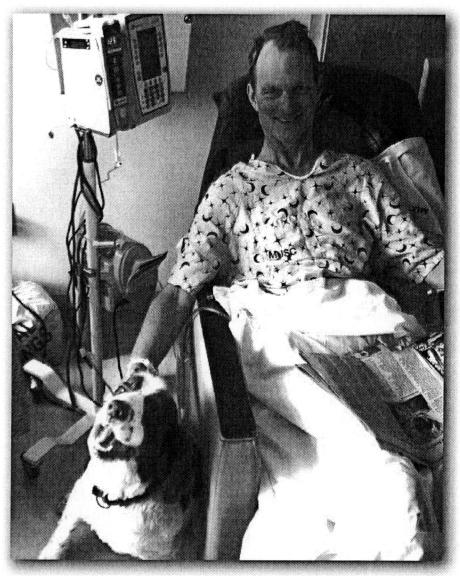

Preston's dog Chester stays beside him during a hospitalization in 2015. Preston and his dog were inseparable; his daughter Olivia arranged for Chester to get a therapy dog collar so that he could sit beside his master.

LIVING ON JESUS STREET

With Advanced Cancer, Facing the Unknown

BY PRESTON HIPP

Editor's note: Preston Hipp has been battling inoperable, aggressive prostate cancer since September 2008. For seven years, hormone therapy and chemotherapy had kept his cancer under control. In May 2015, Preston had an emergency colostomy on the day after his 55th birthday because his cancer had blocked his colon. He also had a stent placed in his left ureter to relieve blockage. Eventually the cancer blocked his urethra, forcing him to use a catheter to urinate. On October 22, 2015, Preston learned that his cancer has begun to grow again. The following are his experiences and reflections as he faces the unknown with faith.

Oct. 27, 2015: Health update --- I found out last Thursday that my PSA levels have risen enough to put me back on chemotherapy. It is not good news. The hormone therapy only works for awhile, then the cancer learns how to feed itself through other means.

God is still lovingly sovereign. He has a plan and a purpose for my suffering.

Oct. 31, 2015: I woke up Thursday with a very high level of blood — including clots — in my urine. Lovely right?

The stent in my left ureter has to be replaced every six months. It is not uncommon for the stents to cause bleeding. I was used to some blood but this level was new territory for me.

When the blood kept clogging up my catheter, I said to myself, "I guess I know what I will be doing this morning. Going to my urologist's office without an appointment."

My urologist had actually told me to go to the emergency room if this happens, but I hate emergency rooms. After a wait at my urologist's office, I finally was placed in an examination room. The nurse did a double take when she saw the urine sample.

Things sped up after that.

There were still a few minutes with just me and the container of red urine sample in the room. That is a moment for reflection. A moment when an active relationship with God is a valuable thing to have.

Heavenly Father, this situation is pretty scary. It would be great if You could hold my hand some. Thanks.

The doctor came in with a large syringe and special catheter to flush out my bladder. While he flushed out and sucked a bowl full of blood and clots from my bladder, he told me great stories about a mission trip he had taken to Indonesia after the tsunami. He was in a very remote village with few resources. A woman with a distended belly and intense pain came to the field clinic. A wall had fallen on her back and caused internal bleeding. She had a lot of blood and clots in her bladder. The doctor told me the woman was the first case of female genital mutilation he had seen.

Suddenly, I did not feel so bad about my situation. God had answered my prayer. The doctor left my catheter in, gave me a syringe for home use and said the hospital would call me with the earliest slot available to swap out my stent.

• • •

Medical treatments for cancer will create a lot of firsts in your life. I remember the first time I used a catheter a few years ago. I had never conceived of the concept, especially for a man in his mid 50s. The female nurse handed me a catheter, told me how to insert it, pointed to the bathroom and said she would help me if needed.

That was strange feeling when the bathroom door shut. You know what you need to do but you sure don't feel like doing it. I did succeed because I was very determined not to need help. So here I am with another first, walking out of the hospital with a permanent catheter. I felt like a cowboy, bow legged and not walking too fast.

But now it is Saturday morning and the catheter is yesterday's news. I am pondering my "to do" list and thankful for another day of life. Thanks be to God.

Nov. 3, 2015: I spent six hours (2:30 p.m. – 8:30 p.m.) in the hospital yesterday only to be sent home with nothing done. That's called a "no hitter" in baseball.

The poor guy before me must have been a train wreck. I did pray mercy and favor for him throughout my stay.

Before going to the hospital, I had a light breakfast of toast and coffee, but I was not allowed to eat or drink after that. Because the procedure kept being postponed, I went about 12 hours without food.

I have a heightened sense of appreciation for good Muslims who do not eat or drink from sunrise to sunset during the month of Ramadan. That takes some focused faith. Gum is helpful. Is that cheating?

As the day passed fruitlessly, the waiting and wondering began to wear on me. There is room for improvement for communication in a hospital pre-op. A surgical unit is a complicated beast with plenty of variables outside of anybody's control, especially the patient's. For a long time they tell you nothing, then transition to vagaries and, as a last resort, tell you what the deal is. It reminds me of an airport when they "don't know where the airplane is".

Really?

The hospital staff wanted to push me back to next Monday. Not an option since I start chemo that day. I am waiting for a phone call to see when they can squeeze me in today.

To be honest, all of this is discouraging and frustrating. I appreciate the prayers of my family and friends.

God is good. *Father, help me trust Your purposes and glorify You.*

Nov. 10, 2015: There is always room for improvement in my attitude of grace under pressure.

It was pouring rain and high tide when my wife and I started for the hospital. In downtown Charleston, high tide and rain cause flooding that paralyses traffic. Miraculously, Laura and I made it to the valet parking at the Hollings Cancer Center by 9:20 a.m. with no problems.

We stepped out of the elevator and a thought crashed into my mind: I forgot to bring even one catheter. That seems impossible since I cannot urinate without one, but you would be surprised how easily you can forget. I was surprised because I had clearly thought about it when I was packing my tote bag for the hospital. They call them distractions for a reason and apparently I had gotten distracted.

Nothing else to do but run back down to the valet parking area and hope my car was still there. It was gone and still pouring rain. The valet folks were not having a wonderful Monday morning.

I told Laura where I keep a stash of catheters in a drawer in the back of my car and went back inside to check in. Laura eventually found me as I was waiting my turn to see my oncologist. She had one catheter in her hand. Apparently the valet did not see the larger bag of catheters and had brought only the one.

I guess it's just going to be one of those days, Lord.

Laura had been working on her tour business and unable to attend my last meeting with my oncologist. He had recommended that I begin a course of chemotherapy for the second time in this battle. Laura needed more information before she could feel good about seeing me go through that again. She had a list of thorough questions that indicated I was going to need that catheter before this was over. Dr. Lilly was very gracious and helpful answering questions and wading through the options.

I cannot overstate the importance of this step. It is hard to have PEACE if you do not KNOW you are using the BEST option.

Two thirds of the way through their discussion, I decided to use my catheter.

I was happy to get out of the room for awhile.

I had resolved this issue about undergoing a second course of chemo-therapy in the last meeting. This meeting was for Laura.

Lord, please give her Your Peace. Amen.

After the meeting I went back to the valet station to get my car keys. Mercifully, it had quit raining.

I had a pleasant walk through the stand-still traffic to my car to get the rest of the catheters. It was noon when I got back to the hospital so I stopped in the café for a bowl of soup.

I enjoyed it on a bench with a view to the street.

People, cars, and buses streamed by trying to salvage their Monday.

I felt guilty not going back to Laura, but the hot soup was in a Styrofoam bowl. She, rightfully, has a long, educated spiel about the evils of Styrofoam that I did not feel like hearing again right now.

The soup and silence were just what I needed.

The day was only half over.

I found Laura and reported to the infusion department to begin the chemical treatment.

One of the hardest parts about the infusion department is seeing the other patients on the tail end of their journey. They wear masks for germs but the masks do not begin to cover their weariness.

They are sick and tired of being sick and tired.

Lord, more hope and strength please. Amen.

I was escorted to my infusion compartment. Hospitals do not have a lot of privacy so you are exposed to whatever is going on around you.

The older I get the more I like silence. Silence allows me to think.

There are a lot of TVs in hospitals, usually tuned into inane game shows like "The Price is Right" with the volume set way too loud. It keeps me up on the prices of major appliances and vacation packages.

The nurse came back with her gear: needle, tubes, and bags.

There are two qualities you want in an infusion nurse: first, that they can get the needle in the first try without a lot of fishing around for your vein.

Second, that they are pleasant.

The first quality is way more important, but the second one helps.

The nurse was great, and I settled into my book.

A contestant jumped and screamed ecstatically over winning a trip to Cancun. My TV neighbor did not notice since he was asleep.

Lord, Help me adjust. Amen.

I read awhile and took a nap myself.

Of necessity, sleep is always interrupted by activity. You go through three different bags of fluid before you get to the chemo. One is for anti-nausea. I forget what the other two are for, but you know when the chemo bag arrives because it comes double bagged and with an extra nurse.

You tell both of them your name and birthday one more time.

They read the information off the bag to each other.

I'm OK with that system. I shudder to think about the mistakes that mandated it.

Lord, keep everyone focused. Amen.

My lifelong buddy, Barre Butler, came by for a visit.

He hasn't missed a session yet. He has an incredible memory, especially for our childhood. Barre remembers every song we learned in kindergarten, even the accompanying hand motions. His visits after my colostomy would kill me because my laughing made my stitches hurt.

Good stories do pass time effectively.

We were back at the valet station by 4 p.m. A long but successful day. *Thank you, Lord.*

• • •

Even though I walk through the valley of the shadow of death, I will fear no evil, for Thou are with me.
Psalm 23:4

Nothing is proven true until it is tested.

Talking about life after death from a distance is a totally different experience than knowing death might be around the next bend. Believing in life after death crushes all of death's power over you.

I still have plenty of angst about my remaining days on earth and the process of dying, but there is no permanence to these feelings of distress. Jesus died for my sins and conquered death. Sharing in His victory for eternity is true joy and freedom.

I do not have a bucket list other than spending time with my family and friends. Part of me can't wait to cast this diseased body aside and go to heaven. No more catheters, colostomy, cancer, chemo, needles, hospitals. In the meantime, my suffering has given me fresh revelation of Jesus' love. Scripture has deeper meaning for me now:

I want to know Christ and the power of His resurrection and the fellowship of sharing in His sufferings.
Philippians 3:10

The very thing we abhor, suffering, is a portal to the depth of Jesus' perfect love we cannot experience from a place of health and strength. Reading and reflecting on Bible verses nourishes me.

Am I perfect? No!

Do I fear? Yes!

Am I comforted? Miraculously so.

There is no fear in love. But perfect love drives out fear, because fear has to do with punishment. The one who fears is not made perfect in love.
I John 4:18

A FEW OF THE READER COMMENTS:

Suzy McCall

You are my hero, brother. I am weeping for your losses, and praying for strength for your journey. I also sometimes long for Heaven, but we would all like to choose the day and the hour, the nature of our lea-vetaking, and the level of suffering involved. These choices are not given to us. Your faith will continue to sustain you and inspire us. May Jesus hold you very, very close. I cherish every hug and encouraging word we have shared through the years, and look forward to more. Shalom.

Betsy Lynch Hodges:

God Bless You Preston, your words are an inspiration, your honesty and love of your family and of God are a model for us all in this often brutal and unpredictable world. I had no idea of your illness; please know that you are a model of love, generosity and a sense of humor in the face of grave adversity. Love to you and your family.

Mark Ables:

Hey Preston, my brother stumbled across this all the way in California so you never know how far and wide your story may reach. God uses stories as a powerful tool to encourage, inspire, and teach, and yours does just that. Thank you for your faithfulness and for pointing towards Christ always.

Stevie Leasure:

Wow what a way to start my day! So sorry to hear of your recurring health issues but so amazed to read your testimony. Life throws so many challenges at all of us, but with faith, family and friends all things are possible….With God, all things are possible!!

Laura Wichmann Hipp:

Only Preston could still seduce any woman he wants while wearing an ice cap! He carries all our hearts together; I'm just the privileged one who gets to wear the ring. Thank you all for loving him with me. He is the man I prayed for in many journals before we met at Rockville on *Mobjack,* my family's sailboat. I just did not know this cancer would be part of the journey. Having been a granola girl even in high school, I thought we were better than this. I pride myself in no shortcuts in cooking, all real whole food. Oh the humbling power of cancer, no respecter of persons. The bottom line is what brought Preston and me together: The Lord God Almighty is worthy of all we endure in this life. In Him we live and move and have our being. We see glimpses of the Eternal in the beauty around us. I said to Preston how wonderful it will be to be free of sin and all that weighs us down and divides us, to love each other wholly and perfectly in heaven. Preston said, "I'll be able to listen to you talk for ever and ever without having to leave to take Chester out for a walk!" He always makes me laugh and not take it all too seriously.

Susan Maguire:
Dear Preston, You and Laura are such testimonies to the power of faith. You both continue to have deep and true joy in life, that which transcends ordinary happiness. You are an inspiration. I am blessed to be friends with both of you. Love, Susan

Joseph Griffith, Jr.:
I want to thank you for your display of courage and grace under pressure. I just happened upon your posts, read them all, and was saddened but inspired. Your faith, attitude, and serenity are amazing. My family will keep you and your family in our prayers.

Catherine Reynolds:
Preston, I think you look quite dashing in that ice hat. Not many men would. Reading about your journey and your faith makes me realize how far away I have removed myself from God. Your words and your strength are incredible. I don't know what to say except you

are a good and faithful servant. I need to stop and reevaluate a lot of things in my life. Thank you. I have always loved Laura, and I am so happy she is there for you.

In response to Catherine:
Thank you for your kind words. Weakness teaches us a lot about life we miss when we are strong. God, family, friends, people are the joy of life. God knew what He was doing when in introduced me to Laura at Rockville in 1984! I pray God's Presence in your reflective search. He is always ready to give us a hand up closer to Him. With Love, Preston

DEC. 15, 2015

THE CHARLESTON MERCURY

Feet in the Vineyard

BY PRIOLEAU ALEXANDER

As part of the *Carolina Compass*, each issue will feature a person doing God's work in the vineyard. Here in our inaugural issue, we can think of no person more appropriate than Charleston's native son Preston Hipp.

In 2008, Preston and his brother were running a very successful real estate development business. In the third quarter of 2008 the real estate bubble exploded, taking the banking business with it. In the same quarter, he was diagnosed with inoperable prostate cancer and in the winter of 2009 began a painful, exhausting and aggressive regimen of treatment. Then, in February of 2010 he lost his brother to cancer.

We believe an unimaginable set of experiences like this would challenge any devout Christian's faith. Not Preston. In the Christian blog *Living on Jesus Street* he wrote, "Trials and hardships are exceptionally good at getting you closer to God. You think you are close to God in times of plenty, but there is always an element of independence and self-satisfaction. This affliction of pride is so subtle you usually miss it, but it can really obstruct your relationship with God. Ironically, it takes a severe trial to grasp in your gut what the Bible means by finding joy in hardship."

Such faith is a rare and wonderful example for all of us to follow … one that can inspire us to reevaluate our relationship with the Almighty and view life in its real context.

Once again, consider the writing in the blog. He quotes Titus 3:4-5, "But when the kindness and love of God our Savior appeared, he saved us, not because of righteous things we had done, but because of his mercy. He saved us through the washing of rebirth and renewal by the Holy Spirit." He then goes on to write, "The washing often feels like God is using a hammer and chisel to carve off the unwanted parts of me. God is carving me out of a block of wood that has been imprisoning me."

Preston serves the Lord everyday, talking to others about his experiences and the faith in Christ that's carrying him through it. Despite the surgeries, loss of muscle mass and overwhelming exhaustion, Preston stands firm in the vineyard, working to make disciples of all nations.

This article was republished with permission of The Charleston Mercury.

Dum Spiro Spero: While I breathe, I Hope

WAITING ON THE MIRACLE

BY PRINGLE FRANKLIN

Tall, blonde, fresh-faced, Preston Hipp looked every inch the heavenly being on Christmas Eve when he donned a long white robe to play the Archangel Gabriel. Preston was only a temporary angel, transformed for the services at St. Philip's Church in downtown Charleston. But afterward, many remarked how much he had fit the part.

The popular appeal of this man went much deeper than his angelic good looks. Preston was a role model for many on how to walk closely with Jesus Christ and remain a guy's guy. For years, he led a committed church group in studying the Bible together on Friday mornings, offering a haven where men could be real with one another, share their struggles without judgment, and receive grounding and encouragement in God's word.

Despite living by the Good Book, Preston was untamed at heart.

He nurtured an unabashed affection for devilish stunts of the sort that Huck Finn might have cooked up. For instance, Preston and his cohorts would slip around the Charleston peninsula like middle school kids and scavenge the dried Christmas trees tossed to the curb during the exodus of the holiday season. When his truck bed was spilling over, Preston and pals would haul away the needled carcasses to a clearing out on Wadmalaw Island, eventually stacking the fir and spruce trees into a towering pyramid.

About a month later, during the dull, cold days of winter, they would ignite the pile before a crowd of awestruck friends. At dusk the orange flames flickered against the deep indigo sky and dry branches cracked and popped as the mass of trees exploded into a powerful blaze, turning the night to day.

For kicks, Preston might wing a few aerosol spray cans over the inferno to enjoy the mini explosions.

Like many Charleston boys, Preston grew up boating and felt at home on the water; not surprisingly, he was something of a thrill seeker. While crossing Charleston harbor in his small pleasure cruiser, Preston was known to open up the throttle in choppy waters, egged on by the bumps, roaring wind, and cold splash of waves.

On dry land, Preston was a man with a wench on his GMC pick-up truck and fresh mud on his bumpers, who sulked when decorum and his wife Laura demanded that he wear ties and sports jackets in lieu of his plaid shirts and comfortable khakis. This was a man who went everywhere, even to work, with one of a series of faithful liver-and-white spotted English Springer Spaniels trotting by his side.

After hardship hit, that man's best friend turned out to be significant. In February 2014, after logging more than five years in the fight against his prostate cancer, Preston would write on *Jesus Street*:

Yes, that crazy man up there at the top of the tree pile is — Preston.

"Loneliness stalks me. While I am extremely blessed with a loving wife, extended family, life-long friends, and a wonderful church community, there are some roads you are forced to walk alone. Sometimes a crowded room is the loneliest place in the world.

"My best therapist is my Springer Spaniel, Chester. He is my constant companion and never says a word. His ministry is one of presence and not advice. Advice usually sounds hollow in a solitary valley anyway."

SHOVELING OYSTERS

This admission was a bit shocking, coming from someone who was often surrounded by friends and admirers. Being in the solitary valley was not his normal habitat; Preston and Laura often entertained at their Tradd Street home. While Laura was known as the Charleston doyenne of polished-silver hospitality, Preston reveled in their backyard oyster roasts.

He was never so happy as when shoveling piles of oysters onto a fire pit and steaming them under the cover of burlap bags on a chilly winter afternoon. Oyster roasts are a tradition in the Lowcountry of South Carolina, and Preston had honed his skills to perfection by years of experience; he knew just when to snatch the gnarled gray shells from the heat and shovel them onto the plywood table while they were still juicy.

Plenty of oyster knives, gloves, and paper towels were on hand for guests in the back garden; Laura and Preston created an easy-going atmosphere with a big cooler of beer and a friendly gathering that always included both unleashed dogs and free floating children. Several generations of families, including grandparents, would mix together happily under the colorful mooring buoys and strings of lights that hung from the twisted branches of their Live Oak tree.

AN UNEXPECTED COMBINATION

In many ways, Laura (elegant, feminine) and Preston (outdoorsy, manly) were an unexpected but delightful combination, like sea salt on chocolate. Friends never tired of recollecting to Laura that many a girl had pined over handsome young Preston during his school days. Yet God heard her repeated prayers for a man with a heart after God and rewarded her chastity and faithfulness.

"Everybody loves him like I do," Laura says. "I am just the lucky girl who gets to be married to him."

Affectionate by nature, Preston often had an arm slung around Laura or one of their three wholesome daughters, Olivia, Delia, and Victoria; he was generous with hugs to the wives of his friends, and he was a tireless and free-spirited shagger who could confidently throw out an open hand and reel in a willing partner at dance parties.

Yet, Preston could be touched by moods, much like a cowboy who needed time alone on the range. When the pitch and tenor of his female-dominated household became too much, Preston would simply disappear, curly-eared dog in tow, and stay gone for hours.

At such moments, Laura would pace the kitchen floor while wearing one of her iconic flowery aprons, wondering what she might have done to upset him. But the storm clouds always blew over. There was not much that a good long walk in the woods and a good long talk with the Lord could not straighten out for Preston.

NO ONE GOT BEAR SLAPPED

The great outdoors spoke to his soul. Preston loved hiking and tent camping in the Great Smoky Mountains with his family and a menagerie of friends; he would encourage all the kids — even the preschoolers — to climb into the bed of his moss green pick-up. About when the last tyke was toppling over the gate into the truck bed, Preston would push down on the gas and the vehicle would take off like a fox chasing a hen, creating a tooth-rattling ride across dirt roads and dandelion meadows. A few of the mommies and daddies would endure bouncing around in the back to keep little bodies from flying out.

One such time, Preston screeched his truck to a halt under the puny branches of an immature crab apple tree. This inadvertently placed the folks in the open bed within spitting distance of a yearling black bear cub who was climbing the tree for fruit. Perhaps the mama bear was not far behind. Surely she could scramble into truck bed and make short work out of defending her young.

"Floor it, Preston. Floor it!" came the alarmed calls from one of the concerned men riding in the rear. But Preston kept the truck idling for several long minutes, enjoying the wildlife show. He was perfectly content inside the protection of the cab and in his certainty that nothing would go wrong.

He was right. No one got bear slapped. Despite taking some risks, Preston was a lucky gambler at life. He had built a profitable career as a real estate investor, enjoyed close relationships with Laura and their girls, was surrounded by a lifetime of devoted family and friends. With his unassuming faith and natural magnetism, Preston looked the picture of health, wellbeing, and fitness.

When the cancer hit in 2008, it caught everyone by surprise, most especially him.

NO CURE IN SIGHT

This wasn't your garden-variety prostate cancer; it was aggressive and inoperable. Doctors offered no cure, but they proposed ways to buy him more time. Over a period of years, Preston and Laura would endure the ravages of his treatments: radiation, hormone therapy, chemotherapy. At five years into his exhaustive battle, Preston had a strange experience that he interpreted as a sign from God.

He ran over a large piece of scrap metal before dawn on the Cooper River bridge; the towering bridge is the worst place in the world for an automobile to break down, as it is impossible to pull over, and stalled cars always create monstrous traffic jams. Preston had no choice as the construction junk was caught under his chassis. Preston and a policemen who happened to be in traffic behind him both stopped and were engaged in a protracted tug-of-war with the twisted chunk before it finally released.

In this struggle, Preston felt he had received a divine message: the scrap metal was symbolic of his battle with cancer. The fight would be hard and perilous, but the Lord would see him through safely to the other side. This promise gave both Preston and Laura immeasurable hope.

Not long afterward in February 2014, Preston wrote on *Jesus Street*:

"Despite my devotion to Christ, I have been wrestling with tough questions. Why me? Had I offended God in some unknown way? Was there some hidden lesson to learn before God would remove the curse?

"Trials and hardships are exceptionally good at getting you closer to God. You think you are close to God in times of plenty, but there is always an element of independence and self-satisfaction. This affliction of pride is so subtle you usually miss it, but it can really obstruct your relationship with God. Ironically, it takes a severe trial to grasp in your gut what the Bible means by finding joy in hardship."

In June 2014, some of us at St. Philip's Church organized a prayer vigil for healing. In a moment of private conversation before we began, Preston asked me to pray specifically for three things: 1) that he would get to walk his daughters down the aisle 2) that he could celebrate his golden wedding anniversary with Laura 3) that he would live to bounce his grandbabies on his knees.

His humble and heartfelt desires brought tears to my eyes. I spent time on my knees, talking to God about the need for Preston to stay with his family. During the time spent in prayer as part of a community of unified believers, I felt the presence of those who have gone before us, those from past generations. I had the sense that Preston's late mother might be watching and joining in on his behalf.

To me, the highlight of the vigil came when Laura stood up in the chapel and pleaded aloud to God for the life of the man she adored, arguing her point by citing scriptures and singing lines from treasured hymns in her sweet soprano voice. Laura's mother was British, and while Laura does not speak with a British accent, there is something in her precise enunciation and dramatic tone that conveys authority.

As Laura stood and talked to God, her determination to save her husband was palpable — and persuasive. I was buoyed by her faith. Surely Preston had more work to do for the Kingdom of God on Earth.

SLOW IN COMING
In God's mercy, death was held at bay. Yet the promised healing tarried, slow in coming. Instead the cancer, temporarily lulled by the various medical treatments, woke up and began to lay claim to more and more of his body.

His digestive system began to fail. Preston underwent emergency colostomy surgery in May 2015. Later he would write of the experience on *Jesus Street*:

"The hardest part of any day in a hospital is the middle of the night.

"The hours tend to blur together. Sleep is elusive. You are in a strange bed, in a strange room filled with strange, noisy equipment. Even though Laura was faithfully by my side trying to get some sleep on a foldout chair, I felt very alone with my thoughts....

"My cancer tormented me. I felt trapped...in a hellish prison. I curled up into a fetal position and felt hopeless.

"Then I saw him.

"I opened my eyes and looked right into the face of Jesus. He was not looking down from Heaven or floating in the room. He was right there, lying in the narrow bed with me. There was no flaw in His features, no crown of thorns on His head. He was regally perfect. He looked directly into my eyes and beamed. His Presence radiated love that vaporized my fears and loneliness. He assured me of his plans for me. He was going to make sure I got out that hospital to fulfill them."

Preston survived, in large part because Laura was striving mightily to make their domestic life as normal as possible.

For her, that meant gardening, cooking from scratch, and inviting whomever turned up to share their lunch or dinner. A local historian and tour guide, Laura draws energy from people, so she continued her habit of offering hospitality to family and friends while maintaining rapt attention to the daily care of Preston.

His appetite was lagging and his once muscular frame had shriveled alarmingly. Laura monitored every ounce of food that he was able to get down and poured highly-focused energy into creating healthful delights. Many friends were assisting in the fight to feed Preston, bringing by locally caught shrimp, buttery pound cake, fresh churned ice cream, and other delicacies that might tempt him to eat. A friend who owns a dairy even brought by fresh goat's milk because Laura was interested in its healing properties.

Sometimes she sent me text messages to report tiny victories: He drank the goat's milk muscadine smoothie that I made for him this morning. In another text, she related her satisfaction at having set up a dinner table in the front yard so their extended family could share supper within view of Charleston Harbor and its reviving breezes.

THE MIRACLE WAS LAURA

To me, the miracle was Laura. She lived in the here and now, thankful for every day that her husband survived, squeezing every drop of happiness out of her time with her beloved. "He lives!" became a common line of rejoicing from her lips and in her texts. Often she invoked South Carolina's state motto like a mantra: dum spiro spero, while I breathe, I hope.

Despite her efforts and plenty of prayers from their church family, the road kept getting rockier. Eventually the cancer had blocked both his colon and his urethra. Something as natural as going to the bathroom had become a humiliating ordeal that involved plastic tubes and collection bags. As if that were not enough, Preston learned in October 2015 that the cancer was active enough to put him back on chemotherapy.

Not long after this, in November 2015, Preston wrote on *Jesus Street*:

"Nothing is proven true until it is tested.

"Talking about life after death from a distance is a totally different experience than knowing death might be around the next bend. Believing in life after death crushes all of death's power over you.

"I still have plenty of angst about my remaining days on earth and the process of dying, but there is no permanence to these feelings of distress....I do not have a bucket list other than spending time with my family and friends.

"Part of me can't wait to cast this diseased body aside and go to heaven. No more catheters, colostomy, cancer, chemo, needles, hospitals. In the meantime, my suffering has given me fresh revelation of Jesus' love."

Preston understood that many people were learning about perseverance in faith by watching him. He began writing daily thoughts in response to Sarah Young's *Jesus Calling*, his favorite devotional. Preston distributed his encouraging messages via email among a wide circle. On Nov. 23, 2015, he wrote:

"Sitting quietly with God is a diminished practice in our digital age. We do not realize how distracted we are by TV, texts, emails, Facebook, etc, etc.

We, as individuals and society, suffer for our lack of meditation with God.

Not hearing God is a common source of frustration for many Christians.

Having a daily Quiet Time is the foundation of our relationship with God."

GOD KNOWS EACH CELL BY NAME

By then Preston was noticeably malnourished; he was walking slowly and deliberately, and he was spending increased stretches of time at home. Preston conceded that God might choose to heal him by taking him to Heaven. But for the time being, he preferred to be restored in the physical world in order to stay with Laura and Olivia, Delia, and Victoria.

During the spring and summer of 2016, Laura seized every moment to celebrate life with her beloved Preston. Here she set up dinner in the front yard in May when the New Dawn Rose was in bloom down the driveway.

Preston was clinging to his way of life, to the people and things that he held dear. His circumstances had forced him to retire from boating or climbing atop piles of burning trees, but occasionally he managed to play bocce on Sullivan's Island with his buddies. He was still driving, working on his remaining real estate projects, and leading the weekly Bible studies. In tandem with their eldest daughter Olivia, Preston and Laura launched a Young Professional's study group in their home on Sunday evenings, and Preston would rest up in advance to increase his chance of being able to lead the Bible teaching.

He was a living example of resilient trust. According to Laura's account, "As Preston told our Sunday night (Yo. Pro. group), 'Never underestimate the power of God to show up at the eleventh hour. It's just like God to show up at the last minute. Never, ever give up hope!' "

A few days before Christmas 2015, Preston wrote in an email based on *Jesus Calling*:

"There are about 37 trillion cells in the human body. That's a lot of cells.

"God knows each cell individually by name. Same with stars, people, etc.

"He has total control over each cell. He knows which ones are naughty and nice.

"The same power Jesus used to give man life (Genesis 2:7) and raise the dead (John 11) is still available today.

"God's love (1 John 4:8) is a consuming fire (Hebrews 12:29) that sooner or later will destroy every cancer cell in my body and restore me to perfect health."

Yet Preston was so gaunt, he looked like he had crawled out of a concentration camp. Well-meaning friends expressed their fears and sympathies to Laura, but she would not tolerate words of death. Throughout her life, once she had set her mind to a task, Laura had been a pillar of resolution. Fortitude was one of her great personality strengths.

Thus endowed, Laura refused to give in to despair. She doggedly maintained her position that God would spare Preston with a miraculous, late-hour healing. In the spring of 2016, she texted:

"We read Psalm 145 this morning @ breakfast with tea & zucchini bread.

'The Lord has compassion on all he has made.

The Lord is trustworthy in all his promises, faithful in all he does.

He upholds all who fall & lifts up all who are bowed down....

The Lord watches over all who love him.

My mouth shall speak in praise of the Lord.

Let every creature praise his holy Name.' "

HOPE FOR BEST, PREPARE FOR WORST
By now I was uneasy. Clearly, Preston had only months, or even weeks, to live. Shouldn't Laura be preparing herself and her household? Wouldn't the pain of losing her beloved be intensified by this refusal to accept that they were down by 37 points with almost no time left on the game clock?

Out of loyalty, I continued to pray for healing; yet I began to add prayers that Preston would would have time to tie up loose ends, that his soul would be at peace, that he and Laura would remain surrounded by loving and supportive friends.

"Thank you for staying in the fight in the heavenly realm for my man," Laura texted.

Somewhere along the way, my prayers for healing became rote, and my prayers for comfort, peace, and support grew longer. Meanwhile, as late spring melted into summer, Laura continued to speak healing over Preston to all who would listen.

But she could not ignore the terminally-ill look which her husband bore. At times it felt nearly impossible to keep visualizing that the miracle would come.

"My anxiety confronts me in the night hours," Laura conceded in a text.

Yet through prayer, music, and scripture, Laura would recenter herself and find the strength for the next day. There is a fine balance between expecting healing and neglecting to prepare for the inevitable. Laura did not wish to act like she lacked faith in God's ability to heal. However, Preston realized that he had to put his affairs in order. He developed a strategy for them to live by: hope for the best but prepare for the worst.

The practicality of this comforted me. I prayed along those lines, hoping daily that no bad news would come.

By midsummer 2016, Preston was spending most of his time sitting in his den, his faithful Chester stretched out nearby. A stream of steady visitors paraded in and out of their home, bringing food, flowers, mementos, or the simple desire to visit. Everyone in town wanted to see Preston before it was too late.

Yet Laura refused to allow her home to be shrouded with the depressing air of mourning.

"Come to say hello, not goodbye," she wrote in her lovely old-fashioned cursive and posted on the front door. "All who believe in miracles are welcome."

That was a difficult command. Hospice nurses had begun to help with pain management, and Preston was soon moved to a hospital bed in their den where he could recline and receive company. His boyish face was emaciated. His skin looked impossibly frail, like a butterfly's wing.

He wanted to talk, but the pain medication made him drowsy, and at times he struggled to stay awake during conversations. But when he rallied, he was the same old guy inside the shriveled shell. His spirit remained strong and his heart remained a cistern of philos love.

Some of his visitors sat by his bedside, trying to work out their own theology, wondering how a loving God could afflict such suffering on such a good man. When he had the strength, Preston was happy to share his thoughts, ever eager to be used by his Heavenly Father to draw others closer to the Light. He seemed to be treading closer to the Light every day.

"God is purifying you so much," I wrote to him in an email, "that when you get to Heaven, you will be in the VIP section down front next to Jesus, and when I get up there, I will be stuck way in the back of the crowd."

"Good thing I am tall so that I will be able to see you," he had replied.

He still had his sense of humor. It felt good to laugh.

Meanwhile Laura pleaded with me to continue to pray for the miracle. To be honest, I struggled with this, as the Lord did not seem to be moving in that direction. My prayers wobbled on shaky legs. When my father was dying of brain cancer in 2000, there was a point when I stopped praying for healing and started praying for his peace and protection as he prepared to cross over to the other side.

Not my will but thy will be done makes a sorrowful but powerful prayer of surrender.

THY SON LIVETH

Then my outlook began to change because of a coincidence of scriptures. Often the Holy Spirit works that way, placing the same scripture in front of us in random ways to get our attention. It started one night in late August; I was reading a devotional before bed and the text covered was John 4:45–54, in which a Jesus grants a nobleman's request to heal his son. Jesus never met the boy, who was languishing at home in a distant town, but when the Master/rabbi uttered his promise, "thy son liveth," the boy's body was immediately healed.

Of course my thoughts turned toward Preston. Had I been wrong to feel it was too late for a miracle? I prayed again, with more vigor, and felt peaceful before falling asleep.

The next day I was working at home when my eyes fell upon another Christian devotional book which I had set aside years earlier. I don't know long it had been since I had read *Streams in the Desert.* For some reason, I felt myself drawn to the little brown book that normally sat unnoticed on my desk. There was a bookmark where I must have left off my reading at some point. Casually I flipped open to the marked page and began to read the selection for January 4.

My eyes grew large. There was the exact same passage, John 4:50, in which Jesus heals the nobleman's son.

The entry read: "When there is a matter that requires definite prayer, pray till you believe God, until with unfeigned lips you can thank Him for the answer. If the answer still tarries outwardly, do not pray for it in such a way that it is evident that you are not definitely believing for it. Such a prayer in place of being a help, will be a hindrance....there is nothing that so fully clinches faith as to be so sure of the answer that you can thank God for it."

These passages aligned with Laura's approach. Apparently my faith had been faltering, as I had been praying for healing in a way that was resigned to failure.

"Okay Lord," I prayed, head bowed. "I don't understand what is going on, but I am convicted of your leading. Of course you can do anything. Maybe we are not done here. I will begin praying with expectation for Preston to be healed."

The next day, I shared my revelation with Laura and promised her that I would join her in praying vigorously for Preston's restoration. She was thankful that God had stirred up my faith. From then on when I prayed, I began asking Jesus Christ to stand beside Preston as he lay in his home hospital bed. I would visualize life energy flowing from Christ and pulsating through Preston. These prayers felt good. The loving peace of God surrounded me.

I don't pretend to be gifted in prophecy; it's too early to know how this saga will end. However, one thing I do know: Laura is right to speak words of life and refuse words of doom. We both believe that God can change the atomic structure of any diseased area of the body and restore it to perfect health. If we are called to pray along those lines, then pray we shall.

Laura's strong will is a testimony of her expansive love for God and her expansive love for her husband. In July 2016, she penned a 17-page handwritten letter to friends and wrote this:

"Am I not blessed to be in love with Preston, still to be on the honeymoon, and to be the one who he loves? There are still many women who would line up for the position. We have received many blessings, both in our marriage and family as well as in our current trial. Thank you for standing in faith with us."

Sadly, Preston Hipp entered into Eternity on Sept. 8, 2016, the day following the release of this story. It was exactly eight years to day after he was diagnosed on Sept. 8, 2008.

Postscript
WHEN THE MIRACLE DOES NOT COME

People may wonder: how does it feel to be praying hard for a miracle, to feel led to pray in this healing direction, only to have your friend succumb to the cancer?

First, let me reassure you: after learning that Preston had died, I sat on my bed, eyes closed, and meditated in God's presence. In that stillness, I felt surrounded by the energy of rejoicing. My heart was filled with this fleeting joy, as I "sniffed" the aroma of an abundant celebration going on in the spiritual realm between Preston and the souls, angels, Son of God, and Father God who have been expecting him in Heaven.

It was a bit like looking at a boisterous party through an open door, glimpsing the laughter, the spread of food, the happy chatter, and feeling a part of what it must be like to be in there, although you were not invited and were merely passing by on the street. One day, God willing, I will step into the circle and link hands with them in love. I trust that in Preston's passing, as in all things, God's timing and care of those who love Him is perfect.

And I cannot overlook the fact that in praying for a miracle, I was able to join Laura in her work to do everything within her power to save her beloved. It is an honor to stand with a friend at such a time.

A FEW OF THE READER COMMENTS
Mark Taylor:
Prayers for the comfort of Laura, Olivia, Victoria and Delia and Thanksgiving for the love and example of all the Hipps. We will all be joined again in Paradise, and Preston will be looking for us from the front. God Speed.

Susan Cale:
Thank you for sharing Preston and Laura's absolute love for each other and God. Very inspirational!

Dorothy Blalock:
Lord, we trust in Your goodness and Your love and concern for Preston and his family. We know that You mourn with them during these season of pain and sickness. We thank You that You are not unfamiliar with our suffering. You entered into the deepest and darkest depths

of our suffering so that we could one day share in Your eternal joy. No matter what this life throws at us, we are resting in the shadow of the cross- we have victory through Your sacrifice and You have given us a hope that nothing can take away.

George Mims

Preston, you are received of the hosts of angel choirs singing, "Glory to God," and you are welcomed by Lazarus, once a poor beggar, into the Holy City, JERUSALEM, City of Peace. The Light of God through Jesus Christ shines on you perpetually. Your finite mind has put on the infinite mind of Jesus Christ. Praise God from whom ALL blessings flow... including this kind gentleman who allowed me the joy of seeing him in angel's wings at St. Philip's Feast of the Incarnation celebration playing the faux trumpet with abandonment in worship of God! Memories never fail of those blessed moments in life, and I am very thankful.

Hungry for the Fruits of the Spirit

Preston's Daily Devotionals
Based on <u>Jesus Calling</u>, by Sarah Young

Preston replaces his Charleston harbor cross on Shutes Folly with the help of his nephew Matt Pridgen and his friend Herman Robinson, Jr., in 2005.

A Virtual Ministry to Preston's Flock: His Keys to Faith

Editor's Note: Preston's idea was for people to read the day's entry in Jesus Calling first, then read his thoughts and personal comments sent via email. If you have a copy of Jesus Calling, you might enjoy reading it as you go through this section. In addition to Preston's daily lessons, you will find occasional email exchanges between Preston and his readers.

Introduction by Preston:
Sarah Young's daily devotional, Jesus Calling, is written from the unique first-person perspective of Jesus speaking to the reader. Throughout history God has chosen certain people with the gift of knowing Him. Then God uses that person as a door for many people to come closer to Him. The central theme of Jesus Calling is experiencing the Presence of God, His Glory. Once you have tasted of the God's Glory, chasing after your glory becomes less important. As you spend more time with God, your "to do" list gets shorter, your worries decrease, your joy and peace increase and your self worth has a new foundation. That's good news.

I encourage everyone to include Jesus Calling in their daily Quiet Time.

November 23, 2015

Sitting quietly with God is a diminished practice in our digital age.
We do not realize how distracted we are by TV, texts, emails, Facebook, etc, etc.
We, as individuals and society, suffer for our lack of meditation with God.
"Not hearing God" is a common source of frustration for many Christians.
Having a daily "Quiet Time" is the foundation of our relationship with God.
Inviting God into our hearts through His Word transforms and renews our minds. (1)
It allows us to hear God's voice above the cacophony of worldly static. (2)
It changes our vision to see God's plan and gifts for our lives.
God's peace is one of the greatest gifts He desires for us. (3)
Sleep is a good indicator of your level of inner peace.
If your peace is lacking, seek more of God.
(1) Romans 12:2
(2) John 10:27
(3) John 14:27

December 1, 2015

When God's everlasting love (Jeremiah 31:3) is your life's foundation, the fickle approval of men becomes less important. When we allow busyness to distract us from God, we suffer for our waywardness. But God's loving Presence gives us proper focus in our successes and strength in our trials. Seeking God's Presence is our greatest investment. Lamentations 3:22-26

December 2, 2015

Peace can only be obtained through security. Isaiah 9:6 foretells the birth of the Messiah, the Prince of Peace. Everyone was looking for the conquering Messiah of Revelation 19. They did not realize Jesus had to be crucified for sins and conquer death. His first words to them after His Resurrection in John 20:19, are "Peace be with you!" Jesus still speaks these words to us every day of our life's journey.

Dec 3, 2015

Today's lesson speaks of spiritual warfare with Satan, the enemy of our soul. Another enemy of our soul is our own fallen nature. Our fallen nature is constantly at war with our soul for control of our will and mind. See Galatians 5:16–25. "Jesus, help me!" works in this battle, too. Our goal is to have "inexpressible and glorious joy" when we bow our knee before Jesus as our Lord and Savior.

Galatians 5:16-25 New International Version (NIV)

16 So I say, walk by the Spirit, and you will not gratify the desires of the flesh. 17 For the flesh desires what is contrary to the Spirit, and the Spirit what is contrary to the flesh. They are in conflict with each other, so that you are not to do whatever[a]you want. 18 But if you are led by the Spirit, you are not under the law.

19 The acts of the flesh are obvious: sexual immorality, impurity and debauchery;20 idolatry and witchcraft; hatred, discord, jealousy, fits of rage, selfish ambition, dissensions, factions 21 and envy; drunkenness, orgies, and the like. I warn you, as I did before, that those who live like this will not inherit the kingdom of God.

22 But the fruit of the Spirit is love, joy, peace, forbearance, kindness, goodness, faithfulness, 23 gentleness and self-control. Against such things there is no law.24 Those who belong to Christ Jesus have crucified the flesh with its passions and desires. 25 Since we live by the Spirit, let us keep in step with the Spirit.

● ● ●

From: Preston Hipp
Sent: Wednesday, December 02, 2015 6:53 AM
To: Butler, Barre (Charleston)
Subject: FW: Dec 2nd

Barre,
If you can't make Bible Study, Jesus Calling is a good resource. You still have a copy right?
Preston

From: Butler, Barre
Sent: Wednesday, December 02, 2015 9:42 AM
To: Preston Hipp'
Subject: RE: Dec 2nd

Preston, thank you for caring. I've had Jesus calling on my desk for over two years and probably picked it up and read from it 10 times. Today, that changes. You know Him. You are one of the doors.
Barre

● ● ●

Dec. 4, 2015

Jesus wants to be our Life Coach, training us for a better life in His Holy Spirit instead of the self focus of our fallen nature. Jesus' help is a precious gift that many people miss because they are not willing to sacrifice any of their time pursuing Him. Blessed is the person who hungers and thirsts after Jesus for they will be filled. Matthew 5:6

Dec. 5, 2015

Genesis 28:11-16 is Jacob's famous "stairway to heaven" dream.
Genesis 28:17 says, "He (Jacob) was afraid and said, 'How awesome is this place! This is none other than the house of God; this is the gate of heaven.' "

What Jacob did not realize is that the "place" was not the gate/stairway to heaven, God's Presence is. Jacob, and everybody who experiences God's Presence, was overwhelmed. The remote, middle-of-nowhere aspect of the "place" enhanced the drama of Jacob's experience. (Think Moses and the Burning Bush, which was God's Presence.) Since God is OmniPresent (everywhere at the same time), we always have His unlimited wisdom and power as a resource in our lives. How cool is that! All we have to do is ask (pray) and focus expectantly for His answer.

Dec. 7, 2015

God: Father, Son and Holy Spirit are <u>omnipresent</u>, which means they exist everywhere at the same time. There is never a time or place they are NOT there. So the <u>power</u> of their <u>Presence depends on us</u>.

If you are not looking for God, you usually do not find Him. God is like a gracious, Southern gentleman. He will not force Himself on you, but sometimes He feels so sorry for our ignorant rebellion, He reveals Himself anyway. I have been the beneficiary of that before. Thank You Lord! Connecting to God's Presence brings a bunch of benefits: Love, Joy, Peace, Patience, Kindness, Gentleness, Goodness, Faithfulness and Self Control. Galatians 5:22-23

Seeking and fulfilling (obedience) God's Plan for our lives gives us a guttural sense of purpose and completion. Chasing after the world's temporal, imitation purpose and fulfillment loses its grasp over our lives. Second Corinthians 4:18 states the wisdom of <u>focusing</u> past the <u>temporal</u> things of this world to the <u>eternal</u> things of God's Kingdom. Think of the things of this world like the Titanic after it hit the iceberg. Everything will be consumed by the sea so quit worrying about it and head for the lifeboat (God). First Corinthians 3 describes the process. Verse 13 states everything will be tested by the consuming fire of God's Presence. Hebrews 12:29

On this date in history, December 7, 1941 – Japan attacked Pearl Harbor to start the Pacific Theater of WWII.

<u>December 8, 2015</u>

Pride, Envy and Self-Sufficiency are the trifecta of death in our relationship with God.
Recognizing our neediness and asking for God's help are the two keys to a beautiful relationship with God.

Tremendous suffering has resulted in man's self-inflicted wounds of trying to find fulfillment from stuff.

God's Presence is the only solution to completing our souls.

The Good News is Jesus (Christ, in whom are hidden all the treasures of wisdom and knowledge. Colossians 2:3) loves us and wants to bless us with a close relationship with Him.

Dec. 9, 2015

I agree with Sarah Young's point on the "safety" of God's "Perfect Will" but would include a lot of negative stuff (such as getting beaten and killed) can happen there, just ask the Apostles, especially Paul. The Spirit will always be in conflict with the World because their goals are 180 degrees apart. The closer you get to Jesus, the further you will be from the World.

The Good News: God is in control of everything. So even in the deepest chaos of the world, God will keep you safe, even if you end up in Heaven in the process. Your fear of the unknown and the future will go away if you live in this Truth. Read the Book of Acts and focus on how God guides the Apostle Paul.

Dec. 10, 2015

Today's lesson requires a whole new value system. Our fallen nature wants to be in control so our lives are predictable and safe. God wants to connect with our Spirit Natures. Genesis 1:27; 2:7

James 1:2–8 challenges us to consider trials and difficulty as joyful because they are God's efforts to break through our fallen nature to release our Spirit Nature to higher ground. I like the saying, "If God is the surgeon, pull the knife in." God loves us and has a plan for our lives. Removing our sin nature is a painful process but it is well worth it in the end. AND, God is with us (Emmanuel) every step of the way. Double Yeah!

Dec. 12, 2015

Most people massively underestimate God's Power and Presence.
God is Omnipresent, Present everywhere at the same time.
Nothing happens without God's awareness and control.
Do not confuse God's tolerance with lack of control.
HUGE amounts of bad things happen outside of God's Perfect Will.
But God has a Plan and He will accomplish His Plan.
Seeking God's Plan for your life is the best thing you can do.

Dec. 13, 2015

Relationship with benefits.
Every relationship requires an investment of time.
God gave us the Bible so we can know Him.
Jesus came to the world so we can know Him.
Jesus told Parables so we can know Him and His Father.
Spending time with God in His Word and prayer transforms us to be more like God.
Galatians 5:22-23 states, "The Fruit of the Spirit is love, joy, peace, patience, kindness, gentleness, goodness, faithfulness and self control."
That's good stuff to be transformed into.
But wait, there's more. Buy today, and you will get peace, rest, and self fulfillment through God.
Ephesians 3:20 says God can do "immeasurably more than all we ask or imagine".
God has a beautiful plan for our lives if we come to Him to be transformed.
That is a relationship with benefits.

Dec. 14, 2015

Meaningless! Meaningless! Everything is meaningless!
This is King Solomon's opening statement in the Book of Ecclesiastes.
King Solomon's problem was he lost sight of God during the middle
section of his life, which is ironic since he asked God for and was
granted incredible wisdom when he became king. Israel achieved her
zenith of power under Solomon but it was all hollow to him without a
close relationship to God. Solomon was wise enough to realize God is
the only source of lasting meaning and purpose on earth.

Trust in the Lord with all your heart and lean not on your own understanding, in all your ways acknowledge Him, and He will make your
paths straight. Proverbs 3:5-6

Seek the Lord in "Deliberate Dependence" and He will be the best
friend you ever had.

Dec. 15, 2015

The key to "Hope" is what it is based on.
Hebrews 6:19-20 says, "We have this hope as an anchor for the soul,
firm and secure. It enters the inner sanctuary behind the curtain,
where Jesus, who went before us, has entered on our behalf. He has
become a high priest forever, in the order of Melchizedek."

The "inner sanctuary" is the Holy of Holies of the Temple of God. It
was separated from the rest of the Temple by a heavy embroidered
curtain. It contained the Ark of the Covenant, considered the Seat of
God. The High Priest would enter the Holy of Holies once a year with
a blood sacrifice to atone for the sins of the nation for the coming year.

In Matthew 27:46 Jesus cried out, "My God, my God, why have You forsaken me?"

Jesus was paying the price for the all the sins of mankind forever.

Verse 51 says, "At that moment the curtain of the temple was torn in two from top to bottom."

The symbolism is the sacrifice of God's only Son, Jesus, which gives us permanent access to God's Righteousness. The spiritual nakedness created by the fall of man in Genesis 3 has finally been cured.

Philippians 2:7 says Jesus laid aside His Glory in Heaven to come to earth as a newborn baby to a carpenter's wife. She laid Him in the manger of an animal stall with only the animals and a handful of shepherds to welcome Him to earth.

That gift is something to hope for. A Merry Christmas indeed.

Dec. 16, 2015

Psalm 46:10, "Be still so you can know I am God."

There are more sources of distraction than anytime in human history.

Smart phones, TV's, Computers, tablets, etc.

These are tremendous resources but if they block you from hearing God you need to adjust your habits.

Matthew 5:6, "Blessed are those who hunger and thirst for they will be filled."

In other words, you generally get about as much God as you want.

God wants a relationship with us but we have to open the door and invite Him in.

Revelation 3:20, " I stand at the door and knock. If anyone hears My voice and opens the door, I will come in and eat with that person, and they with Me."

God's Presence and Glory make life better. Amen

Dec. 18, 2015

Pretty often God reduces the power of "Stuff" and "To do" lists over your life by giving you a problem.

All of a sudden the "Stuff" and your "To do" list do not seem that important.

All of a sudden asking God for help seems real important.

It is perfectly acceptable to pray to God for healing or relief from a problem but make SURE you remember to ask God to teach you what you need to know from the problem.

Our nature is to focus on the temporary and lose sight of the eternal.

God wants us to learn from the temporal to our benefit for the eternal.

Dec. 19, 2015

"Stuff" and your "to do" list are enormous distractions away from God.

Everyone has "stuff" and a "to do" list. That is not the problem.

The key is not letting your "stuff" and "to do" list dictate who you are and what you are about.

The key is to carve out some time, even brief moments, when you focus on God.

You have to be willing to give up your "to do" list for God's.

Heads up. That is not always convenient.

But, trust me, God has a better plan.

When God asks you to give up some "stuff" or a "to do" list, He will give you something better.

<u>Dec. 20, 2015</u>

Jesus is Omnipresent (exists everywhere at the same time, even through time) but His Glory can only be seen by people who are looking for it.
Blessed are those who hunger and thirst after righteousness for they will be filled. Matthew 5:6
Jesus performed many miracles during His 3 year ministry, including raising the dead.
Luke 23:34-35 Jesus said, "Father, forgive them for they do not know what they are doing". And they divided up His clothes by casting lots. The people stood watching, and the rulers even sneered at him. They said, "He saved others, let Him save Himself."

Yikes! I would not like to be that guy on Judgment Day.
Romans 14:12 says, "So then, each of us will give an account of ourselves to God."
The "Good News" is Jesus paid the price for our sins so we can have a relationship with God.
That gives you something to proclaim as you sing about God's goodness to mankind. Amen

<u>Dec. 21, 2015</u>

God's Plan - Your life.
Sounds good but It's enough to give you indigestion.
God has some real curious pacing issues.
Usually He is way behind the schedule of your plan.
Waiting, Waiting, Waiting.
Lord, when is ____ going to happen?
Then one day you look back over your shoulder to see if God is making any progress and He is not there.

You look ahead to see God looking over His shoulder saying, "Are you coming or not?"
You have to rush to catch up.
Summary: You have to pay attention to God or you will miss the point and the blessing.
Your weakness is a door out of your self-sufficiency into God's Kingdom.
Look with eyes of faith to see miracles of God's Glory.

Dec. 23, 2015

The King of Kings and Lord of Lords is full of His dazzling bright light of Glory ready to hold your hand as your guide, companion and friend. Ready to live within you and supply all your need. Ready to use your life as a channel of blessing and light to share with the people around you. That is good stuff. Jesus is the Pearl of Great Price; the Treasure Hidden in a Field. He is worthy of all our praise and sacrifice. Whatever we give up for Him, He gives us something better in return.

Dec. 24, 2015

Jesus created the world and all things. John 1:3
Every person has some of Jesus' divinity. Genesis 2:7
Our sin is like the shell of a nut around Christ's divinity within us. Genesis 3
God is helping us reconnect with Him to fulfill our destiny in life. The whole Bible.
The "Good News" is God did all the work.
All we have to do is surrender our "Control" and listen for God's voice of guidance.
May the Presence of Emmanuel (God with us) bring you great joy this Christmas.

<u>Dec. 26, 2015</u>

Understanding the depth of Jesus' love is challenging beyond the point of comprehension.

Our "Fallen Nature" wants to be acceptable (equal) to God through our own efforts.

This is totally ridiculous because we cannot even come close to God's righteousness.

God's love is available 24/7/365. (Every day, all the time.)

The goal is to get our soul closer to receiving God's love.

Step one to approaching God's love is admitting our 100% need of it.

Step two is putting down your "performance expectations".

Step three is clearing your mind and seeking God with humble praise and thanksgiving.

Blessed is he who hungers and thirsts after righteousness for he will be filled. Matthew 5:6

I John 4:17, "Herein is our love made perfect, that we may have boldness in the day of judgment: because as He (Jesus) is, so are we in this world."

Christianity is the ONLY religion where the followers came claim with "boldness" their acceptable status before God, because our acceptable status is achieved through the work of Jesus the Christ and not of ourselves.

<u>Dec. 29, 2015</u>

Trust Me with every fiber of your being!

What I can accomplish in and through you is proportional to how much you depend on Me.

Smooth sailing can lull you into the stupor of self-sufficiency.

Personal reflection and health update:

Our family had a wonderful Christmas and Boxing Day.

I woke up to pee at 2:00am Sunday morning and had a high level of blood in my urine.

The blood continued through the night and then started producing clots.

By 6:30am the catheters quit working.

I packed a bag and headed for MUSC's ER.

I will spare you the details but the process of flushing and sucking the blood and clots out of my bladder is gnarly.

I spent a day and a half in the hospital finishing the process.

Take home message:

As I packed my bag for the ER, I thought, Lord, I am not sure how this fits into Your plan, so help me "trust You with every fiber of my being." My prayer and hopes are that my added dependence on God will produce more good fruit for His Kingdom.

My other prayer is that I do not become a frequent flyer for this process.

• • •

From: Dustin LaPorte
Sent: Tuesday, December 29, 2015 10:34 AM
To: Preston Hipp
Subject: Re: New Year's Day 2016

Thank you, Preston, for making time to share your heart and your pain and struggles. The words God gave you encourage my heart. I am truly blessed to have you in my life and to be able to share in your struggles and pain with you.

• • •

Dec. 30, 2015

Your "soul" existed before you were born.

God matched up your DNA to give you all your characteristics, even the weak and less desirable ones.

God knew your parents, where you were born, when you were born, all the circumstances of your life, etc.

God already knew the "Good Works" He wanted to accomplish through you.

Fulfilling God's destiny and producing good fruit* depends on our level of surrender to God's love and plan for our lives.

Nine Fruits of the Holy Spirit: Galatians 5:22-23, "Love, Joy, Peace, Patience, Kindness, Gentleness, Goodness, Faithfulness and Self Control."

Good News – God has a custom made plan for each one of us.

God is the ultimate "Life Coach".

His power is unleashed when we reduce our focus on ourselves and increase our focus on God and others.

Dec. 31, 2015

Peace and rest cannot be obtained unless all your enemies have been conquered.

Only God has the power to accomplish this.

The 23rd Psalm is laden with this concept.

Because the Lord is my Shepherd:

I will not want. (Lack anything I need.)

My "soul" is restored by God's righteousness.

I can even walk through the Valley of the Shadow of Death without fear because God's rod and staff protect me.

Death has no hold on me because of Jesus' victory over death by His resurrection.

Sin no longer separates me from God because Jesus paid the price for my sin on the cross.

I can eat at a table in the presence of my enemies because of God's protection.

When God anoints my head with oil, my cup of peace overflows.

God's goodness and mercy follow me all the days of my life.

In gratitude I will worship God in His church all the days of my life.

That's enough to make you say Happy New Year!

Jan. 1, 2016   Happy New Year!

Everyone has a relationship with God but most of them are not going too good.

God works 24/7/365 to improve His relationship with you.

God can literally "transform you by the renewing of your mind". Romans 12:2

In the process, God will invade more and more of your heart, the root of your mind.

The Love of God transforms you into a "Living Sacrifice" that is pleasing to Him. Romans 12:1

Jeremiah 29:11 is an often quoted verse about God's "plans to prosper you and not to harm you, plans to give you hope and a future".

That's good stuff because God totally means it.

The irony is the setting in which the verse was given.

Around 600 BC Israel had been behaving poorly for quite a while.

God eventually got tired of it and raised up the Babylonians (Iraq) to conquer Israel and haul them off as slaves.

That always gets your attention.

The cool part is verse 10 where God says, "When seventy years are completed for Babylon, I will come to you and fulfill my gracious promise to bring you back to this place." True to His word, God raised up the Medes and Persians (Iran) to conquer Babylon and send Israel back to their land.

Moral of the Story: Life works a LOT better when we earnestly seek God with a teachable spirit.

<u>Jan. 2, 2016</u>

In Luke 10:38–41 Jesus visits the home of His friends Lazarus, Martha, and Mary.

In three verses, a core truth of a relationship with God is communicated. The older sister, Martha, is focused on "proper" hospitality for their honored guest, a worthy goal.

Her sister, Mary, is focused on soaking in every word from the Savior and is no help to Martha.

Recipe for a cat fight. Martha brings the issue to Jesus but does not get the answer she was hoping for.

"Martha, Martha", the Lord answered, "you are worried and upset about many things, but few things are needed – or indeed only one. Mary has chosen what is better, and it will not be taken away from her."

Notice, Jesus does not say Martha's goal of hospitality is bad.

He tells Martha do not let the better take the place of the best.

Boiled down: Do not let your focus on "Stuff" get between you and God.

This is particularly important in the morning.

God invented time for our benefit.

Every morning is a fresh start. Yeah!

Before you get out of bed say, "Lord, Thank You for giving me this day. I give it back to You. Lead me to Your custom designed plan for my life."

Spend some time with God like He is your best friend. (Because He is.)

The Bible, spiritual devotionals, prayer, meditation, even Youtube your favorite songs of praise and worship.

This sacrifice of time pleases God and strengthens you.

That is a wise investment worthy of #1 on your "to do" list.

Jan. 3, 2016

The Gospel of John concludes with these words in 16:33, "I have told you these things so that in Me, you might have peace. In this world you will have trouble. But take heart I have overcome the world."

Trouble in this world. That is the understatement of the day.
There is trouble at every turn. You can't get away from it.

Every human being lives in two worlds simultaneously.
The fallen dog-eat-dog world and the righteous world of God's Kingdom.

God's solution to trouble is His Peace, which passes all understanding.
Philippians 4:7
The only place you can find God's Peace is in His Presence.
The irony is God is Omnipresent, present everywhere at the same time.
The key to "Finding" God's Presence is looking for it.
This is not hard stuff.
The problem is a whole bunch of people do not want anything to do with God's Kingdom.
They prefer being their own "god" in their own world.
These people win a lot of battles but they have already lost the war.
Jesus' death and resurrection have overcome the world and all its troubles. Amen

Jan. 4, 2016

I trust you, Jesus. Piece of cake when things are good.
Requires a lot of focus when life is NOT going your way.
God's love and power are the 1 – 2 punch for strengthening our faith.
God loves us and is unfolding a uniquely crafted plan for our lives day by day.
God has wisdom outside of time.

God has already seen our whole life.
God's sovereign power controls EVERY thing.
So where is the problem?
The problem is God has different goals than we do.
God's goal is to purify us so we can get closer to Him.
The problem is this process can be painful, and we hate pain.
The key is to see pain as a vehicle to move closer to God.
We are on our way when we can say, "I trust you, Jesus." in the midst of pain.

Jan. 5, 2016

God's goals are different than our goals.
We like being independent. (Our own gods.)
God wants us to be dependent on Him.
God knows that the benefits of depending on Him far outweigh the suffering of trials and defeats.
Second Corinthians 4:17 says, "For our light and momentary troubles are achieving for us an eternal glory that far outweighs them (troubles) all."
It's perfectly normal to look for the "exit door" of pain and suffering but, on the way, ask yourself what God is trying to teach you and accomplish in your life through the situation.
Saying "I trust you, Jesus." affirms your faith in God's sovereign love for you.

Jan. 6, 2016

God's power is unlimited, beyond our ability to imagine.
If God loves us and is all knowing, all present and all powerful, then why doesn't He use His power more often, right?
Apparently He is trying to teach us something or use our circumstances in someone else's life.

God uses two different kinds of time.

Kronos time is the 24 hours in a day kind.

Kairos time is an appointed time for something to happen.

Sometimes we allow the passage of kronos time to discourage us that a kairos time for the solution to our problem does not exist.

Sometimes God allows our problems to fester to get our attention. Instead of letting the building pressure separate us from God, we should let it drive us to God with expectations for a miracle.

Read Exodus 14 about the crossing of the Red Sea.

Focus on verses 19 and 20. The pillar of cloud by day and fire by night went from leading the people of Israel to a rear guard protection of Israel by becoming a curtain of light to the people of Israel (you) and a curtain of darkness to Pharaoh's army (your problem).

Open your heart to the things of God, and your mind and eyes will follow.

Jan. 7, 2016

The Parent/Child relationship should be modeled after the God/Person relationship. Imagine that.

The Parent works hard for the child and really appreciates when their child expresses appreciation for the blessings they receive.

The thanks and praise flow pretty easily with gifts like $$$, phones, cars, etc.

The thanks and praise can get overlooked with gifts like insurance premiums, mortgages, power bills, etc.

The thanks and praise get harder when the parent and the child are on different pages.

The child might think things like chores, school, and how you spend your time are an inconvenience or downer.

This analogy is real hard when you get into real life and the school of hard knocks.

When you are sick, lose your job, lose a loved one, etc, it is easy to lose sight of God's love for us.

It's interesting that Sarah Young chose as one of the scripture verses, Psalm 22:3, "Yet you are enthroned as the Holy One, You are the One Israel praises."

Psalm 22 is the prophetic description of Jesus' crucifixion.

Psalm 22:1 says, "My God, my God, why have you forsaken me? Why are you so far from saving me, so far from my cries of anguish?"

This is the moment God the Father placed the sins of all mankind on His Son, Jesus.

It would be easy to think the Father and the Son were on different pages but they were not.

Jesus knew the "end game" when He laid aside His glory and left Heaven to be born in a stable 2016 years ago.

Jesus knew His Father loved Him more than anything, but His Father had a really hard, important chore for Him to accomplish.

Jesus' obedience to His Father's love is the gold standard we aim for (even though we will always fall far short).

That is why Job could lose everything and proclaim in worship, "Naked I came from my mother's womb, and naked I will depart. The Lord gave and the Lord has taken away, may the name of the Lord be praised." Job 1:21

Jan. 9, 2016

Once again we have some conflicting information that needs further explanation.

Seeking Jesus is a delightful, privileged treasure hunt.

But the way to Jesus is filled with difficulties and hardships carefully dosed with tenderness.
Trust me, this is a matter of eternal perspective.

Second Corinthians 4:17 claims, "Our light and momentary troubles are achieving for us an eternal glory that far outweighs them all."

I have been in some "light and momentary troubles" when 15 minutes seems like an eternity.
My difficulties do not seem carefully dosed with tenderness.
In my pain, frustration and anger, I have even screamed some really negative things at God.
News flash: God has seen it all and considers our crazy rants as part of the process of purifying us.

Athletic coaches work their athletes to their breaking point to increase their stamina and skills.
God pushes us to our breaking point to increase our faith and love for Him.
If you can focus on the beneficial aspects of affliction (Spiritual Growth), then you will begin to see afflictions as favored gifts from a loving God.

Jan. 10, 2016

What we choose indicates our value system.
God thinks a good relationship with us is really important.
He wants to spend time with you in His Word (Bible), church, worship, prayer, meditation, and in our thoughts throughout the entire day.
Time is one resource that cannot be renewed or created.
We honor God when we spend time with Him.
We usually have to give something up to make time for God.

God says He will give you His favor to accomplish as much or more for the time you give to Him.

Having the Creator and Sustainer of the universe on your side is a ridiculously good deal.

The affairs of this world are astoundingly good at distracting us away from God.

2016 has the most distractions in the history of mankind.

I could make a long list but I think you get the point.

Pay attention to your use of time and make room for God.

If something else has to go, then get rid of it.

Nothing in your life is more important than knowing God.

God wants to know you, teach you, lead you, bless you on earth and for eternity in Heaven.

Hallelujah! Amen and Amen.

Jan. 12, 2016

> Your "fallen nature" NEVER wants to surrender control of your life to Jesus. BUT, you cannot move forward in your spiritual relationship with Jesus until you do.

EVEN if you do not FEEL like giving up control of your life to Jesus you can pray,

"Lord, help me give up control of my life to You. You are the true source of life."

Jesus not only knows your whole day, He knows your whole life.

He loves you. His living Presence desires to lead you in a path of transformation.

Grab hold of Jesus' hand and hold on.

Cry out to Him any time you feel afraid or confused.

He will answer you and show you great and mighty things you do not know. Jeremiah 33:3

January 13, 2016

Try to view each day as an adventure; a precious, unrepeatable gift; never dull or predictable but full of surprises.
Resist taking the easiest route and be willing to follow Jesus wherever He leads.

I Peter 2: 21-22, "But if you suffer for doing good and you endure it, this is commendable before God. [21] To this you were called, because Christ suffered for you, leaving you an example, that you should follow in his steps."

The NIV study note says, "Jesus' experience as the suffering Servant-Savior transforms the suffering of His followers from misery into a privilege."

Yikes! This is going to take some faith and focus.
Suffering is never wasted in God's economy.
Suffering weakens our love of self and the world and strengthens our need and love for God.
Suffering is dreadful but Jesus meets us at our point of need and uses suffering as a portal into a whole new world filled with His Presence.

January 14, 2016

The prophet Samuel is on a mission from God to find a king for Israel. Samuel is looking for the usual features people want in a king: a strong commanding leader with a dominant physical appearance.
Samuel thought he had found a good candidate, but when he asked God about it …

I Samuel 16: 7 states, "But the Lord said to Samuel, 'Do not consider his appearance or his height, for I have rejected him. The Lord does not look at the things people look at. People look at the outward appearance, but the Lord looks at the heart.' "

God's greatest desire is to purify our hearts so we can have a better relationship with Him.

Rejoice in the relief that God already knows all your weaknesses and dark thoughts.

God has the power to transform (Romans 12:2) us into new creations. (II Corinthians 5:17)

Then we are ready to receive the grace and peace of God's Presence.

Jan. 17, 2016

I, Jesus, want you to rejoice today, refusing to worry about tomorrow.
Great concept. Way easier said than done.
It boils down to control.
Do you really believe God is all-powerful, in control, loves you, and has a plan for your life?
"There is no fear in love. But perfect love drives out fear." I John 4:18
Fear and worry are close companions of trouble.
We expect fear and worry from cataclysmic events but sometimes the day-to-day drudgeries of life are surprisingly good at shaking our faith in God.
Miracles happen a lot more often when you are looking for them, expecting them, praying for them.
Thanking God in good and bad times releases His Presence in your life.
God's Presence brings peace, because it destroys fear.

"He who does not long to know more of Christ, knows nothing of Him yet."
Charles Spurgeon

Jan. 18, 2016

Jesus is leading us (pay attention/stay close) on the "high road" to "snow-covered peaks" (Heaven) in the "distance" (our lives).

Jesus wants to direct your paths. (Requires loss of control)
He does not want you to take shortcuts. (Easy way of convenience)
Jesus will disrupt your routine (comfort zone rut) with trials. (when things go wrong)
Decision time.
Do you trust Jesus' sovereign (all knowing) love for you enough to consider your trials to be blessings for your eternal benefit?

16 Therefore we do not lose heart. Though outwardly (world) we are wasting away (wearing out), yet inwardly (spiritually) we are being renewed (strengthened) day by day. 17 For our light and momentary troubles (needs perspective) are achieving for us an eternal glory that far outweighs (major benefits) them all. 18 So we fix our eyes not on what is seen (the world), but on what is unseen (Heaven), since what is seen is temporary (will eventually be destroyed), but what is unseen is eternal (forever). Second Corinthians 4:16–19

Jan. 19, 2016

Jesus is omnipresent (everywhere at the same time) but you have to ask for His attention to see His Face.

In other words, it is hard to have a relationship if you are ignoring the other party in the room.

Jesus created us to be in relationship with Him. Genesis 2:7

The nature of the relationship was for Jesus to pour blessings into our lives. (Eden: Genesis 2:8-25)

This relationship blew up with the Fall of Man. (Genesis 3)

Jesus has been trying to get our attention ever since.

When "lesser goals" distract us from Jesus, we suffer a great loss. (Meditate on this)

Good news! Jesus is always ready to restore our relationship. (Prodigal Son)

Moral of the story: Be God-Seekers and receive the blessings of knowing Jesus.

Jan. 20, 2016

Who is the boss of your plans? Always a good question.

God wants to be boss, but His goals do not always match up with our goals.

"As the heavens are higher than the earth, so are My ways higher than your ways and My thoughts higher than your thoughts." Isaiah 55:9

We want a comfortable routine we know and control.

God wants to purify us of our sinful nature so we can have a better relationship with Him forever. (Eternity)

God uses disruptions to our plans to get our attention.

The next time your plans blow up, start asking yourself what God is trying tell or teach you.

Good news: God has a plan in your blown up plans. That is His plan.

"For I (God) know the plans I have for you", says the Lord, "plans to prosper you and not to harm you, plans to give you hope and a future. Then you will call on Me and come and pray to Me, and I will listen to you. You will seek me and find Me when you seek Me with your whole heart." Jeremiah 29:11-13

Who is boss of your plans?

Are you seeking God and His plans?

Are you willing to trust (Faith) God, even when your plans blow up, that He is working out a better plan?

Can you imagine that God uses your suffering to connect with His Son's suffering to create love and spiritual power in your life?

That suffering reduces our self-sufficiency and opens a door to the Kingdom of Heaven?

When you find yourself struggling with these relationship issues, cry out, "I trust You, Jesus!"

This act of faith releases spiritual power into your life. Yeehaw! God is good.

Jan. 28, 2016

Nothing impure exists in God's Presence. Death and sin are consumed. Hebrews 12:29

The Gospel of Matthew and Jesus' Great Commission end with His promise, "I am with you always, to the very end of the age." Matthew 28:20

"... all the pieces of your life fall into place." Disclaimer: This does not mean your problems go away or even diminish.

FYI: "the age" is the period of time sin and death exist in the world.

Eventually Jesus returns and throws both into Hell and takes His true church to Heaven.

The heart desires, the will chooses, the mind justifies.

When you invite Jesus into your heart (Revelation 3:20), your world view changes.

Your life is no longer based on glorifying your "self" for a few decades on earth.

Your life is based on glorifying Jesus forever, which is what we were created to do.

Then your life will have true meaning and fulfillment along with love, joy, peace, patience, kindness, gentleness, goodness, faithfulness, and self control.

Jan. 31, 2016

Psalm 112:7 "He (the person who trusts the Lord) will have no fear of bad news; his heart is steadfast, trusting in the Lord."

"No fear of bad news" is not possible without God.

It is next to impossible with God because it requires a measure of faith that is difficult to maintain.

It's like swimming.

We start out strong but then our arms (faith) get weak and gravity starts taking over.

It's like Peter walking on the water.

Peter started out fine when he stayed focused on Jesus but he started sinking the moment he shifted his focus to the waves.

Moral: we are goners until we learn to trust Jesus' sovereign love in all circumstances.

Worshipping Jesus is a miraculous cure for fear. (I John 4:18)

The next time you feel fear overwhelming you, stop what you are doing and spend some time thanking Jesus. Thank Him for His love for you, His good plans for you, His miraculous power over you, all the good things He has done for you.

Before you know it, you will be holding His hand walking on water.

Feb. 1, 2016

God operates outside of time and physics.

This is why Jesus says, "We should live by faith, not by sight." Second Corinthians 5:7

Jesus performed miracles for two reasons.

First, He loves people and wants to heal them of their infirmities.

Second, He wants to prove to people He operates outside of time and physics.

Jesus raises His friend, Lazarus, from the dead in the Gospel of John 11.

John 11:6 says Jesus stayed where He was for two days when He heard His friend died.

Jesus delayed His trip to raise Lazarus from the dead to prove He operates outside of time and physics.

Jesus works outside of time and physics now.

He can even insert energy into your mind, body and spirit.

Psalm 18:29, "With Your help I can conquer a troop of soldiers, with my God I can scale a wall."
God can make a way where there is no way to be found.
Seek His Presence, stay close, and enjoy the view.

Feb. 2, 2016

Romans 12:2, "Do not conform any longer to the pattern (ways) of this world, but be transformed by the renewing of your mind. Then you will be able to test and approve what God's will is – His good, pleasing and perfect will (plan)."

Fear is the opposite of faith.
Fear testifies to doubting God's love and power over your life.
Perfect love makes fear disappear. I John 4:18
Remember: God is greater than you and all your problems.
The key is to invite God into your life and stay close to Him.
God's power is in His Presence.
Nothing impure can exist in God's Presence.
For our God is a consuming fire. Hebrews 12:29
Sin, sickness and death cannot exist before God.
Our sinful nature (Pride/Shame) draws us away from God.
We want to "fix" our problems ourselves and our way.
This is a hopeless exercise in futility.
Be a God Seeker, tell Him your problems, and He will rock (transform/renew) your world.

Feb. 4, 2016

Weakness is a good thing in God's Kingdom because it elevates our need for God.
Self-sufficiency is a bad thing in God's Kingdom because it does not recognize our need for God.

These two opposites can be boiled down into, "Who is in control of your purpose in life"?

Self-sufficiency elevates our focus on self-glory. Imagine that.

Our weaknesses open the doors of our heart to God's Presence.

God's Essence (Fruit of the Spirit: Love, Joy, Peace, Patience, Kindness, Goodness, Gentleness, Faithfulness and Self Control. Galatians 5:22-23) always accompanies God's Presence.

It is not uncommon for God to diminish or remove our worldly support systems to expose and increase our need for Him.

Instead of cursing the difficulties of our circumstances, praise God for the spiritual blessings He is pouring into your life through them.

This requires a lot of focus on God's love for you and His sovereignty over your circumstances.

For example: I received Round 5 of chemotherapy last Monday.

I spent yesterday in the Emergency Room getting blood clots flushed out of my bladder.

I do not feel well. I am really tired. I have a lot of frustration.

I also have an amazing peace that God loves me, has a plan and is going to work this out.

I bring my physical weakness to God so He can transform it into spiritual strength.

It's like turning lead into gold. Only God can do that.

I am thankful for God's love and trust His sovereign power. Amen

Feb. 6, 2016

As usual with Jesus Calling, there is a lot going on in a few words.

Come to Me and rest, be blessed and restored.

Cling tightly to My hand while I teach you a difficult lesson learned only by hardship.

Whoa!? Do those sentences belong in the same paragraph?

Yes and here's why.

Our "Sin Nature" (Pride, Self-Sufficiency, Control) grasps just about everything but God.

God's love for us allows hardship to weaken our grasp on things and cling to His hand.

Once you have done that (Humility, God-dependency, Turned over control to God), then you can enjoy the benefits of God and His Kingdom: Peace, Rest, Light, Joy, etc.

OK but why all the hardship?

Because our "Sin Nature" is more stubborn than a mule.

The only way to really get rid of our "Sin Nature" is to get close to God.

Our "Sin Nature" is consumed in the fire of God's Presence. Hebrews 12:29

That is why Jesus can say, "Come to Me, all you who are weary and burdened, and I will give you rest. Take my yoke upon you and learn from Me, for I am gentle and humble in heart, and you will find rest for your souls. For my yoke is easy and my burden is light." Amen and Amen.

Feb. 12, 2016

Our Heart desires
Our Will chooses
Our Mind justifies

This process is a self-fulfilling feedback loop.

Negative desires and choices create negative thoughts that produce more negative desires and choices. It is a vicious downward spiral.

God gave us His Word (Bible), Jesus gave us His testimony, and the Holy Spirit gives us His power for the process to work for our benefit.

Godly desires and choices create positive thoughts.

God created mankind to worship Him, but Satan tries to hijack our worship away from God.

Marketing companies bombard and seduce us to their products.

Our "Sinful Nature" is a willing accomplice.

That is where the trouble starts.

Jesus offers us a way out.

If you focus on Jesus, He will wash and transform the desires of your heart.

Feb. 14, 2016

Isaiah 41: 13, "For I am the Lord, your God, who takes hold of your right hand and says to you, Do not fear; I will help you."

God's offer of help is a mega-awesome deal, however, the pride of our sin nature always wants to be self-sufficient. Even when we recognize our need for help, we are prone (understatement) to fear and worry because our image of God is too small and our focus is on our problems, not on Jesus. When we get to Heaven and see how BIG God is we will feel foolish about our fears and worries.

February 15, 2016

"The bottom line is that I (Jesus) am taking care of you; therefore, you needn't be afraid of anything."

For the last 100 years, the modern Western mind has shifted to technology solving our problems to the detriment of our relationship with God. God is not opposed to science. (He created it!)

God created man to worship Him and be in relationship with Him.

Humans are famous for replacing God with idols, which can take a staggering variety of formats.

You will never conquer fear and find true peace while you are in "control of your life" through your created idols. Peace, safety and rest can only come by giving up "control of your life" to God.

<u>Feb. 19, 2016</u>

Habakkuk 3:17–19

Though the fig tree does not bud
and there are no grapes on the vines,
though the olive crop fails
and the fields produce no food,
though there are no sheep in the pen
and no cattle in the stalls,
[18] yet I will rejoice in the Lord,
I will be joyful in God my Savior.
[19] The Sovereign Lord is my strength;
He makes my feet like the feet of a deer,
He enables me to tread on the heights.

Habakkuk wrote his short book in the days before Babylon invaded Israel.
Israel had strayed from God and His desires for them.
Life in Israel was unjust and chaotic.
God gave them over to their sinful desires and got pretty quiet.
The book of Habakkuk is man crying out for God's mercy and intervention.
Habakkuk concludes his book with a bold statement of faith in God's goodness despite the dismal circumstances.
He will rejoice and be joyful for God's strength that enables him to tread through the difficult season to a better day.

<u>Feb. 21, 2016</u>

I Peter 5:5–7 "God opposes the proud but shows favor to the humble."
6 Humble yourselves, therefore, under God's mighty hand, that he may lift you up in due time.

Cast all your anxiety on him because He cares for you.

Jesus' greatest desire is to be our Savior, Lord and Friend.
To be Jesus' friend we must first lay aside our worldly pride and self-sufficiency.
Jesus' holy purity will literally burn up our imperfections as we get closer to Him.
This process is not easy, pretty, or comfortable.
A lot of Christians are not willing to venture too far into this process.
Jesus gives us the freedom to choose.
It is not a one-time decision.
We must choose Jesus 1,000 times a day for our whole lives.
Making the right decision requires focusing on Jesus on a regular basis.
Good news! Knowing Jesus has a bunch of benefits.
Love, Joy, Peace, Patience, Kindness, Gentleness, Goodness, Faithfulness and Self Control. Fruit of the Spirit. Galatians 5:22-23
Throw in a large dose of Provision and Protection and you have a deal worth striving for.
Oh, don't leave out an Eternity in Heaven with all the loved ones who have gone before you.

Feb. 22, 2016

What a good word for me this morning.
Today is another round of chemotherapy.
I have considered and delved into self-pity, self-preoccupation, and giving up.
The cumulative effect of all I have been through has taken its toll on me physically and mentally.
I attribute the good health I do have to all the prayers of friends and family.

I agree with Sarah Young that worldly neediness can be a portal into tremendous spiritual growth.

I have never been so aware of the Presence of God in my life.

John 16: 24, "Ask and you will receive, and your *joy* will be complete."

Jesus can meet us at our point of need because no human has suffered at a deeper level than He did for us.

When Jesus' Presence shows up, your neediness decreases and your joy increases.

I can testify and guarantee it.

Feb. 24, 2016

"Whoever does <u>not</u> love does <u>not</u> know God, because God is love." I John 4:8

Jesus coming to earth to die for our sins is the culmination of the Father's love.

Sin, sickness, death, etc. cannot exist in Jesus' 100% Presence. (Heaven)

Our sinful, worldly bodies cannot endure Jesus' 100% Presence so He gives us enough to draw us closer to Him. Our sin nature (Pride, Envy, Self-Sufficiency, Hatred, etc.) is consumed by the Holy Fire (Hebrews 12:29) of Jesus' love. This process is filled with the awe of experiencing Jesus' love and the suffering of having our sin nature destroyed.

The last sentence states, "For now, the knowledge of My loving Presence…"

There is head knowledge and heart knowledge.

When Jesus' love (Presence) connects with your soul; (Genesis 1:27), that is heart knowledge.

That is where miracles happen on a regular basis.

● ● ●

Preston with his favorite sidekick, Chester. (February 2014)

<u>Feb. 25, 2016</u>

There is no death, sickness, sin, hate, etc. in Heaven.
Jesus' Presence is a mobile Heaven.
Jesus is like a mobile dog washer that comes to your house to give your dog a bath to get all the dirt and smells off.
In case you missed it, we are the "dog" in that analogy.

The closer we get to Jesus, the more He can wash away all the negative things in our lives.
One really hard step in this process is releasing "control" to Jesus.

Your "fallen nature" (Genesis 3) NEVER thinks that is a good idea and will fight it to the day you die.

The best way to claim victory is to praise God with thankfulness for the His goodness in your life.

Praising God sucks the energy out of our sin nature and pumps it into our spirit nature.

As I like to say, "Ba-BOOM". Take that, sinful nature.

• • •

From: "Barre Butler"
To: "Preston Hipp"
Sent: Thursday, February 25, 2016 10:14:50 AM

Woof-Woof!

• • •

March 1, 2016

Anxiety and worry usually involve conflict and scarcity.

The world (Our "Flesh"/"Fallen Nature") tries to solve anxiety and worry with "Peace and Prosperity".

The problem is the "world" operates from a dog-eat-dog, pride and envy, competitive spirit.

That is why "Peace and Prosperity" are hard to come by and harder sustain.

An enormous danger of the world's economy is a spirit of self-sufficiency that thinks it does not need God. (God laughs at that one. Psalm 2:4)

God's Kingdom operates from a totally different economy.

God spoke everything into existence.

He still speaks things into existence.

God continually offers us His eternal "Peace and Prosperity".

The hard part is trusting God enough to turn away from the world's economy.

The premise of Psalm 23 is God is our Provider and Protector.

True Peace comes from faith and trust that God loves us, has a plan for our lives and works all things together for our good.

Do not be anxious about anything, but in every situation, by prayer and petition, with thanksgiving, present your requests to God. Philippians 4:6

March 2, 2016

Where does your "significance" come from?

Sarah Young gives a few categories from a potentially long list.

The real question is what is temporal and what is eternal?

The mistake a bunch of people make is leaving the eternal out of the decision process.

The "Good News" is Jesus offers us abundant, eternal life for free. **

** The catch is you have to "take My yoke upon you", which means surrendering your desires of Pride and Self-Determination into loving God and your fellow man.

Your "fallen nature" will hate you for it, but your Spirit Nature will soar to new heights of unspeakable joy and glory. Hallelujah! That's a good deal!

March 11, 2016

Today's meditation is based on the two Kingdoms: the Natural and the Supernatural.

The Natural Kingdom focuses on power, control (self determination), comfort, pleasure, etc.

The Supernatural Kingdom focuses on God's Power and Mission. This Kingdom operates out of weakness, submission, hardship, self denial, etc.

Jesus' discussion with Pilate is a great example. Pilate had never met a King like Jesus with no army or power.

Jesus told Pilate in John 18:36, "My Kingdom is not of this world. If it were, My servants would fight to prevent My arrest by the Jews. But now My Kingdom is from another place."

When Jesus was arrested in the Garden, one of His disciples cut off the ear of one of the servants of the High Priest. Jesus healed the severed ear and told His disciples not to resist. In Matthew 26:53 Jesus says, "Do you think I cannot call on my Father, and He will at once put at My disposal more than twelve legions (72,000) of angels?" Jesus submitted His will to His Father's will to be an eternal sacrifice for our sins.

The "steps of faith" in today's Jesus Calling devotional is anything that glorifies God by serving others. We usually feel inadequate for such missions. God tells us to stay close to His Power and Presence and we can walk on water. Miracles happen every day. Ask God for a miracle and keep your eyes peeled for opportunities.

March 12, 2016

Psalm 27:14, Wait for the Lord; be strong and take heart and wait for the Lord.

Waiting is one thing modern Americans hate to do.

We have trained to expect things right away.

God does not make us wait just to mess with our heads.

God uses waiting to increase our faith in Him.

Waiting usually involves something we need.

An object, an opportunity, a change in a relationship, etc.

God wants us to live in the Spirit trusting Him for our provision.

When we get tired of waiting and our faith weakens, we start operating in the flesh manipulating circumstances with our own power.

Negotiating a balance between living in the Spirit and the "world" requires focus.

Step 1: Prayer: Lord, I look to You for guidance. Give me Your wisdom on how to deal with this issue to Your glory and to the benefit of others. Then trusting and waiting on the Lord does not seem so onerous.
Pay attention because God probably wants to teach you something in the waiting.

March 13, 2016

Jesus says in John 16:33, "I have told you these things, so that in me you may have peace. In this world you will have trouble. But take heart! I have overcome the world."
We look at trouble like a boxer in a ring.
Trouble is right in front of us ready to punch us in the face. (Again)
It's a challenge to "live above our circumstances" under these conditions.
Unlike a boxing coach, Jesus can actually change the circumstances in the ring.
Jesus brings an "eternal" perspective to our problems.
All problems immediately get smaller from an "eternal" perspective.
Jesus' Presence overshadows all problems.
Getting close to Jesus replaces our fears with peace and our frustrations with joy.
It does not necessarily remove our problems but transforms them.

March 16, 2016

Every animal does its best to hide any weakness.
Weakness makes you vulnerable and less attractive.
Weakness is a blessing in God's Kingdom because it makes us look to God for provision and protection.
Our "fallen nature" loves independence (being your own God) and never wants to submit to God.

God continually says, "Hey, I am the Creator and Sustainer of everything. Maybe you should give Me a chance. I might surprise you with some blessings you could never obtain on your own."

Our "fallen nature" is very serious about projecting perfection, not weakness.

God says, "Lighten up, give it a rest and try enjoying life and Me more."

This is always MUCH harder to sustain in a crazy world.

Jesus says, "Call out My Name. I am eager to help you overcome your fears."

True peace can only be found in Jesus' Presence.

• • •

From: Shep Davis
Sent: Friday, March 18, 2016 10:57 AM
To: Preston Hipp
Subject: Re: March 16
Thanks Preston.
You are a good man
Love ya

On Mar 19, 2016, at 07:00, Preston Hipp wrote:
Shep,
Thank you for the encouraging feedback.
It is amazing how little I get.
I don't need it for my ego.
I just wonder if it is scratching anyone's itch out there.
Love, Preston

• • •

<u>March 17, 2016</u>

God knows us better than we know ourselves.
God matched up our DNA when and where He wanted for a reason.
He knows our weaknesses and loves us (Grace) anyway.
The Word of God (Bible), the blood of Jesus and the power of the Holy Spirit can transform us.
If we are willing, we can become fountains of God's love overflowing to the people around us.

Psalm 139: 1, "O Lord, You have searched me and You know me."
Read all of Psalm 139. It will bless you.

Psalm 139 English Standard Version (ESV)

Search Me, O God, and Know My Heart

To the choirmaster. A Psalm of David.
1 O Lord, you have searched me and known me!
2 You know when I sit down and when I rise up;
you discern my thoughts from afar.
3 You search out my path and my lying down
and are acquainted with all my ways.
4 Even before a word is on my tongue,
behold, O Lord, you know it altogether.
5 You hem me in, behind and before,
and lay your hand upon me.
6 Such knowledge is too wonderful for me;
it is high; I cannot attain it.
7 Where shall I go from your Spirit?
Or where shall I flee from your presence?
8 If I ascend to heaven, you are there!

If I make my bed in Sheol, you are there!
9 If I take the wings of the morning
and dwell in the uttermost parts of the sea,
10 even there your hand shall lead me,
and your right hand shall hold me.
11 If I say, "Surely the darkness shall cover me,
and the light about me be night,"
12 even the darkness is not dark to you;
the night is bright as the day,
for darkness is as light with you.
13 For you formed my inward parts;
you knitted me together in my mother's womb.
14 I praise you, for I am fearfully and wonderfully made.
Wonderful are your works;
my soul knows it very well.
15 My frame was not hidden from you,
when I was being made in secret,
intricately woven in the depths of the earth.
16 Your eyes saw my unformed substance;
in your book were written, every one of them,
the days that were formed for me,
when as yet there was none of them.
17 How precious to me are your thoughts, O God!
How vast is the sum of them!
18 If I would count them, they are more than the sand.
I awake, and I am still with you.
19 Oh that you would slay the wicked, O God!
O men of blood, depart from me!
20 They speak against you with malicious intent;
your enemies take your name in vain.
21 Do I not hate those who hate you, O Lord?
And do I not loathe those who rise up against you?

22 I hate them with complete hatred;
I count them my enemies.
23 Search me, O God, and know my heart!
Try me and know my thoughts!
24 And see if there be any grievous way in me,
and lead me in the way everlasting!

March 19, 2016

"…the depths of your being." Is your Soul.
Genesis 1: 27 says God made men and women in "His own image".
This is not about one head, two arms and two legs.
This is about our Soul and the character of God.
Genesis 3 describes how Satan tricked Adam and Eve into seriously disrupting their relationship with God.
Satan has been doing that ever since and one of his favorite tools is religiosity.
Satan tricks people into thinking they can approach God through their own efforts of obeying the law. (That's religiosity by the way.)
Spoiler Alert: This approach NEVER works. All it produces is frustration, defeat, and a negative attitude for the church and God, which is Satan's goal, so DON'T fall for it.
Jesus always comes to us in love, not condemnation.
Romans 8:1-2, Therefore, there is now <u>no condemnation</u> for those who are <u>in Christ Jesus,</u> [2] because through Christ Jesus the law of the Spirit who gives life has <u>set you free</u> from the law of sin and death.
There is a biometric trick you can use for victory over condemnation from "religiosity".
As you take a deep breath, say I am breathing in the love of Jesus.
As you breath out say I exhaling any condemnation of "religion".
This prepares you for Jesus inhabiting your thoughts, words, and behavior.

<u>March 20, 2016</u>

Today is Palm Sunday. The start of Holy Week.
The one day Jesus was publicly recognized as the Messiah.
Luke 19:37–40
When Jesus came near the place where the road goes down the Mount of Olives, the whole crowd of disciples began joyfully to praise God in loud voices for all the miracles they had seen: "Blessed is the king who comes in the name of the Lord!" "Peace in heaven and glory in the highest!" Some of the Pharisees in the crowd said to Jesus, "Teacher, rebuke your disciples!" "I tell you," he replied, "if they keep quiet, the stones will cry out."

Jesus knew He was worthy of the praise (Thanksgiving) which He was receiving by the crowd of worshippers. The Pharisees (Religiosity) told Jesus to rebuke (Stop and Correct) His disciples. Jesus said if they stop, the stones on the ground will cry out in worship to Me. The stones represent all of creation. The first chapter of the Gospel of John declares Jesus created everything. (Genesis 1 & 2) So even the inanimate objects recognize Jesus as their Creator and will praise Him.

It is easy to forget to be thankful in modern America. Drinkable water comes out of our taps. Toilets flush our waste away. We get in our cars, go to the grocery store, come back and put our food in a refrigerator or two. The parent-child relationship represents our relationship with God. (by design) We like it when our children express thanks for our sacrifices of time and money. We get annoyed when they receive the gifts with no recognition or thanks. God is the same way. (We were made in His image. Genesis 1:27)

The Holy Spirit is the second most important gift God has given us. (Jesus is #1) Without the POWER of the Holy Spirit, we would not achieve much victory over our sinful nature. That is why the Apostle Paul cried out in Romans 7:24, "Oh, wretched man that I am! Who will save me from this body of destruction? (Fallen Nature)" The answer is the blood of Jesus to cleanse our sins, the Word of God (Bible) to show us what to aim for and the power of the Holy Spirit to actually do it.

Victory comes through focus. As the saying goes, "A man is what he thinks about."
Make a Holy Week goal of thanking God for His love for you, His plan for you and His provision for you.
That will make God very happy. Yeah!

<u>March 22, 2016</u>

Trusting Jesus' love when things do not go your way.
I went to hospital for another round of chemo yesterday.
Step 1 is giving blood so the doctors can verify your body is ready to receive it.
Your "PSA" indicates the activity level of your prostate cancer.
My PSA has been floating around 27 through all the treatments.
After intense healing prayer sessions at the Men's Conference and another at a Spiritual Gifts Conference, I was really hoping to see a dramatic reduction in my PSA.
Instead, my PSA went up 55% to 42 since my last treatment 3 weeks ago.
The chemo killed one strain of the cancer, but the cancer mutated into another strain that the chemo was not killing.

"Rejoice and be thankful!" would be a challenge but....Jesus is not surprised or caught off guard by these developments.

He still loves me and has a plan that works all things together for good. (Romans 8:28)

I am still one miracle away from being healed.

Holy Week reminds us of Jesus' tremendous obedience and sacrifice to give us victory over sin and death. (Including all diseases.)

I thank Jesus for today and trust Him for tomorrow.

I am humbled by His love for me and for the world.

Psalm 95

1 Come, let us sing for joy to the Lord;
let us shout aloud to the Rock of our salvation.
2 Let us come before him with thanksgiving
and extol him with music and song.

March 23, 2016

Invitation to the Thirsty: Isaiah 55
"Come, all you who are <u>thirsty</u>,
come to the waters;
and you who have <u>no</u> money,
come, buy and <u>eat!</u>
Come, buy wine and milk
without money and without cost.
² Why spend money on what is not bread,
and your labor on what does <u>not</u> satisfy?
Listen, listen to me, and eat what is good (eternal),
and you will delight in the richest of fare.

John 14: 12–14, Truly, Truly I tell you, whoever believes in me will do the works I have been doing, and they will do <u>even greater </u>things than these, because I am going to the Father (and sending you the Holy

Spirit). [13] And I will do whatever you ask in my name, so that the Father may be glorified in the Son. [14] You may ask me for anything in <u>my name</u>, and I will do it. (Jesus came to do His Father's Will. His name equals His Father's Will.)

God loves the "Long Shot". The shot no one else can make. God loves to prove His abilities to His faithful followers.
Come to God in "joyful expectation" in submission to His Will, and anything is possible.

<u>March 26, 2016</u>

We can't wait for _____ to happen!
The longer we wait, the more tempted we are to "help" the circumstances to obtain what we want.
A famous example of this is Abraham and Sarah waiting for the birth of their God-Promised son, Isaac.
Because of Sarah's advanced age, she suggested Abraham have a child with her handmaid, Hagar.
Their impatience created a disaster you can read about in Genesis 16.
God visited Abraham and Sarah and restated His promise of a child. Genesis 18: 1–15.
After the birth of their son Isaac, which means "He laughs", 90-year-old Sarah says, "God has brought me laughter, and everyone who hears about this will laugh with me." Genesis 21:6
It is fun to laugh at yourself in hindsight but clearly we need to focus on God to have the strength and patience to wait in the future.

Isaiah 40:26 -31
Do you not know?
Have you not heard?
The Lord is the everlasting God,
the Creator of the ends of the earth.

He will not grow tired or weary,
and his understanding no one can fathom.
29 He gives strength to the weary
and increases the power of the weak.
30 Even youths grow tired and weary,
and young men stumble and fall;
31 but those who hope in the Lord
will renew their strength.
They will soar on wings like eagles;
they will run and not grow weary,
they will walk and not be faint.

Psalm 16: 11
You make known to me the path of life;
you will fill me with joy in your presence,
with eternal pleasures at your right hand.

March 28, 2016

Philippians 2:17
But even if I am being poured out like a drink offering on the sacrifice and service coming from your faith, I am glad and rejoice with all of you.

"...I (God) search for people who are able to receive in full measure."

Who are these people and what are they receiving?
These people are the ones motivated to do God's will.
Jesus repeatedly said, "I and the Father are one."
They are not one in position. God is the Father and Jesus is His Son.
They are one in purpose. Jesus came to earth to show us the Father.
Reread any of the Gospels if you are unclear about God's intentions for anyone's life.

Surrendering your will to the Father's will does not mean you have to become a missionary or a robot. There is tremendous freedom within God's Kingdom. Motivation is always at the core of one's will. Are you asking God what He wants you to do or do you forget and do whatever you want to do all the time?

There are a bunch of benefits to knowing and following God.
Galatians 5:22 tells us the Fruit of the Holy Spirit is Love, Joy, Peace, Patience, Kindness, Goodness, Gentleness, Faithfulness and Self-control.
Other benefits are increased faith, hope, strength, and miracles.
God wants to pour all these qualities into your life, but you have to pay attention to what He wants you to do to receive them in "full measure".
If you feel like you are missing it, just ask God for guidance.
He will give it to you. He is searching for people to bless.

March 29, 2016

A Time for Everything: Ecclesiastes 3:1-2

1 There is a time for everything,
and a season for every activity under the heavens:
2 a time to be born and a time to die,
a time to plant and a time to uproot, etc, etc.

There are two kinds of time.
We live in Chronos time.
24 hours in a day, 60 minutes in an hour, etc.
This is the root for chronological order.

Kairos time is the coming of an event, like a woman getting pregnant, or getting a job, etc.

We cannot rush a season, and more often than we want to admit, we cannot rush an outcome.

This reality can produce anxiety, fear and even distrust in our relationship with God.

If this is the case in your life, take each issue one at a time, and lift them up to God.

"Lord Jesus, I know you love me and have a plan for my life so I hand _____ over to You. Please give me Your wisdom and power to want Your will on this issue. I trust You to work it out. Amen."

Jesus promises your peace will increase if you do this.

John 16:33 "I have told you these things, so that in me you may have peace. In this world you will have trouble. But take heart! I have overcome the world."

April 2, 2016

"I have promised to meet all your needs according to My glorious riches."

Jesus definitely has glorious riches.

He spoke creation into existence.

He could speak a large pile of gold coins into existence if he wanted to.

Yes Lord, think of me.

"According to" is where we need to pay attention.

We crave comfort and security.

God's goal is to get rid of our sin and have a better relationship with us.

Spending a "Quiet Time" with Jesus in His Word (Bible), in prayer and in meditation is where miracles take place.

Romans 12: 2, ...but be transformed by the renewing of your mind."

Titus 3: 5, "He (Jesus) saved us through the washing of rebirth and renewal by the Holy Spirit."

Jesus washes, renews, and transforms us when we spend time with Him.

If you are not doing this every day, you are missing a tremendous blessing.

God also uses trials to drive us closer to Him.
This is a carrot-and-stick technique.
God's love for us is always the core motivation, so try not to get frustrated or angry with God. (Easier said than done.)
God uses trials to get rid of the Curse of Genesis 3: Envy, Pride, Self-Sufficiency, Selfishness, etc.
Our tendency in trials is to jump, shout and look for the closest exit door. That is a mistake.
The key to any trial is to ask, "Lord, what are You trying to do here? What do you want me to learn?"
Thank God that He loves you enough to want you closer to Him.
This will not get rid of the trial, but it will give you peace about it.
Peace in our cacophonous world is a major blessing. Amen

April 3, 2016

Genesis 1:27, "So <u>God created</u> man in <u>His own image</u>, in the image of God He created him; male and female He created them."

When Jesus created us (John 1), we were perfectly complete and had everything we needed. (Genesis 2)
Our rebellion in Genesis 3 wrecked our relationship with God.
God has been trying to "fix" us ever since.
Our lack of cooperation is the problem in the relationship.
We are pretty attached to Self, Pride, Envy, etc., "debris and clutter".
God's grace feeds our inner "yearning" to have a good relationship with Him.
If we are willing to move closer to God, He will bless us. (Prodigal Son Parable/23rd Psalm)
Do not let the crazy chaos of the world fool you into thinking God is not in control.

God always has the last word, and He will accomplish His purposes. One day, God will throw Satan, Sin, Disease, and Death into Hell and shut the door.

Then our Genesis 2 relationship (Pre-Rebellion) will be restored and we will spend eternity in God in Heaven. Oh Happy Day!

April 4, 2016

"Here I (Jesus) am! I stand at the door and knock. If anyone hears my voice and opens the door (of their heart), I will come in and eat with that person, and they with me." Revelation 3:20

"...looking for one whose heart is seeking Me."

The "seeking" has to be based on who Jesus is and what He is about. Plenty of people want to seek Jesus for His favor over *their* plans. Jesus is not into that.

He is looking for people who want to submit to Him and fulfill His mission statement.

Love the lord your God with all your heart and with all your soul and with all your mind. Love your neighbor as yourself. Matthew 22:37-38

The best way to talk and listen to God is in a quiet place with a clear mind, not jumbled with to-do lists, etc.

If you actually hear His voice, you are in a super minority (or crazy).

Pay attention to the thoughts that come into your mind as you pray and meditate.

Not all your thoughts are from God, but plenty are.

Jesus will pour out His favor on the people who seek Him in the fullness of His Truth. Amen

For the eyes of the Lord range throughout the earth to strengthen those whose hearts are fully committed to him. Second Chronicles 16:9

April 6, 2016

It is hard not to hyper-focus on the problems in your life.
It is like a white garment with a large, dark stain.
The world (and ourselves) give us a constant supply of large, dark stains.
Jesus challenges us to rise above the stains by focusing on Him.
Giving thanks to God shifts our focus away from the stain.
Giving thanks to God transforms us into a better person.
Getting close to Jesus' Presence consumes the large, dark stain from our minds.
All the more reason to give Him thanks and praise. Amen

I John 1:7, But if we <u>walk in the light</u>, as he is in the light, we have fellowship with one another, and the blood of Jesus, his Son, <u>purifies us from all sin</u>.

April 7, 2016

The modern Western mind grossly underestimates God's desire and abilities to guide every aspect of our day. We mistakenly trust in ourselves and our inventions more than God.

"The opposition you feel may be from Me, or it may be from the evil one," Christ says in today's <u>Jesus Calling.</u>
That is a statement worth pondering.
God's loves us, wants to be in relationship with us and wants to spend eternity in Heaven with us.
As a parent corrects a wayward child, God tries to draw us closer to Him.

He starts with a gentle love call. If we ignore Him, He increases the intensity of His call until He gets our attention.

This truth is a common thread in many people's spiritual testimonies. If we submit to God's love and seek His guidance, He will transform us into a beautiful new creation.

The key is to desire an active relationship with God.

Isaiah 64:8, Yet you, Lord, are our Father. We are the clay, you are the potter; we are all the work of your hand.

April 8, 2016

Opening our heart to Jesus.

Our "Spirit" loves it.

Our "Fallen Nature" wants to keep Jesus out because it knows Jesus will kill it.

Self, sin, disease and death cannot exist in Jesus' Presence.

Jesus' love consumes them like a fire consumes wood.

Even though we know this to be true, it is extremely hard to consistently deny the "Fallen Nature"..

As our "Fallen Nature" is diminished, it cries out for its own way.

Like our stomachs denied food, the "Fallen Nature" wants to command our attention.

Jesus is the answer.

Getting close to Jesus gives us power we cannot muster on our own.

Cry out to Jesus and invite Him into your heart.

Revelation 3:20, Here I am! I stand at the <u>door and knock</u>. If anyone hears my voice and opens the door (to their heart), I will come in and eat with that person, and they with me.

April 9, 2016

To the modern Western mind, releasing control of our lives to God does not make any sense. We are trained that education, technology and work will solve all our problems. Releasing a problem to God does not mean you will not be involved in solution. You will. The difference is you are honoring God as the Source of all power and wisdom in your life. Submitting to God's will, come what may. Your pride and self-sufficiency will never agree to this. Submitting to God is a lot easier when you are in a crisis and all your efforts are not working. It takes a conscious act of your will to submit to God during good times.

The key is simple. Stay focused on Jesus is God, that He loves you and has a plan for your entire life.

In Exodus 33:14-15 Moses is having a heart to heart conversation with God. Leading the Israelite nation to the Promised Land is an overwhelming task. God assures Moses that His Presence (Power and Wisdom) will go with him. Moses said, "Good, because if it does not, we are goners."
The Lord replied, "<u>My Presence</u> will go with you, and I will give you <u>rest</u>."
[15] Then Moses said to him, "If your Presence does not go with us, <u>do not send</u> us up from here."
That should be our position in our relationship with God. Lord, if you do not go with me, I am a goner.

Bonus Points: Praising God in worship has dynamic power in your spiritual life. YouTube has an enormous range of Christian music. Type in your favorite music style, and spend some time worshiping Jesus. It is guaranteed to make you feel better and the problems in your life feel smaller.

Footnote from Laura on April 8, 2017: Victoria and I heard "For King and Country", an Australian Christian band at LIBERTY University. She listens to them daily now. This was Preston and my anniversary weekend. In one of

their songs, they sing: 'We were born to run wild, live free, and love strong'.
This is the essence of Preston.

April 10, 2016

"Nothing is random in my Kingdom"
Stated in the positive.
"I have sovereign control over everything in My Kingdom."
God's Kingdom includes you and all the circumstances of your life.
If you are having a hard time believing that statement, your God is not BIG enough.
The human body has around 35 trillion cells. (That's a lot of cells!)
God knows and has control over every cell in every body.
It's hard to raise people from the dead unless you do. (Lazarus, etc.)
So why are hospitals so full?
The answer to that question requires a lot of faith.
God loves us and has a plan for our lives.
Being "Fallen" people living in a "Fallen" world creates an endless supply of trouble.
God protects us from most of it but He allows some trouble to come our way.
Romans 8:28, "And we know that in all things God works for the good of those who love him, who have been called according to his purpose."
This is where the faith needs to come in.
God has a purpose in your difficulty.
He is trying to teach you something, teach somebody around you something, etc. etc.
(Hint: He is usually trying to teach us to live closer to Him.)
There are many reasons for difficulties we will not understand until we get to Heaven.
The key is to love God and look for His will and purpose in all things.
Then God will bless you with the "Peace that passes all understanding".

That is a beautiful place to live. Amen

April 11, 2016

"The best way to handle unwanted situations is to thank Me (Praise!) for them."
That's a tall order from Jesus.
The key is to think about God's purpose in the difficulty.
In the Book of Genesis, Joseph was sold into slavery by his brothers.
After a season of great success, he was thrown into jail on false charges.
He was miraculously assigned to the highest position in Egypt under Pharaoh.
Because of a severe famine, his brothers came to him to buy grain.
Only then (Genesis 45) did Joseph realize the purposes of God.
Because Joseph recognized God's sovereign plan, he was able to forgive his brothers (release resentment) for selling him into slavery. (No small feat)
The final result was Joseph's 70 member family moved to Egypt.
Over the next 400 years they grew into a nation of over 2,000,000 people.
Your story will be lesser in scale, but the principles are the same.
Joseph stayed faithful to his God in a foreign culture with many other gods. (Like the USA in 2016)
Trusting God (Living in His Presence) reduces our resentments of the past and our fear of the future.
Then we can rejoice and be glad despite the circumstances.

In Second Corinthians 12:10 the Apostle Paul proclaims, "That is why, for Christ's sake, I delight in weaknesses, in insults, in hardships, in persecutions, in difficulties. For when I am weak (in Self), then I am strong (In God's Spirit)."

April 12, 2016

"You are forced to choose between trusting Me intentionally or rebelling, resenting My ways with you."

This problem has existed since the Fall of Man (Genesis 3).
The root of our Sin is Pride, Envy, Self-Sufficiency and Self (Being our own god).
God wants to remove the Sin Qualities from us.
It is not always a pretty process.
It usually involves some suffering to get us to realize how much we need God.
The process requires our cooperation.
Our Sin Nature never wants to cooperate because it knows the process will diminish its hold over us.
We have to use our will to choose the Path of Life that leads to God.
It is not an easy path but the rewards (Now and Eternal) are well worth the difficulty.

The lesson from Exodus 15 portrays a pattern God often uses.
God blesses us. We get a little heady that we are awesome.
Then God gives us a trial to prove we are not as self-sufficient as we think.
We fuss, grumble and cry out to God for mercy.
God is merciful and helps us with our problem. (Often miraculously)
The goal is to reduce the fussing and increase the thanksgiving.

The Waters of Marah and Elim: Exodus 15

22 Then Moses led Israel from the Red Sea and they went into the Desert of Shur. For three days they traveled in the desert without

finding water.23 When they came to Marah, they could not drink its water because it was bitter. (That is why the place is called Marah. 24 So the people grumbled against Moses, saying, "What are we to drink?" 25 Then Moses cried out to the Lord, and the Lord showed him a piece of wood. He threw it into the water, and the water became fit to drink.

April 15th & 16th

Trusting God's love and sovereignty is difficult on many fronts.
We live in a "Fallen World" of pride, greed, suffering, accidents, disease, and death. (Just to name a few)
God's goals are often the opposite of our goals.
God wants to prepare us to meet Him in Heaven.
God wants us to serve others and glorify Him during our brief time on earth.
We like comfortable, constant routines that insure our safety and provision. (Self-Sufficiency)
We like being our own gods and calling all the shots.

This is a tremendous conflict that has to be sorted out.

God Seekers must be willing to fight through the conflict.
Step 1 is trusting God's loving plan for your life.
When negative circumstances arise, (there is an endless string of these) cry out, "I trust You, Jesus!"
Resist the temptation to "fix" the situation and run through the closest exit door.
If you hang on to trusting God, He will open the door to a new world for you. (Glory to Glory)

To add to the challenge, God wants us to give Him *thanks* for our trials.

You cannot give thanks for trials unless you are convinced of God's loving sovereignty.

When you catch yourself criticizing and complaining about your life, turn to God with praise.

Praising God's goodness in the midst of trials calls down His Glorious Presence.

God's Presence transforms and renews your mind to God's Kingdom. (Romans 12 :1 -2)

That is God's ultimate goal.

Isaiah 12: 2, 3;
Surely God is my salvation;
I will trust and not be afraid.
The Lord, the Lord himself, is my strength and my defense[a];
he has become my salvation."
3 With joy you will draw water
from the wells of salvation.

Second Corinthians 3:18
And we all, who with unveiled faces contemplate[a] the Lord's glory, are being transformed into his image with ever-increasing glory, which comes from the Lord, who is the Spirit.

April 17, 2016

Humans have more distracting stimuli in 2016 than any time in the history of mankind.

It is no wonder our relationship with God suffers for it.

This calls for an act of your will.

God's desire is to have a running dialogue with you throughout the day, just like a friend.

Some prayers can be conversations.

Lord, do You think this is a good idea?

Lord, I lift this day up to You and ask for Your help.

Lord, help lower my stress level so I can have a better relationship with _____.

Etc., Etc.

One resource is to carry an index card with a Bible verse on what is troubling you.

Your favorite internet search engine should generate a healthy list of verses on most subjects.

Read the Bible verse throughout the day.

A relationship with God will decrease your burdens and increase your peace.

That is a pretty good deal.

Matthew 11:30

For my yoke is <u>easy</u> and my burden is <u>light</u>."

John 16:33

"I have told you these things, so that in me you may have <u>peace</u>. In this world you will have trouble. But take heart! I have <u>overcome</u> the world."

Psalm 112: 6, 7

Surely the righteous will <u>never</u> be shaken;

they will be remembered forever.

⁷ They will have <u>no fear</u> of bad news;

their hearts are <u>steadfast</u>, trusting in the Lord.

Isaiah 41: 10

So do <u>not fear</u>, for I am <u>with you</u>;

do <u>not</u> be dismayed, for I am <u>your God</u>.

I will <u>strengthen</u> you and <u>help</u> you;

I will <u>uphold</u> you with my righteous right hand.

April 21, 2016

The mind (and the heart) have two categories.
God gave us some of His Spirit when He created us.
Satan gave us some of his spirit when he convinced us to rebel against God.
Social graces teach us to control our tongue. (In theory)
Our minds are another matter altogether.
Thank God people cannot read minds, because it would cause a lot of trouble.
God wants to control our minds. Not like a robot but as a goal to pursue.
If we recognize God's goodness and power, and invite Him into our hearts and minds, amazing things will happen.
One of the best side effects is having peace with yourself, God, and the world.

Genesis 1:27
So God created mankind in <u>his own image</u>,
in the image of God he created them;
male and female he created them.

Genesis 3: 4, 5 "You will not certainly die," the serpent said to the woman. "For God knows that when you eat from it your eyes will be opened, and you will be like God<u>, knowing good and evil.</u>"

Romans 8:6, The mind governed by the flesh is death, but the mind governed by the Spirit is life and peace.

April 23, 2016

The first step in seeking God's will is surrendering your will.
It is human nature to want to play both sides of the fence.
We like the idea of having God on our side providing for and protecting us.

But we will resume our control to suit our needs.
You have to keep God in control if you want His direction and power.
That's just how it works.

We also need to spend time with God.
This means prayer, reading the Bible, and praising God.
YouTube has an incredible variety of hymns and modern songs.
I'm not much of a singer so I sing in my mind while I listen.
God's very nature responds to our desire for friendship with Him.
Don't give up if your time with God does not seem "delightful" at first.
Like anything, it takes a little practice to get your groove on.
The eternal benefits are worth the effort.

Psalm 16:11
You make known to me the path of life;
you will fill me with joy in your presence,
with eternal pleasures at your right hand.

• • •

From: Pringle Franklin
Sent: Saturday, April 23, 2016 10:24 AM
To: Preston Hipp
Subject: Re: April 23rd

Preston,
Great and worthwhile message in this devotional note today. If only more people would catch on. Time spent seeking and worshipping God is the foundation of sincere faith and yet many are satisfied with simply being "saved" without actually loving God.

You are an exceptional role model for other men, who both like and admire you and are therefore going to take your words more seriously. The idea came to me recently that you are being intensely purified and empowered with the Holy Spirit for eternity. I was reading <u>The Divine Conspiracy</u> by Dallas Willard and he explained that humans do not morph into higher beings after death. The opportunity for growth in character and spiritual connectivity happens here on earth, and we enter the next life with whatever we have won or earned while living in the flesh. I find that highly motivating.

Honestly I wish things were easier but you are winning a powerful spiritual battle and demonstrating to many both on earth and in heaven that the soul is victorious when aligned through love to God's will.

Your sister in Christ,
Pringle

RE: April 23rd
Sent By:
Preston Hipp On:Apr 04/24/16 8:16 AM
To: Pringle Franklin

Hi Pringle,
It is good to hear from you again.
Your spiritual insights always bless me.
This one is no exception.
I often thought of heavenly rewards but never could figure out how they work.
Dallas Willard's premise makes perfect sense.
My health is a peculiar spiritual tool.

This fall will be 8 years of fighting the cancer. I have been slowly losing through the whole process. Yet I know God's hand is upon me.

My PSA increasing dramatically after the trip to Bethel, Men's Conference and the Grace Center's Healing Conference was truly discouraging.

I have been in a no-treatment holding pattern for the last 4 weeks while my insurance company drags their feet.

My health is the worst it's ever been, but I still feel like God is going to give me a miraculous healing.

I am very touched to be a source of spiritual encouragement for some people in the meantime.

It is a great honor and privilege.

I look with great expectation into each day.

Waiting for the Lord is monotonous.

But when He shows up, you need to be ready to go.

With all my love and appreciation for you, Preston

• • •

April 24, 2016

Resting in stillness and waiting are not great American attributes.
We want it now and have become too used to constant overstimulation.
For all His enormity and power, God usually speaks in subdued tones.
He can speak with tremendous volume if the occasion calls for it.
He uses His small voice most of the time to see who wants Him and is paying attention to what He has to say.
Responding to God with trust automatically establishes a relationship with Him, because that is what God is looking for.
As our trust of God's loving sovereignty grows, our fears diminish and are replaced with peace.

Psalm 46:10
He says, "Be still, and know that I am God;
I will be exalted among the nations,
I will be exalted in the earth."

Health update: it turns out my kidneys have been creating the majority of the ill effect in my life for the last few weeks.

I do not fully understand all the nuances but the combination of past stress, current stress and stent performance added up to a problem.

I saw a PA last Friday, Oncologist on Monday, had my right stent replaced on Tuesday, got IV fluids Wednesday and went to the ER last night for blood clots.

I am very thankful for MUSC but was glad to miss a day.

In the meantime, I have not been able to start my new cancer drug, Xtandi.

I am very thankful for all of your prayers for faith, wisdom, strength, healing, and God's Presence.

<u>April 27, 2016</u>

April 27th was very appropriate for me.

Come to Me with empty hands and an open heart, ready to receive abundant blessings. I know the depth and breadth of your neediness. Your life-path has been difficult, draining you of strength. Come to Me for nurture. Let Me fill you up with My Presence: I in you, and you in Me. My Power flows most freely into weak ones aware of their need for Me. Faltering steps of dependence are not lack of faith; they are links to My Presence.

<u>May 1, 2016</u>

Today's message is good for me.

Health challenges always feel random, especially when you know how many variables are involved.

Accepting poor health as part of God's "plan" is another challenge.

I do not think God initiates poor health.

God is the God of life, healing, etc.

But God does allow poor health to exist and will use it to accomplish His purposes.

It is not an indicator of judgment or punishment, just the opposite.

God uses health challenges (all challenges) to purify us so we can have a better relationship with Him.

Part of the process is to let go of any ill will of the past and all our worries about the future.

Instead, focus on God's Presence in the present.

Doing this actually works.

If we can open our hearts to connect with God, the past and the future tend to fade into the background.

Then God's love, peace, joy, patience, kindness, gentleness, goodness, faithfulness and self-control floods into our very being.

That will improve any situation.

Luke 12:22-26

[22] Then Jesus said to his disciples: "Therefore I tell you, do not worry about your life, what you will eat; or about your body, what you will wear. [23] For life is more than food, and the body more than clothes. [24] Consider the ravens: They do not sow or reap, they have no storeroom or barn; yet God feeds them. And how much more valuable you are than birds! [25] Who of you by worrying can add a single hour to your life[b]? [26] Since you cannot do this very little thing, why do you worry about the rest?

May 5, 2016

Today's lesson is easy when everything is going well in your life.

It is no wonder the "health, wealth and prosperity" gospel is popular.

But what do you do when your life starts spinning out of control?

Or worse, when chaos comes crashing into your life from outside sources?

Then you start wondering what "control" even means.

When you admit that your strength and control have serious limitations is where your spiritual life starts getting interesting.

God has unlimited resources and He shares most of them freely.

The rain falls on the just and the unjust.

God does reserve some treasures just for the people who are seeking Him.

Faith and thankfulness are two of the key ingredients.

God wants us to trust in His character more than our circumstances.

If your circumstances are dreadful then pray, "Heavenly Father, I thank You for Your Sovereign Love. I thank you that there is a reason for this situation and that You have a plan to get me through it. Help me to glorify You, learn more about You and serve my fellow man. Amen"

If you can do this, you will obtain a peace that passes all understanding and confidence about the future.

I John 1:5–7 This is the message we have heard from him and declare to you: God is light; in him there is no darkness at all. 6 If we claim to have fellowship with him and yet walk in the darkness, we lie and do not live out the truth. 7 But if we walk in the light, as he is in the light, we have fellowship with one another, and the blood of Jesus, his Son, purifies us from all sin.

May 9, 2016

"Don't be so hard on yourself"

Being human means a steady stream of mistakes.

"Your failures can be a source of blessing, humbling you and giving you empathy for other people in their weaknesses."

In Second Corinthians 12:8–10, the Apostle Paul writes, "Three times I pleaded with the Lord to take my thorn away from me. But He said to me, My grace is sufficient for you, my power is made perfect in (your) weakness. Therefore, I will boast all the more gladly about my weaknesses, so that Christ's power may rest on me. That is why, for Christ's sake, I delight in weaknesses, in insults, in hardships, in persecutions, in difficulties. For when I (my flesh) is weak, then I am strong. (in the Spirit)"

In other words, our strong, independent, self satisfied condition hurts our relationship with our loving Father.
Mistakes, challenges and weakness open the door of our hearts to God.

Revelation 3:19–21, "Those whom I love I rebuke and discipline. Here I am! I stand at the door and knock. If anyone hears My voice and opens the door, I will come in and eat with him; and he with Me."

Romans 8:28 is a good memory verse!
God works all things together for good.

May 13, 2016

"Thank me in the midst of the crucible."
A crucible is a heavy pot used to melt ore to create metal.
The primary intent is to take out what is impure and leave in what is pure.
The end result is a pure metal suitable to be shaped into an object with a purpose.

Life always has its challenges but sometimes it is an outright crucible filled with pain, destruction, frustration, and crushing disappointment. God does NOT cause bad things to happen to people but He does allow them to accomplish His purposes.
God wants to decrease our self-sufficiency and increase our love relationship with Him.
God wants to give us His favor and blessings but not as an "add on" to our own plans. God wants to direct us to His plans and purposes, because they are better than our own plans.

When you find yourself in the midst of suffering, cry out to God to show you what He wants. Thanking and worshipping God in the midst of a trial releases God's power over the situation.

That is when things start to change for the better.

• • •

From: Preston Hipp
Sent: Monday, May 16, 2016 9:51 AM
To: Butler, Barre (Charleston)
Subject: RE: Jesus Calling

Barre, your visits always lift my spirit.

```
Thank you for your sacrifice of time to
bring love into my life.
```

Preston

From: Butler, Barre (Charleston)
Sent: Monday, May 16, 2016 11:16 AM
To: 'Preston Hipp'
Subject: RE: Jesus Calling

It works both ways. The time I'm giving you is the time you're giving me. The love I bring into your life is equal to the love you bring into mine. That being said, I get THE bonus of you sharing your faith in Jesus with me. I'm blessed.
Barre

• • •

<u>May 19, 2016</u>

"I want you to know how safe and secure you are in My Presence."
Evil, chaos, crime, selfishness, disease, Mother Nature, Murphy's Law, substance abuse, rebellion, etc., etc.
It does not take long to put together a list that challenges your faith in God's Sovereign Love.
God claims to be 100% sovereign (in control) regardless how we feel about it.
God knows trusting His sovereign power through "eyes of faith" is a challenge.
One day God will reveal Himself to us in the fullness of His Glory.
He will take Satan, death, disease, sin and everything imperfect and throw it all into to Hell for Eternity.
That's when the eternal party in Heaven starts.
In the meantime, the best thing we can do for ourselves is make a conscious effort to get as close to God's Presence as we can.
That is how we can transform negative emotions in our lives like fear into the Fruit of the Spirit. Galatians 5:22-23.
Love, Joy, Peace, Patience, Kindness, Gentleness, Goodness, Faithfulness, and Self Control.
That is where you want to live your life.

For now we see only a reflection as in a mirror; then we shall see <u>face to face</u>. Now I know in part; <u>then I shall know fully</u>, even as I am fully known. I Corinthians 13:12

<u>The Lord gives strength</u> to his people; the Lord <u>blesses</u> his people with <u>peace</u>. Psalm 29:11

Health Update: I am going MUSC this morning to get a shot of Radium 223. This is nuclear material specifically designed to attach itself to the cancer in my bones and kill it. Pain goes down, length of days and quality of life go up. I get a shot a month for six months. I am pretty excited about it. Pray for success.

May 22, 2016

Believing in God is pretty easy.

The overwhelming diversity of the earth and all life on earth points to a Creator.

Believing God has everything on earth under His Control is a more challenging faith issue.

The other end of the spectrum is that God created everything, is doing the best He can (but is overwhelmed) and will figure everything out in the end.

This one issue will determine what kind of relationship you have with God.

Good news: God loves You and wants you to see Him in all of His Fullness and Truth.

Being humans with emotions, we find ourselves all over the map.

One minute we are standing on Christ the solid rock, the next minute we are running around like Chicken Little thinking the sky is falling on our head.

Fortunately, God has a sense of humor and a LOT of patience.

The key benefit to believing in God's Sovereign Love is everything has a purpose.

Romans 8:28 states, "And we know that in <u>all</u> things <u>God works for the good</u> of those who love Him, who have been called according to <u>His purpose</u>."

This one concept is a game changer for your life.

Satan is the source of all things negative in life: Sin (Rebellion), Disease, Death, Greed, etc., etc.

God is a bazillion times greater than Satan and limits him and his influence.

The key is to not get distracted by Satan or worse yet get sucked into his power.

The way to do this is to stay as close as possible to God and His purposes for your life.

God is the best Force Field protection system there is.

Having a good relationship with God takes focus and effort, but it is the best investment opportunity you will ever have. Amen

May 28, 2016

One of the greatest blessings of my battle with cancer is all the people who have prayed with me.

A lot of people have anointed me with oil in combination with their prayers.

It is very encouraging and powerful so I welcome it every time.

One time my nephew Matt wanted to really bless me, so he poured the small bottle of oil over my head.

We laughed at the mess it made but appreciated the representation.

Jesus wants to anoint us with His Presence here on earth.

Revelation 3:20 says, Here I am! I stand at the door and knock. If anyone hears my voice and opens the door, I will come in and eat with him and he with Me.

A lot of people want to let Jesus into their Living Rooms but not the rest of the house.

They like the thought of having Him "nearby" in case something "comes up".

They do NOT want to welcome Him into their whole house because He might want to "change things".

We can get so busy shaping and controlling our lives that we miss the opportunity to be friends with the Creator of Life.

James 4:7-8,

"<u>Submit</u> yourselves, then, to God.

<u>Resist</u> the devil and he will flee from you.

<u>Come near </u>to God and He will come near to you.

<u>Wash</u> your hands, you sinners, and <u>purify</u> your hearts you double-minded."

<u>June 4, 2016</u>

Trust produces Peace.

James 1:2 states, Consider it pure joy, my brothers and sisters, whenever you face trials of many kinds.

Having "joy" in many different kinds of difficulties seems beyond our reach.

It is like loving our enemies. We know it is a worthy goal but sometimes we do not have the energy (or desire) to go there.

Zooming out to God's perspective is crucial to having victory in both of these pursuits.

We are playing a game of 100 year checkers. This game can produce a lot of worry.

Do I have enough money? Do I have all the right stuff? Some of my stuff is broken and needs repair. Am I receiving all the honor and privilege I deserve?

Most of your concerns in 100 year checkers are about your own sufficiency and preservation.

This is a direct result of the Fall (Rebellion against God) of Mankind described in Genesis 3.

God is playing Eternal Chess, and He is really good at it.

The key to chess is to stay a few moves in front of your opponent and being willing to lose some minor players to win the game.

The loss of "minor players" is much more dramatic to someone playing 100 year checkers.

This is where you have a decision to make.

You can focus on your loss or you can focus on God's love.

Sometimes the loss is so large we do not think we have the strength to endure it. Guess what. You don't.

The solution is to cry out to God for help and stay as close to Him as you can. (That's where the Power is.)

God loves you and has a beautiful plan for your life.

Surrender your will to His and you will receive peace (and even joy); glorify God and be a blessing the people around you.

God is looking forward to spending eternity in Heaven with us and He wants to accomplish great things through us on the way.

You will keep in perfect peace those whose minds are steadfast, because they trust in You. Isaiah 26:3

June 16, 2016

God the Father did not send His Son, Jesus, to die for our sins so we can do whatever we want waiting to spend eternity in Heaven with Him.

God created every human being to be unique, like a snowflake.

God built a "Destiny" of service to Him into our lives before we were even born.

True fulfillment, peace and joy come from getting close to God like you would with your best friend.

You share life together. What is on your hearts and minds. What are your challenges. What are your successes. How can I help you? How can you help me?

God can do miracles anytime He wants to and most of the time He uses people.

Sometimes God asks us to do something great. Usually it is something small that means a great deal to the person you are serving.

Warning: Most of us spread ourselves too thin. Knowing and serving God often requires letting go of something.

Are you willing to do that? It's worth it.

Ephesians 2:8-10

For it is by grace you have been saved, through faith, and this is not from yourselves, it is the gift of God and not by works, so that no one can boast. For we are God's handiwork, created in Christ Jesus to do good works, which God prepared in advance for us to do.

Micah 6:8

He has shown you, O mortal, what is good.

And what does the Lord require of you?

To act justly and to love mercy

and to walk humbly with your God.

Health Update:

I received two units of red blood cells yesterday to prepare me for my 2nd nuclear bone shot. The nuclear medicine does a good job of killing the cancer in my bones but some blood gets damaged in the process. It's still a great trade off and I am excited to get the shot. I still repeat my mantra, "I am one miracle away from being healed!"

Second Corinthians 4:16- 18 and 12:9-10 are a couple of my "Go To" verses. Your prayers, love and support carry me.

Love in Christ, Preston

2 Corinthians 12:9-10New International Version (NIV)

9 But he said to me, "My grace is sufficient for you, for my power is made perfect in weakness." Therefore I will boast all the more gladly about my weaknesses, so that Christ's power may rest on me. 10 That is why, for Christ's sake, I delight in weaknesses, in insults, in hardships, in persecutions, in difficulties. For when I am weak, then I am strong.

2 Corinthians 4:16-18New International Version (NIV)

16 Therefore we do not lose heart. Though outwardly we are wasting away, yet inwardly we are being renewed day by day. 17 For our light and momentary troubles are achieving for us an eternal glory that far outweighs them all. 18 So we fix our eyes not on what is seen, but on what is unseen, since what is seen is temporary, but what is unseen is eternal.

<u>June 18, 2016</u>

It's hard not to want to know the details of your future.
Jesus says to not worry about the future but to focus on the present.
The more we trust God with our future, the more we can enjoy our relationship with Him in the Present.
The less baggage we bring into the relationship the better.
God will meet us wherever we are, so if we have a lot of baggage, He will help us get rid of what we do not really need.
The key is always to ask God what is on His heart and how you can accomplish the purposes He has for you.

3 Praise be to the God and Father of our Lord Jesus Christ, who has blessed us in the heavenly realms with every spiritual blessing in

Christ.4 For he chose us in him before the creation of the world to be holy and blameless in his sight. Ephesians 1:3-4

"For I know the plans I have for you," declares the Lord, "plans to prosper you and not to harm you, plans to give you hope and a future. 12 Then you will call on me and come and pray to me, and I will listen to you. 13 You will seek me and find me when you seek me with all your heart. 14 I will be found by you," declares the Lord. Jeremiah 29: 11 -14

The Fight to Stay Alive

With Chester on the Battery, May 2016, about four months before the end.

Emails, text messages, & correspondence

From: Preston Hipp
Sent: Sunday, July 13, 2014 10:47 AM
To: Olivia Hipp; Delia Hipp
Cc: Preston Hipp
Subject: Summer Lowcountry Boating

Hello my sweet daughters,
We had a most excellent day boating yesterday.
My best high school buddy, Richard Hollowell is in town from China.
My other best high school buddy, David Schools, joined us.
The older you get, the more you appreciate these rare days of fellow-ship with old friends.
The rest of the crew was your mother, Victoria, Victoria Hanham and Hugo Chaplain's nephew, Harry.
And of course Chester and Dottie.
It was a classic Lowcountry "scattered showers" day with some BIG thunder heads in the mix.
It was raining lightly as I loaded the cooler.
We came close to pulling the plug on the trip but decided to forge ahead.
I packed lots of rain coats because the chances of us getting nailed were pretty good.

But as I have said your whole lives, "Hey, it's not raining battery acid. It's just water."

There was a bad rain cell over the city heading our way as we left the cyc dock.

We took off anyway and headed for "dynamite hole" below the jetties.

Fortunately, the ocean was pretty calm so it was pleasant cruising.

We had the bonus of seeing two shrimp boats trawling, which is way too rare these days.

One boat had just pulled up its nets and was throwing the by-catch overboard with the usual swarm of seagulls attacking the waters around the boat for an easy meal.

I cruised by as close as possible. What a beautiful Lowcountry scene!

Next, we set our sights on the lighthouse.

It was dead low tide so the water was thin but with an abundance of sand bars for a calm, easy anchorage.

We were approaching the lighthouse when Chester did his obligatory plunge off the bow of the boat.

The only problem was he jumped about two hundred yards from the beach.

We accused him of premature ejection and kept going.

Eventually we felt pity on him as his head go smaller and smaller on the ocean surface.

He would have made it but we turned around to get him anyway.

He was grateful but jumped off again when we got within striking distance of the beach.

He just can't help himself.

Amazingly we were the ONLY boat in sight, which always enhances a beach experience, especially in mid-July.

The scenery was exotically beautiful. The sky was slightly overcast with a huge array of clouds on the horizon.

We could see the rain pouring out of monster anvil-head cumulus clouds pounding

different parts of the mainland. We never got a drop rain the whole day.

Victoria and Harry swam/walked across the two hundred yard lagoon to the base of the lighthouse.

Some dolphins worked their way within 10' of them.

The other events were pretty typical of our trips.

Lots of ball throwing for the dogs, bocce, beer, food, swimming, talking, laughing, enjoying being alive in the Lowcountry.

Two other boats showed up after a couple of hours but we ended up knowing both parties so that added to the fun.

We HATED to leave but an invitation to the Donaldson's in the Old Village of Mt P for a full moon dock party required we move on.

The standard afternoon sea breeze never kicked up because all the rain was keeping the mainland cool.

The ocean was a mill pond with some rolling swells. Very rare conditions for a July afternoon.

We ran back to town just off the beach bathed in the afternoon sun. So peaceful and mellow.

We smiled as we passed Cummins Point near Ft. Sumter with the usual crowded boat circus in full swing. No thanks.

The jet dock proved its worth one more time for ease of boating.

We hosed the dogs and boat down and loaded the dock cart.

There was a buzz of activity in the CYC basin as everyone was concluding their day.

A fisherman was cleaning a large cobia at the fish station. What a treat for him.

We walked through it all thinking, "If anyone had more fun than we did, they had a hell of a day."

The only thing that would have made it better is if the two of you were with us.

And we needed Becca and the GoPro to do another awesome documentary.

Lord God, We thank You for Your goodness to us. Amen

Laura added her thoughts:

What makes me remember this boat outing is the intense purple thunderheads and Preston's expertise in hanging out around the rows of rocks of the jetties where one false move or whip of a rising storm could nail us. It was actually the most sheltered position in which to be. Only the Prince of Tides would have been thinking that the dangerous looking jetties were the safe haven. The resulting great day was Victory grabbed from the jaws of defeat! We met up with the Kulzes on the back side of Morris Island. It is that inner pride in who I was married to that I remember the most. Preston was proud of having circumnavigated James Island as well. He was in his element, and I as I had grown up. I was living in the manner to which I had grown accustomed, never a dull moment on the water.

● ● ●

Sent by: Preston Hipp
To: Pringle Franklin

Jan. 1, 2015

My health is doing OK. No major issues like chemo or surgery but between using a catheter to pee, ostomy to poop and scar tissue pulling on my gut all the time I am constantly reminded of my mortality. I choose to use it as a spiritual "hair shirt" to remind me of my dependency on God. It works really good.

I am on two different testosterone blocking drugs. Thankfully I do not have 95% of the potential side effects.

I do feel puny, get dizzy occasionally and my toes usually feel numb but it keeps me focused on God.

God does meet you at your point of need. I feel spiritually blessed!

Love, Preston

Sent By:
Preston Hipp
To: Pringle Franklin

On: 01/30/15 3:47 PM

God continues to move here. More men coming to Bible Study.

One cool story. Matt Miller, a fellow from Bible Study, has been going through a challenging time financially.

He has been a "Seeker" and God's hand is mightily on him.

I grabbed Matt and another friend after Bible Study and asked Marnie (Kerrison) if we could sneak into the prayer room for 5 minutes while she waited on the rest of her crew.

I knelt at the altar, asking Matt to join me. I asked the other man to pray over Matt.

When we were done, Matt said he felt a lot of heat coming from our friend's hand through his heavy coat into his shoulder. Matt said his knees were healed of chronic pain he has had for many years after tearing them up playing college basketball.

The really cool part was we did not know his knees bothered him and not a word/prayer was said about his knees.

We serve an awesome God! Amen

Love in Christ, Preston

• • •

From: Preston Hipp
Sent: Saturday, March 7, 2015 7:26 AM
To: Matthew Miller
Subject: The gift of today

Matt,
I was thinking about you as I helped clean out Laura's mother's house yesterday.
It is difficult work emotionally and physically.
I pray God's favor over you.

I had a wonderful quiet time setting this morning.
The rising sun illuminated the setting full moon.
I prayed God would give you a day as beautiful.
Love in Christ, Preston

● ● ●

FW: Chemo report
Sent By: Preston Hipp On:Dec 12/22/15 12:42 PM

Here is the "Day in the Life" of Round 3
Chemo Update : Round 3

Laura had a conflict of a tour for ten people so her brother, Bunky, was my handler for the day.
He picked me up at 7:45am sharp.
Delia and Victoria said they wanted to go but I had my doubts since they are not morning people.
I was having a "Quiet Time" (Good head preparation) in my office when I heard Delia's alarm go off, a deep groan and the bed covers peeling back.
She even managed to get Victoria out of bed. No small feat.

Victoria was pretty comatose and grumpy but was trying hard to be a trooper.

We checked in and waited for my turn in the blood lab. The waiting room was already full.

Once you give blood you have an hour to kill, so we went to the café and got some breakfast, which was a nice break.

Thank You Lord for daily bread.

Then back to the waiting area to see my Oncologist, Dr. Lilly.

My good friend and fellow St Philippian, Susan Clarkson Keller, was filling in for Dr. Lilly's nurse, Carol.

Crossing paths with a "Super" Christian like Susan is always a good omen and source of strength.

Thank you Lord for that blessing.

It was wonderful to have Delia and Victoria to hear Dr. Lilly.

Their confidence in the "Plan" increased hearing Dr. Lilly's wisdom and competence.

I just had another CT Scan last Friday to clarify an inflammation issue I am having with my left ureter.

The CT Scan is chopped into about 30 slices of your body.

The doctor can literally scroll through your body with the roller ball on his mouse.

You can't make heads or tails of the images unless the Doctor tells you what's what.

The slides look like a series of inkblot tests a psychiatrist would use.

You get a little nervous scrolling through the images because you might inadvertently blurt out some dark secret hidden behind a locked door in your subconscious.

The inflammation was still there. Dang it, no perfect solution.

They called my Urologist for his opinion. Kidney numbers look good. No action - future monitoring.

I was OK with "future monitoring" because replacing the stent in my ureter was an option.

No thank you. Been there; got extra T-shirts.

My lifelong buddy Barre Butler was patiently waiting in the hallway keeping his perfect attendance intact.

We checked in at the Infusion Lab and did some more waiting.

The Infusion Lab presents a problem for my entourage because they have a one-visitor-at-a-time policy.

Victoria came back with me. We got an end unit with a window and a little more privacy.

My Infusion Nurse, Mary, was a wonderfully pleasant veteran who made the process look easy.

Thank You Lord for those blessings.

Victoria and I had a great visit. Then she went to go get Delia.

Delia and I had a great visit. Then she and Victoria walked home.

Thank You Lord to live within walking distance of our hospital.

Barre and Bunky came back for a visit. We tried hard but were not particularly quiet.

Bunky and Barre are two of the funniest, upbeat people I know.

86 years of combined friendship provided plenty of laughs.

The nurses do their best to bend the rules but they know their supervisors are not deaf.

They eventually say someone has to go and it can't be me.

Bunky takes a turn in the waiting room and rolls back in after an appropriate wait.

More stories and laughing. I think I hear one of my neighbors turning up the volume on "The Price is Right".

I had to go to the bathroom which requires unplugging and rolling your infusion stand with you.

My neighbors look at me with curiosity. Who is this person doing all the yakking and laughing in the chemo lab?

My oldest daughter shows up during her lunch break to maintain her perfect attendance.

Lord, Thank You for all three of my daughters being with me today.

The day flies by. It is time to go home before you know it.

I do get a shot in my arm and a shot in my ass as parting gifts. Life's a package deal, folks.

God, family, friends and the dedicated souls at the hospital have seen me through another session.

PS: There are about 37 trillion cells in the human body. That's a lot of cells.

God knows each cell individually by name. Same with stars, people, etc.

He has total control over each cell. He knows which ones are naughty and nice.

The same power Jesus used to give man life (Genesis 2:7) and raise the dead (John 11) is still available today.

God's love (1st John 4:8) is a consuming fire (Hebrews 12:29) that sooner or later will destroy every cancer cell in my body and restore me to perfect health. Eden in Genesis 2. The New Jerusalem in Revelation 22.

Thank you for your prayers for healing in the here and now.

Merry Christmas! Emmanuel (God with us) is born in Bethlehem.

Laura's PSS on why she was not with me :

A lady on Laura's tour whose lack of warmth and off-putting attitude in the beginning of the tour later texted her that among many things she admired was the way Laura was able to weave faith and history up to the present and into the future with quotes from the Founding Fathers and scripture. These were unchurched folks with teenage daughters with whom Laura had a breakthrough by the Holy Spirit. This return on her sacrifice of not being with Preston was the feedback that compensated for the separation. Romans 8:28

• • •

From: "Preston Hipp"
Sent: Monday, January 25, 2016 5:03:20 PM
Subject: FW: Bethel Church

Laura and I made a last minute dash out to Bethel Church in Redding, California for a healing conference. Here is a brief description. Love, Preston

Subject: Bethel Church

Report from Redding, CA:

We have taken over the one bedroom apartment of two transplanted Charlestonians, Zac Arnold and Edwin Smythe. They gave us their bedroom and relegated themselves to their sleeper sofa. Laura and I considered a B&B but wanted to spend as much time with these guys as possible. Edwin has cooked a full breakfast both mornings so it has been a B&B.

I have not been cured of cancer (yet) but I have been blown away by the power, spirit, teaching and miracles of Bethel Church. We were double blessed to come the weekend of a large Healing Conference held in Redding's Civic Auditorium with speakers Randy Clark, Tom Jones and Bill Johnson. (God had a plan even in our spontaneity.) Their wisdom and testimonies of healing are mesmerizing. Redding's Auditorium holds 4,000 people and it was packed. The worship music is superb and the level of enthusiasm is hard to describe. Bethel's School of Spiritual Healing has around 1,700 students from around the world. Their hunger to know God and be healing ministers of His power is intense. Everyone is upbeat, encouraging and expecting miracles. Lots of miracles did occur at the conference.

In addition to the conference, anyone can come to Bethel Church every Saturday to be prayed for. We arrived at 9:30am and the parking lot was packed. There were lots of volunteers and everything was beautifully organized. The students that prayed for me were a young man from Germany and a girl from Switzerland. They poured their hearts into me and I could feel God's love and power.

We went to the pizza restaurant where Edwin works for lunch. It is owned by a member of Bethel Church who encourages the employees to minister to the customers. They pray over the dough and food. Praying and spiritual discussions are normal activity. There are many stories of miracles of healing for gluten and dairy intolerance.

We are going to dinner tonight at Zac's host family's home.

We are looking forward to seeing everyone soon. Love, Preston

• • •

RE: February 2nd
Sent By: Preston Hipp
On: 02/02/16 9:03 AM
To: pringle franklin

I did Round 5 of chemo yesterday.
Each experience is so different.
I was in an infusion room with 3 other patients.
One was a female red neck from the country near Moncks Corner.
She was there with her daughter.
The African American man across from her was a delightful, old-school scoundrel from James Island.

Their conversation comparing notes on cigarette and alcohol usage was extensive.

Then they got into peculiar things they have eaten before: snake, squirrel, raccoon, etc.

Laura came in later and got in the middle with all her favorite garden and God stories.

Everyone got along beautifully. It was a lot of fun and helped pass the time.

It was a slow day. We did not finish until 4:00pm.

The pharmacy will not start mixing your chemo until you finish the 3 pre-bags.

That alone takes an hour.

I feel fine. We are going to try skipping my shot that tricks my body into making white blood cells.

The side effects of the shot are as bad or worse than the chemo, so I am happy to try it.

Pray my body will keep a reasonable amount of wbc's (white blood cells) around and not get an infection.

I was sorry to hear of your mother's purse snatching but was VERY impressed with her mental acumen to describe her attackers and their getaway car.

Yay! For the police to apprehend them so quickly. Remarkable! Thank you Lord! Use this experience to change the path of these young men.

When do you come home? They are wrapping up Colonial Lake. Yay!

.....Gotta' run. Love in Christ, Preston

• • •

From: Butler, Barre
Sent: Thursday, May 12, 2016 3:21 PM
To: Preston Hipp
Subject: I Long For Serenity

I know, seems like a strange subject line. My father-in-law's password to get on his computer was "I long for serenity." Of course, Fran and Dixon think that was a dig about their mom, Tut. Nothing is serene when Tut's about. Why am I going on about this? Because Ian Walker told me yesterday how he happened to drive by your house just as you were sitting down on the porch to have your lunch. He told me he had a wonderful visit for almost an hour.

All I could think of was how I wouldn't want somebody watching me eat, for an hour.

I'm sure it was all ok to good to great, but sometimes, a little peace and quiet and/or solitude can fill that need of "longing for serenity." Bottom line, I hope you have those moments when they're needed the most. I love you and I'm praying for you, right now.
Barre

From: Preston Hipp
Sent: Thursday, May 12, 2016 3:27 PM
To: Butler, Barre (Charleston)
Subject: RE: I Long For Serenity

Ian is a good friend. No trouble at all. He is a character but one of the more interesting people you will ever meet. Ask him about hitchhiking around the world. Thanks for watching out for me. Love, Preston

From: Butler, Barre (Charleston)
Sent: Thursday, May 12, 2016 3:39 PM
To: Preston Hipp' Subject:
RE: I Long For Serenity

Glad to hear it was all good. As for Ian, I agree. He is a character and I enjoy his company. I don't know him well enough to know any hitchhiking stories, but if you recommend it, I'll ask him next time I see him; which will probably be lunch tomorrow at the Back Bar. Speaking of which, I want to go to lunch with you. I can pick you up or I can bring it to your porch. But, you have to tell me when it's good for you!
Hug-Hug!
Barre

• • •

From: "Preston Hipp"
To: "franklin pringle"
Sent: Thursday, August 11, 2016 2:08:17 PM
Subject: RE: prayer for you

It's a season, not a sentence....has been helpful to me lately.

God still loves me and is using my suffering for His purposes.
Thank you for your prayers and encouragement. Preston

• • •

Text message conversations between two old friends: Preston and George Kanellos. There are gaps in the correspondence because often they spoke on the phone. However, the texts say a lot.

August 20, 2015

From Preston: Thank you for your love and support. I appreciate your steadfast friendship and never wavering commitment to the cause of Christ.

From George: Two way street Brother.

From Preston: Pure Grace.

• • •

Nov 16, 2015

From George: My thoughts turn towards you this morning, Preston. As we face the day and the things that lie ahead, let us look with confidence to the one who created us, with an unworldly assurance that He is with us and will do in us that which He pleases. My continuous prayer for you is that your cancer treatment will be effective and that God will fight the internal battle for the cells that are destructive.

This summer you mentioned your boat being out of commission and thought the lack of it in your life would give you more focus on the Lord. The joys of life grow dim in light of the eternal. Enjoying the pleasures of life and being steadfast in our faith continue to vie for our attention and affection. We can rest assured that God is working His purpose in our lives at this moment at 7:35 AM and will be at 7:50 and at 8:00 and always.

Further my prayer is that despite cancer, you will regain wellness, that you will mount up with wings as eagles, that you will run and not be weary and that you will walk and not faint.

• • •

March 26, 2016

From George: Preston, I have been thinking about you today. The intensity of the Resurrection moves me to my knees. I am humbled at the birth in a stable and now this: death on a cross... nails, wounded side, gall to drink.... This Jesus, King of the Jews. How Divine and how it moves His followers to continue on. What a good life we have following Jesus, serving God and having the Spirit breathe in us new life every day, every moment, every breath.

I am grateful for your breathing by the goodness and mercy of our Father....rejoice, this Jesus will not be here in the tomb tomorrow, He will be risen. We have the same hope. Love to you, Laura and your three graces.

March 27, 2016

From Preston: Amen Brother! Your message reminds of the time we spent together in our 20s. Happy Easter!

●　●　●

April 25, 2016

From George: Count it pure joy, Preston, when you face these trials.... This testing of your strength is producing for us the observer, a wealth of fortitude. Your strength becomes ours.... This humble observer leans more fervently on the cross as do a multitude. I am aware of how frustrating this process, this course you are enduring... Be strong brother.... Your endurance is an everlasting testimony... I praise God for you and your light in a dark world. At a point, the Father's light will be the brilliance ... The perfection.

I do not wish to be a fool as Job's advisors.... Lending foolish words to you....Only a dull friend who loves Jesus. ... and you.

April 26, 2016

From George: Praying that your procedure goes well today and that you will feel much better.... Love to Laura and your 3 graces.

From Preston: Thank you Brother. Tough stretch of road.

• • •

May 23, 2016 -- (Preston's birthday)

From George: Preston, I find myself waiting for Terminix to spray the house. They may be late, and it will cross over to your evening fête. One of the main reasons that I traveled here today was to see you on your birthday. May I visit you tomorrow ... mid morning? I am sending you the happiest of good wishes.

> `Your presence in my life is one of my greatest blessings. You are my closest friend.`

I love your Godly attitude.... it enriches me and so many others beyond what small or shallow words I could write. I breath prayers for you through my days for your wellness to return. I pray we can cook fish for breakfast on the beach next year and think on that Galilean who did the same many years ago. Into His hands do I commit my petitions for you, and I raise my own in praise to the Father in thanks for the man Preston Hipp...

May 24, 2016

From George: I am praying for you.

From Preston: Thank you Brother. Taking more pain meds and feeling better.

• • •

May 28, 2016

From George: Mark 5 is my prayer for you today.... "a certain woman,
which had an issue of blood twelve years, And had suffered many
things of many physicians, and had spent all that she had, and was
nothing bettered, but rather grew worse, When she had heard of
Jesus, came in the press behind, and touched his garment. For she
said, If I may touch but his clothes, I shall be whole. And straightway
the fountain of her blood was dried up; and she felt in her body that
she was healed of that plague. And Jesus, immediately knowing in
himself that virtue had gone out of him, turned him about in the
press, and said, Who touched my clothes? And his disciples said unto
him, Thou seest the multitude thronging thee, and sayest thou, Who
touched me? And he looked round about to see her that had done
this thing. But the woman fearing and trembling, knowing what was
done in her, came and fell down before him, and told him all the
truth. And he said unto her, Daughter, thy faith hath made thee
whole; go in peace, and be whole of thy plague."

See you at noon. George

From Preston: Thank you Brother. Looking forward to seeing you for
lunch.

From George: Preston, thanks to you and Laura for a lovely day. I will always hold dear to my heart these times we have together. I am at Folly with the house shedding rain as it has for so long and reading Pringle's book… What a perfect combination. Your friendship is life affirming… I love your pragmatic approach to the things of today and tomorrow…this more than fortuitous; meeting with you in your study gives me hope. You are a bright diamond that shines in the dark night for me.

From Preston: I am glad we could spend some time together in my Prayer Room at home. It is a great spot to draw close to God. Our Spiritual Pilgrimage continues. I will pray for healing for you in the areas we discussed. All my love, Preston

May 30, 2016

From Preston: Good morning Brother, Sorry I missed your call. Try again.

May 31, 2016

From George: Preston, I am at the airport and will soon be blasting off to work…. straight to the office. It was exceptional spending time with you, brother.

There are dark clouds on the western horizon this morning, promising cleansing rain. As with you, dark horizons are so eternally bright. Going back to Noah, people mocked his insight. Floods came as did the rainbow and new life and exciting prospects. As Noah and his family came through the storm, it is my prayer for you today. I could say it was against all odds that Noah, et al, pulled through, but it was God's intent all along. I await with anticipation, the dove and the olive branch being delivered to your extended hand. Grace, peace, love, and healing to you.

From Preston: Thank you Brother. Christian fellowship is always sweet and encouraging. It was good to catch up and know how to pray for you and your family. Love in Christ, Preston

• • •

June 2, 2016

From George: Hi Preston, I had a decaying tooth pulled today... Infected but relieved to be rid of it.... Point being, when the body is not as it should be, there is pain, as my tooth was being extracted I had this picture of your cancer being radically pulled from your body. I am praying for that radical extraction of the cancer in your body. Your devoted friend and prayer partner, George

From Preston: Even now the pain is only a part of the healing. The Fellowship of Suffering with Christ. It is humbling to say the least.

From George: Yes it is and I pray for the pain to lead to a glorious healing in your body...for the all-powerful Spirit to breath life into you as God breathed in Adam's nostrils and he lived.
I pray it for you and that the testament of your renewed body will cause those who live on the periphery of knowing God to be moved to loving the Eternal and Divine. I pray that your life will rock the core of so many. I pray that it is as radical as the splitting of stones. I ask it in The Name of Jesus.
Hang on brother and let the wonder of God and his work astound the world.

From Preston: Ba-Boom!!! Yes Lord.

• • •

June 7, 2016

From George: Hi Preston. How are you feeling today? With you in prayer.

June 8, 2016

From George: Perhaps there is no such things as chance phone dialing. Your brief call a moment ago is only affirmation of the goodness of God, the joy of celebrating Delia's birth in her twenty-first year and an enormous blessing to me.

From Preston: Amen Brother! Never underestimate God's Sovereign love.

June 10, 2016

From George: Hello Preston. The work week is now past. There is still something leftover from childhood that makes the weekend magical. I am thinking about you and have wondered how I could have a friend in my life like you. So grateful ... So blessed and so hopeful for a friendship that will continue into our old age.

Do give Delia my love especially and tell her how glad I am to see this dear and beautiful child blossom into such a lovely young lady....she was stunning as a young girl and has matured in the most delightful way. As long as I live and breathe, your girls (all 4) will be precious to me.

June 12, 2016

From Preston: Hi George, God has blessed me with girl power. I have learned so much from them and am a better person for it.

• • •

July 8, 2016 *(Editor's note: exactly two months before Preston would pass away.)*

From George: Hi Preston, I am glad you are home. Although your hospital stint was necessary, it is very weakening to the body as well. Being home is such a comfort and is the best therapy. God's plan for quiet resting place: My people shall dwell in a peaceful habitation, and in sure dwellings and in quiet resting places. (Isaiah 32:18).

I have been blessed beyond measure in having you as my friend. I have not grown weary in pleading your cause to God returning you to health... I have grown ever closer to God because of your condition and the eternal bond I have in your friendship is refined. I love you dear brother.

As you go through your day and in the night watches, may the peace of God bring you even more joy, and as the hart pants for the water-brooks...so may your soul pant even more for God. You are setting an example for us, your family and friends.

I am praying for your life as I breathe.

From Preston: Thank you Brother. This has been an arduous journey. Thank you for your prayers and love.

• • •

Laura wrote two lengthy handwritten letters, giving detailed updates to their support community in June and August 2016. The following are excerpts:

June 8, 2016

Dear friends:

As our miracle baby, Delia Joyce Wichmann Hipp, turns 21 this day, I am so excited that my beloved lives! Preston at 6'3" is admittedly in desperate need of weight, teetering between 156 and 160 pounds, but he is up and about some, getting priorities accomplished. A body in motion stays in motion! When he eats and is up, I am up, singing songs of victory! "Let the people be glad! Our God reigns!" Victoria, a rising senior in high school, is 18; Olivia, in her own Charleston apartment, is 23.

"He trains our hands for battle." I use my hands to prepare food for Preston that he will enjoy, for which he will have an appetite. He does not want to chew too long or have food too long in his mouth as "it turns to cardboard".

● ● ●

Heaven has become more real to me, and my sense dreams have become more vivid. The veil grows thinner between this world and eternity. Scriptures have become alive and applicable as if they were saying, "Put me to the test." They have become windows into the greater reality of the Kingdom of God, the keys to unlock victorious living in earthy trials. Not that I would have said yes to any of it, if asked: it is no picnic! But gardens are not made by singing "oh! how beautiful" while sitting in the shade.

Somehow the pruning we experience is to teach us greater love and relationship with our Lord. "He must increase; I must decrease," as realized by John the Baptist. It must be our heart cry as we age and lose our youth. These shortcomings of bodily functions remind us we are nearing Heaven's shores. Preston says he can't wait. I say, "Lord, you can have him for eternity. His three daughters Olivia, Delia, and Victoria need him for these transitional yard to adulthood. I need to be with my husband and father of my children, for whom I prayed and fasted and journaled for years before we were married and before I even knew him."

It is plain to see that opposites attract. Preston and I are living examples. He can take only so much animation and exuberance from me. "Indoor voice," he says, when I get too excited. It is hard to keep a lid on it when you are programmed to proclaim the great things the Lord hath done. Preston likes to hear it but in less detail and in lower volume. I am still in training as a newlywed; we have been married only 28 years!

The great thing is we are still on the honeymoon! I see it as a miracle, the biggest part being that Preston Hipp loves Laura Wichmann, asked me out of all the world to marry him, and still prefers my company despite our different personalities. I still feel honored and surprised when he reaches for my hand. He repeats, "in sickness and in health" in thanksgiving that I am there for him. It is as if that line of our vows is being proofed in the Refiner's Fire.

Preston's body is like Michelangelo's sculpture depicting Jesus in Mary's arms, the *Pieta* in St. Peter's. We were very moved by this work when we toured the Vatican when our children sang there with St. Philip's choir. Like Jesus, Preston is all skin and bones, angular and sculptured. Beautiful. Moving. Pitiable. To be honest, when he gently caresses me in the night, I have a momentary shudder, not recognizing the feel of his limbs. He has lost fat all over, even his lips. He has lost muscle tone. He is like a shadow of his former self. Yet he is alive and has come through critical weeks where we were on the tight rope of life praying he would HOLD FAST!

....The fruit of the labor of all Preston's loved ones who pray for him, who bring in wonderful food, who visit to cheer and to bless, is that Preston lives! He has returned from the brink several times with kidney issues, then liver issues, then a troubling red blood cell count, and fevers and crushing pain. The day after he turned 57, it was as if the pain doubled. He had no appetite and had trouble keeping down the little food he would eat. The oncologist allowed him to double his pain medication, which has helped get it under control.....Where we really are that matters is more spiritual than medical. We know that our God is worthy of whatever Refiner's Fire we go through here. He is also Mighty to Save.

.....No matter what, I willfully intend to bless the Lord at all times. His praises shall indeed continually be in my mouth. When I seem boastful, let it be known that my soul shall boast in the Lord!...As Renny Scott said, I am a proclaimer!

It is a choice of focus...."Have I not commanded you? Be strong and courageous! Do not be terrified. Do not be discouraged. For the Lord thy God will be with thee whithersoever thou goest." Joshua 1:9

> ....Am I not blessed to be in love with Preston, still to be on the honeymoon, and to be the one who he loves?

There are still many women who would line up for the position. We have received so many blessings, both in our marriage and family, as well as in our current trial. Thank you for standing in faith with us.

Love always,

Laura Wichmann Hipp

August 2016

Dear friends:

Preston is at Bible Study this morning. This outing is stupendous as you would realize if you could see him. The Friday morning Men's Bible Study has been perpetuated for 25 years by Preston as the facilitator at St. Philip's at 7 a.m. Once they reach 20 men, they divide in two with the understanding that a cell is not healthy unless it reproduces by dividing. There are many men's cell groups Bible Studies at St. Philip's consequently.

….This morning, I was reading my 1984 journal to Preston and came across a handwritten letter from my mother in her beautiful, very English-style cursive. She wrote:

> I have worried about you, so much, for so long and now, suddenly, Jesus has blessed me with the knowledge, (I mean the real knowing and believing) that He does indeed have your life in His hands, and that He *will* give you the very best.

That was tucked into my 1984-85 journal where I poured my heart out writing about my realizing that Preston might be "the One". I wrote of going on a retreat to Kanuga in Hendersonville, N.C., where I had been a counselor at the camp and where I met Joanna Drake. Joanna

Laura Wichmann and Preston Hipp, during their engagement, 1988. In her letter written in the summer of 2016, Laura wrote that she and Preston were "still on the honeymoon".

Drake, John Macmurphy, and Preston Hipp later worked together at the Charleston County Tax Assessor's Office. Joanna invited Preston onto our family boat, *Mobjack,* to meet another Christian girl at the Rockville Regatta 1984.

I wrote (of Kanuga), "Joanna and climbed to High Rocks…..I wore my red ankle weights which my loving boyfriend gave me to remind me that he loves me and cares about my body. "I love your body. I love your body too much. I just think you need more exercise." Preston told me if he were to marry me, he'd whip my body back into shape after having a baby! I told him he should not tease me like that about marriage or he would have me thinking in that vein. "Lord, keep me from thinking, planning, or anticipating marriage with Preston," I wrote. "I don't want to marry a non-Episcopalian anyway. I don't want to think about it."

When he did ask me to marry him Christmas Day 1987, I answered that I would have to think about it. He was incredulous. "What have you been thinking about for four years? Don't tell me you haven't been thinking about it."

But when we went to his parents for Christmas Dinner and they had me booked to go with their family to the Cayman Islands, I had to tell them I was still thinking about Preston's proposal; Big Charley respected that response from me and said, "It *is* something to think about."

I am glad I did not think about it longer than Christmas Day. Little did either of us envision that Preston's strong and healthy body would be the one to deal with being racked with pain and sickness. We are in the season of marriage where the vows "to love and to cherish in sickness and in health" are transforming our lives together. As Terrell Glenn said in counseling before our marriage, the vows cover all the

Preston with his parents, Delia Joyce Preston Hipp and Charles Rucker Hipp, Sr., on his wedding day, April 9, 1988.

variables. It is marriage that makes the love, not love that makes the marriage. The commitment of marriage makes that love, even though the seasons vary and the tide ebbs and flows.

Believe it or not, this is a high tide of love. "Sweeter and sweeter as the days go by; oh, what a love between my (husband) and I. I keep falling in love with him, over and over, and over and over again." I hear the words of praise and appreciation that in dating my romantic heart longed to hear. God always answers prayer. Preston taught our Young Professionals Bible Study that there are four D's to answered prayer. God may DO it, DENY it, DELAY it, or DO IT DIFFERENTLY. This deeper love and words of affirmation that I looked for early on in our relationship I am now receiving as I nurse him, read to him, prepare and cut his food for him, pray and weep with him — I do most of the weeping. But I sing to him and to the Lord as well.

Preston told our Young Professionals Bible Study that every one of the Wichmanns in my family has as their love language "words of affirmation". That is how we give love. But I said for Preston it is "gift giving", like his father Big Charley who paved a well-worn path to Croghan's Jewel Box on King Street for Joyce in which path Preston has followed. But for Preston his love language is also "acts of service". As a Southern Gentleman and a Christian man, love, duty, providing and protecting are so closely interwoven that there cannot be one without the other in Preston Hipp. He has worked hard to go to the office in the morning, putting one foot in front of the other, an amazing feat theses last few months as his body grows more frail.....

This season of our lives where the love is at high tide is, consequently, God answering prayer *differently.*

Preston is on the receiving end of "acts of service" on a deeper level, which registers to him as receiving love. He, therefore, responds more deeply with "words of affirmation and appreciation", my love language.....

Praise God that I have the opportunity to show Preston love by "acts of service".....With his body being encumbered by clogging nephrostomy tubes and a colostomy and the accompanying bags that render life a burdensome and troubling load, Preston says he "can't wait" for Heaven. And yet, when I asked him alone what he would say if the angel asked if he was ready to enter into the pearly gates, he said without hesitation, "No, I need to go back for Laura. She waited for me." Only those like my mother and father and brother, and my Salt & Light Bible study friends from college and high school and my single years know how diligently I prayed for "the One". My diary knows.

I simply cannot do without Preston. I talk with his mother in Heaven and ask how she can be in Heaven where there is no sorrow and yet see her son racked with pain and true baggage of this world. I clearly heard her answer: "It is part of your love story." She sees the beauty being produced out of this Refiner's Fire, what is pure and of good report.

.....As strong and as ever-present our faith is to help in times of trouble, nothing prepares us to see our beloved Preston looking so frail and thin. Morphine helps but renders him sleepy. He has spells of staying awake while I read to him....If Preston can keep holding onto life until cooler weather, maybe he will revive. *Dum Spiro Spero*, While I breathe, I hope, is our South Carolina motto.

Thank you for believing, loving, and reading!

Laura Wichmann Hipp

• • •

From brother-in-law Bunky Wichmann, August 2016 (written before
Bunky departed on a trip to Italy, about a month before Preston died.)

P-Tone,

I enjoyed our short visit yesterday --- even with all of its interrup-
tions. I am sorry that I didn't make better use of the short time we
had together, realizing now that it very well may be our last time
on this earth together. I suppose I left things undone and unsaid
in hopes that you would be here when I return. I should have said
more and I should have let you know that you are one of the THE
most influential people in my life. You have helped to shape me
into the person I am today. I should have hugged you longer, I
should have told you how special you are to me and how much I
truly love you.

Believe it or not I pray for things. I mostly pray that God will help
me to overcome my own failings and inadequacies (It's almost always
about me). Lately my focus is slightly different - though there is still a
strong emphasis on me when you get right down to it. I pray that God
will be kind and gentle with you. I pray that Laura will continue to be
resilient and strong -- as she has been.

I pray that the time you have left remaining with us will be spent with
the people YOU wish to be with and doing the things you can do, and
want to do. I pray that your girls will have the faith and the trust in
God that you and Laura do. I also pray that I will see you again.

I can't help but feel completely selfish and guilty for taking off to
Italy to have FUN while I leave you here to suffer and wither. I am
leaving you to carry this burden without my tiny hand to help lift
and ease your load - and it is not fair. To help ease my conscience,
I bathe myself in the memories of all the many good times we have

had together and how VERY important you have been to me for more than 32 years now. Truly, from the moment we met I knew you were special and I selfishly wanted to have you in my life. Right then -- on that very day in Rockville, God answered many of our prayers by showing you the way to *Mobjack* and into our lives. The Wichmanns don't often hit home runs -- but that one was a grand slam, and it went WAY out of the park.

You have blessed me with a friendship, which is the closest I have ever had to actually having a brother. You have ALWAYS been there for me --- to offer a hand and a shoulder. I am a selfish bastard and I do not want to go through the rest of my time with only the memories of what we have done, and the places we have gone together. I want you to stay --- not to leave me alone to finish my days without you. Yet, I know you must go and be with your Father as well as your parents, sister, and brother. I pray that God will take your pain away in the only way that is left for Him to do it. I pray that you feel full and realize that your cup does indeed runneth over. The throngs of people you have touched and helped is incredible.

There are SO, SO many people who look up to you and believe that THEY are your best friend, because that is the way you make everyone feel --- like your best friend.

Your faith and relationship with God and Jesus are more than an inspiration. You do not preach in the traditional sense, but you are a minister because of the man you are and how you live your life.

```
You live your life in the manner in
which God intended; not as a saint, but
as a man who knows he is a sinner and
takes comfort in his faith that Jesus
died for our sins.
```

Instead of shoving religion down people's throats, you show people the way by simply living your life as a Christian and leading by the amazing example of being a man of God. You will leave many legacies, but I believe this one will be atop the list.

When I am really struggling with your ultimate death (as I am now) I comfort myself with a quote that I've taken the liberty to modify ever so slightly. With apologies to Pat Conroy and Jimmy Buffett: "Heaven knows, but God decides, just when to take the Prince of Tides".

I love you, my brother. Have peace in knowing that you will be in my heart for as long as I live.

Bunky

The Last Day

Sept. 8, 2016

Across the years and generations, the Hipp family stayed close. Pictured in July 1996: Preston is flanked by his big brother Charley Hipp, (holding Olivia) and his big sister Dee Hipp Pridgen.

By Dee Pridgen

I remember the entire day so well. I had spent much of the morning with Preston, and he was weak but so very alert, and we had very normal conversation.

He asked me what I was planning to do that day and I said, "Not one thing but be here with you."

I had absolutely no idea it was to be his last day. I asked him if there was anything I could do to help him and that is when he said it would be nice to have clean sheets. That prompted a lot of discussion about what sheets to use and where they were stored. I remember Hartley Watlington and Clark Hanger moving Preston. It was very difficult to move Preston because he was so thin and frail. But they got him seated, and Laura and I changed the sheets.

I think because we were still acting as though everything was fine and Preston never complained that I was refusing to see and accept what was happening. Even in his frailty, Preston had a presence of strength and calm.

When Preston began to slip into unconsciousness I remember talking to him rather loudly and holding his hand to try to rouse him. I told him to take some deep breaths, which he did, and it seemed to awaken him enough that our eyes locked. I so wanted to encourage him to hang on until Delia could get there, which he did. We were all so grateful for every second that Preston was with us.

● ● ●

By Pringle Franklin

It must have been the Holy Spirit that led me to 194 Tradd Street that afternoon; it had been three days since I had been by to check on my dear friends Laura and Preston. I felt anxious with dread about what I would find; when someone is terminally ill, a day apart can feel like an eternity.

During recent weeks, Preston no longer looked ill; he looked like a dying man. His cheeks, eyes, and temples were deeply sunken; it was difficult to look at him without feeling immense sorrow and trepidation.

Laura expressed her hope that, if Preston did go to Heaven, the Lord would heal him in the River of Life and send him back, restored and ready for more happy years on earth with her. We've all heard stories of people being raised from the dead, in Bible days and in contemporary time. Is it wrong to hold out hope against all evidence to the contrary?

Many faithful friends were still praying for a miraculous healing; and yet here was Preston, resting in a hospital bed downstairs in the den. Some days earlier, he had been moved from the sofa to this contraption in order to be more comfortable.

When I entered the room, Preston did not respond to my greeting. This was a big change for the worse. In my recent visits, Preston had managed to smile weakly and to exchange a few words. On his good days, we'd managed to achieve five minutes of meaningful conversation.

```
Now he did not lift his head or open his
eyes -- it was as if he already had one
foot in Heaven.
```

I soon learned that Preston had worn himself out that morning when his family accommodated his request for clean sheets (see Dee Pridgen's story, above). When I showed up, it was after 3 p.m. Preston was lying prone in the bed, adrift in a state of semi-consciousness.

There was nothing to do but simply be present. Laura and I sat in chairs stationed nearby and quietly talked. Preston's sister Dee came into the den and stood at the foot of the hospital bed; when his big sister called out to him, Preston recognized her beloved voice. He started like a newborn whose slumber had been momentarily disturbed. Preston opened his eyes, looked in Dee's direction, and blinked several times.

He struggled to stay awake in order to speak, but he could not muster the energy. Within moments he had fallen back into his hazy state. Dee wrung her hands, and she and I reassured ourselves that it was the pain medication, and not an impending demise, carrying Preston off into this deep slumber.

After a while, Preston and Laura's friends Diane Arnold and Patricia Estes came by. Diane and Patricia are some of those extra Spirit-filled people who can see into the ether in special ways. As we held hands and prayed for Preston, Diane and Patricia sensed the presence of angels in the room. In fact, they each described heavenly beings that they could see, including an enormous angel standing beside Preston, guarding him.

I wanted to see the angels, and even asked the Lord to open my eyes, but I could not. However, during our prayer I had felt a sudden movement of air near the bed. The sensation that something significant was happening around us was palpable.

I wondered: what might the visitation of angels signify?

Before long, another visitor could be heard at the front door. Laura left the den, and the others drifted out. I was left alone with Preston; his face was impassive and his eyes were still closed. I reached over and touched the semi-conscious man on the shoulders, trying to let him know that I was there. He did not move. I leaned in closer so that I could whisper directly into his ear. I felt it was important to reassure him that, if this were his moment, he should not feel guilty about making his exit.

"You have done such a good job," I said. "You have fought so hard; you have fought the good fight. But don't be afraid to go on. We will see you on the Other Side." Tears were running down my face. "It won't be long; before you know it, we will all be together again. Laura, you, the girls, all of your many friends…everyone. It won't be long."

Patting him, I stepped away, feeling relieved. For months, there had been so much expectation of a miracle, both at healing services and from many prayerful friends, that I had begun to feel the weight of this hope like a tether tying Preston to his sickly body. I had prayed for a miracle too, of course, and yet, it just seemed like Preston might need permission to fly away when the final boarding call came.

A few moments later, Laura and Diane returned to the den. We sat down to wait for whatever unfolded next. No one was expecting anything specific. Perhaps Preston would open his eyes; perhaps he would ask for a sip of water. Laura was a champion at getting him to take some little sip of nourishment. This had been the general pattern on other such afternoons.

Suddenly, I had a deja-vu moment. Something about the way that Preston was breathing transported me back to the hospital room in Charlotte where my father had taken his final breaths. As my mother, sister, and I sat beside my father, the rhythm of his breathing had faltered, then his intake of air had grown more shallow. Now some part of my brain recognized the same pattern of sound coming from Preston. A sense of clarity washed over me.

"Laura," I said solemnly. "It's time."

In recent months as Preston's body had grown more sickly and skeletal, Laura had vigorously forbidden any pessimistic talk in her presence. This was her effort to stay strong and hopeful. Now she looked directly at me, her greenish gray eyes growing wide. She did not chastise me for giving into despair but grasped the sincerity of my diagnosis. A short discussion followed between Laura, Diane, and myself, about whether or not Laura should call the girls home. Were they really at this point?

Delia was up in Columbia at the University of South Carolina, where she still had another class that afternoon. Olivia was at work, and Victoria was busy with an after-school activity. No one wanted to send out a false alarm. But we all felt the urgency to alert them.

Before long, Laura had contacted each girl. Family friend Martha Vetter also dropped by that afternoon, and as the sense of death's approach grew stronger, she and I sat on the front porch awhile, trying to give Dee and Laura some privacy, yet wanting to stay nearby until one of the girls got there, in case Laura needed someone to fetch something, fix something, or comfort her with a hug. When the first daughter arrived, Martha and I took our leave.

Around 10:30 p.m., Laura and the three girls were surrounding their beloved husband and father, singing the 23rd Psalm, when Preston took his final breath. The angelic voices of Preston's "four graces", as their dear friend George Kanellos refers to them, were the last earthly sounds that Preston heard before leaving his body and crossing over to the other side.

The three graces — Victoria, Delia, and Olivia, at home with their father in 2014.

Psalm 23

1{A Psalm of David.} The LORD is my shepherd; I shall not want.

2He maketh me to lie down in green pastures: he leadeth me beside the still waters.

3He restoreth my soul: he leadeth me in the paths of righteousness for his name's sake.

4Yea, though I walk through the valley of the shadow of death, I will fear no evil: for thou art with me; thy rod and thy staff they comfort me.

5Thou preparest a table before me in the presence of mine enemies: thou anointest my head with oil; my cup runneth over.

6Surely goodness and mercy shall follow me all the days of my life: and I will dwell in the house of the LORD for ever.

A Vision of Preston in Heaven

SEPT. 8, 2016, SHORTLY
AFTER PRESTON'S DEATH
AS TOLD BY EDWIN SMYTHE:

This is what happened the Thursday evening I found out Preston had gone:

I had arrived at my apartment when I received the text from Laura and immediately went to the prayer house at Bethel Church. The floor is a compass so I faced south east toward Charleston and got on my knees and prayed.

I knelt still for about a half hour praying and I thought I heard his voice.

"Preston," I said.

"Hey man," He replied.

"Where are you?"

"I'm in Heaven man."

"What's it like?"

«Beautiful.»

"Are you coming back?"

"I don't know....I don't think so."

"Is it up to you?"

"Not really sure."

At this point I experienced God's palpable presence in His comfort and love, and began to see visions of Preston in Heaven.

The first vision I saw was two angels flying down, each one grabbing Preston by the upper arm and then flying upward from darkness into sunlit clouds.

The next was a mountain in the distance, with sunlight peeking from behind. My perspective was from the valley below. The sun rose from behind the mountain and painted the valley with a glorious burst of color. I saw two feet with sandals and the lower part of a walking stick facing the valley and the mountain behind it. He then took a step into the valley.

After that I saw Preston standing in the middle of a large plain with rolling green hills. Next to him was a large windmill with a stone tower. He just stood there gazing into the distance.

Then I saw him ankle deep in a stream casting a fly-rod back and forth. (I thought this was interesting because Preston did not fly fish here).

Jesus then emerged from the tree line and sat down on a rock near Preston as he continued to cast. Jesus smiled behind a thick beard and played with a stone as He and Preston talked. I could not hear what they were saying but it was a beautiful encounter and I wanted to be part of it. In fact I was jealous.

Then I saw Preston at a beach, body surfing in clear blue water. He stood up and ran his hands through his hair and I noticed he looked young. He walked up to the beach and lay down in the sand and let the sun shine on him. He looked like he did not have a care in the world.

The final thing I saw was a cliff with long green grass that over-looked an ocean. It was very windy and Preston was at the edge of the cliff crouching down and gazing out toward the ocean. The salty breeze was blowing his hair....which was considerably thicker than I remember. Jesus approached from a distance and Preston looked at him and smiled. Jesus walked over and crouched next to him. I could not tell if any words were spoken as the two looked at the distant horizon.

I continued to kneel and wept for the wonderful things Preston was experiencing. I wanted to be where he was and I wanted to stay there forever. I called out to him again.

"Preston....Preston."

"Yeah."

"Preston, you need to come back....Preston."

"Leave me alone, man. I'm in Heaven."

I continued to call out but that was it. I knew Preston had gone to be with Jesus. I sat there wishing I could return to Heaven and see and feel it again. I am weeping now just thinking about how wonderful the experience was. Words cannot describe the how beautiful it was to see Preston in Heaven, full of life and talking with Jesus.

Remembrances Delivered at the Service

Tuesday, September 13, 2016, St. Philip's Church
Charleston, South Carolina, at 10 a.m.
(listed in speaking order)

One Proud Daddy: Preston with young daughters Olivia and Delia.

By OLIVIA HIPP

For anyone who doesn't know me, I'm Olivia, the oldest of Preston's three girls followed by Delia and Victoria. That psalm we just read, Psalm 27, is particularly important to me, because it is my birthday psalm. "What is a birthday psalm?" you may ask. Well, it is some combination of your birthday numbers and the psalms, for me October 27. At breakfast on our birthday, we would read our psalm during our morning devotional over tea and whatever homemade treat my mom put together. And that is so indicative of how my sisters and I all grew up.

My dad made such an effort to put in time with each of us. He took Victoria on a ski and snowboarding trip to Colorado just two years ago to his sister Dee's condo, and he loved seeing Victoria, the most athletic one in the family, take on the harder slopes even as a novice snowboarder.

He took Delia to look at colleges, and he was so proud to see her thriving at his alma mater, USC. He took her to get her first car just last year and made sure to test drive it himself and make sure it was what she wanted.

And before that, when I didn't have a car and I'm afraid didn't really drive, he would drive the 14 hours to Memphis, TN to drop me at college and pick me up every year, taking the time to get to know my friends, even when his health was quietly failing him. And when I graduated he told me, "You know, I'm really going to miss our drives together."

It never mattered how many friends I had in school, because my family were my best friends, and we would hang out all the time. Going out on the boat, tubing for hours, listening to Bob Marley and dancing, making drip castles, rock climbing, playing cards and Rummikub, watching one of my dad's favorite shows, "America's Funniest Home Videos" " – which is so redneck but he made cool – he had such a young, boyish, mischievous spirit. My dad loved to laugh, and once he got started, he couldn't stop. He loved pranks and old cartoons, as his sister Dee remembers from when he was a little boy, and he would laugh at AFV until his cheeks and nose puffed up and he was red in the face and tears were streaming down his face. He never lost that humor either.

He was completely infectious. And he was my best friend. But one of the amazing things about Preston Hipp is that he had the ability to make everyone feel that way. He knew just how to listen quietly and respond perfectly in a way that always put you first. And if you didn't feel like you and Preston were best friends, man you wished you were! He was born with an effortless cool.

The first year they dropped me off at college in 2010, we took the longest road trip with the whole family to get there – the kind of cooped up family time that should have made us sick of each other, with the minivan and bubble on top of the car packed to the gills.

We went to my dad's cousin Charlene's lake house in Hot Springs, Arkansas where we went out on the boat to try out water skiing. My mom and sisters and I flopped around in the water with our skis splaying out into a pizza as we just tried to stay up – with the exception perhaps of Victoria, who as the athlete would resent me for saying that.

My dad, though he really hadn't skied since he and his friend John Burrous lived in Colorado after college and hadn't water skied in even longer, decided he'd hop out after we'd finished and "give it a shot".

He, of course, popped up immediately, leaning back on the skis, knees bent, back straight, and he started gliding in and out of the wake, then dropping a ski and slaloming, throwing up a huge spray of surf behind him. He was a natural at everything. And he had an unshakable twinkle in his eye for adventure. He always squeezed every ounce of life out of each day.

Recently, Victoria Hanham told me that after I was born, my dad told her, "Well, we better not have a bunch of girls, or Laura will waste the rest of her life ironing bonnets!"

After my youngest sister, Victoria, who everyone thought would be a boy, was born, my mom looked at Dad and said, "Looks like God decided you needed to be loved by yet another woman."

Not too long ago, my dad and I were hanging out, and I told him that, for his sake, I was sorry he never had any sons, because he would have been such a good boy dad! Hunting, boating, football, all of that. And he looked at me so seriously and calmly without missing a beat and said, "You know, I think God gave me daughters to make me a better man."

It wasn't just the obvious or wild things that made him cool, though, as many of you can attest, there is no shortage of those. He made driving big truck seem cool. He made Goombay Smash and bocce under the moonlight cool. He made wearing a dress on TV after Hugo as the Angel Gabriel in the St. Philip's Christmas Eve service cool. He made hanging out with your parents every weekend cool. But he also made the Young Professionals Bible Study cool. He made Quiet Time with God cool. He made *constant* prayer cool. He made humility cool.

My mom was my dad's partner, cheerleader, and right hand to whom he addressed every card and letter he ever wrote to her, "To the Love of My Life". But she had to share him with many people, and she always says,

"You could not know Preston but to love Preston."

And anyone who knew him knew he was somehow both the dynamic life of every party and a stoic man of few words; an endless fount of wisdom and the goofiest guy on the dance floor; a type-A business-man and an imaginative inventor; a simple man and a deep thinker; a cool guy with a cocky attitude and the most humble servant whose love language was quiet acts of service; an introverted man who loved to commune with God in the peace and quiet of nature, and an exu-berant lover of people's souls.

And somehow, battling cancer for the past eight years never consumed his identity but rather strengthened the very best parts of his charac-ter. He worked on himself. His New Year's resolution in 2015 was to dance more – and did he ever! He miraculously became even more carefree, even more compassionate, even more humble, even more wise, even more holy.

He once told us in our Young Professionals Bible Study that if God had given him a choice before all of this to stay exactly as he was, or to push a button and get cancer but be opened up to all of God's saving glory the way he was able to be during his trials... "Man, I tell ya, I'd be pretty tempted to push that button."

And it pained me to hear that. Because I already miss him so much. I've never met anyone who changed so many people's lives as my dad did, and the past few days have been such a testament to that. He and I had a good understanding, and I would tell him most everything. And one time when I was venting to him about someone that was annoying me, I remember he paused and looked at me and said, "You know, I try not to focus on the things I don't like about people. I like to look at my favorite parts of them and then try to emulate that." And how blessed are we to have known someone like Preston Hipp, the Prince of Tides, to try to emulate in our lives and whose life was shaped by all of us?!

My dad is all around me in each of you and in everything I see. As his faithful friend Malcolm Rhodes said when we were putting wreaths on my dad's crosses in the harbor, I cannot go anywhere in the Lowcountry without seeing my dad – out in the country, on the water, in the water, in the marshes, in the birds flying overhead.

When my mom and dad were dating, my dad told her he wanted to be a bridge tender. Like the guy whose job it is to sit in that little box alone all day long and just wait for a tall boat to come by. But he just wanted to sit in God's creation and pour over God's Word, and that seemed like the perfect job to have in order to spend your whole day doing that. I sit in my dad's office with his real best friend Chester guarding the door. I look across the Coast Guard and through the marshes to the white cross he put up 19 years ago, when we moved to 194 Tradd. I can hear him in his home office spending hours preparing for his Bible study lessons. He had an android phone and he would use it to look things up. I can just hear him in his office: "Hey Google, what are the fruits of the Spirit?" And when he would get frustrated with that daggum phone it would sound more like, "HEY. GOOGLE. LOOK UP BIBLE VERSES ON JESUS HEALING PEOPLE!!"

Eternity always terrified me, as it does many people. How could I want to do anything forever?? And yet I feel like 1,000 years wouldn't have been enough time with my dad. I could hang out with him forever and not get tired of it, not learn everything I wanted to learn. How much greater then must our Heavenly Father be?? If being in Heaven is anything like hanging out with my dad forever, I think I'd like to go there.

Each of us will carry Preston Hipp's light in our hearts for the rest of our lives. But he has paved the way ahead of us and sailed on past the bridge tender to a more beautiful and serene creation than we can imagine. He is on a wild adventure that isn't limited by fear or pain or frustration. For him, the dream is over. For him, it is the morning.

**Preston and Barre, friends for life. Pictured here in 2015. Barre did
not miss one of Preston's chemotherapy treatments but showed up to
help his buddy pass the time.**

By BARRE BUTLER

Let's begin with a story I told in a toast at Laura and Preston's wedding rehearsal dinner 28 years ago:

When Preston and I first met, we were half-clothed, incoherent, and behind bars. Of course, we were 3 months old and "the bars" kept us in the crib.

I've always said that public speaking is easy when you speak from the heart. So this SHOULD be easy. But I've never had to speak about a brother, my brother – my brother from birth who is no longer here.

Early on, the signs of loyalty, leadership and strength were evident from Preston's actions. When we were 7, the neighborhood bully and his "gang" forced me to eat some orange berries which burned my mouth – I cried like a 7-year-old. Preston walked me like a wounded soldier back to his house. I wanted to give up, but Preston said, "No. We have to fight the bully." Sure enough, Preston planned our defense and avenged their dishonorable deed. My friend became my hero.

We fought bullies together, we watched cartoons together, we built tree forts together, we drove to school together, we went to summer camp together, we played football and ran track together, we sailed Sunfish sailboats together, we laughed, we cried, and then eventually we prayed together.

My whole life has been around the Hipps, and why wouldn't it be? Growing up, the Hipps were "the cool family." They had cool modern houses with upstairs-to-downstairs laundry shoots. They had ice makers and trash mashers. They had outboard boats and even a Florida Everglades air boat. They had pool tables and ping pong tables, surfboards and jeeps. And two gorgeous daughters, foreshadowing the three gorgeous daughters Preston would one day have. No wonder I practically lived in their homes.

When we were in junior high school, Preston's mom got a Jaguar. His parents were going on a trip and told Preston and me at their front door as they were leaving, "Don't drive the Jag." Two minutes later, we were in the Jag on the way to Ye Olde Fashion for ice cream. Seven minutes later, we were fine, but the Jag was totaled.

When we were in high school, Mr. Hipp gave Preston one of his used company trucks. It was white. So, what did Preston do? By himself, he painted it CAMO. Now, I'm not saying he had the first camo-painted pickup truck, but I'm sure it was the first one that was permanently parked South of Broad on Murray Blvd.

College and adulthood arrived – and life physically separated us for years.

One day, a Saturday, my home was struck by lightning and pretty much burned to the ground. We lost 90% of the "things" we had. That afternoon, after the firemen left, many of our friends and family had an impromptu celebration in our front yard – celebrating that all were alive and there were no injuries.

The next day, Sunday, I was there at the scorched and stinking rubble of what used to be our home – I was alone; I was in despair. And all of a sudden, Preston was there. He held me; he prayed for me – like no one else could do.

Preston didn't just touch my life – it's hard to describe, but he grabbed it.

He grabbed my life, my spirit, and helped me to be a better man. Just as he grabbed yours.

Richard Hollowell flew 28 hours through 12 time zones from China twice to be with his dear friend, first while he was still alive and second to honor him today. What kind of man does that? A man whose heart and spirit have been grabbed by another.

This summer, Malcolm Rhodes got about twenty of us together – those of us lucky enough to spend an afternoon at Laura and Preston's house remembering good times we'd had. We laughed about what a powerful—almost startling—figure Preston was as the angel in the St. Philip's pageant. Although we knew he was supposed to represent Gabriel, God's messenger, we all agreed that to us he better represented Michael, the leader of God's army against evil, just as he had fought against the bully when we were seven years old.

Someone said to me that there are a thousand people who would have been honored to carry this casket. It sounds like an exaggeration, but it's not. There is a void in our world. A man is gone: A really, really good man is gone. It will take a hundred good men to fill that void.

When Preston spoke, when he prayed – you listened, you heard, you learned, and you remembered. A couple months ago Preston emailed me, "Your visits always lift my spirit." I replied, "And selfishly, my visits with you lift my spirit, but I get the added bonus of having you share your faith in Jesus with me."

The impact Preston made-- on his family, his friends, his strangers, his church – rolls through every pew and down every street and now up to Heaven. There's a pillow in my house that says "I wish I could be the man my dog thinks I am." Preston WAS that man – to Chester and to all of us.

Tomorrow, we'll still think of Preston, who he was and what he did – hopefully we'll go a step further and BE a Preston – and make a difference.

The Rev. Brian McGreevy and Preston in service at historic St. Philip's Church, Charleston, S.C.

By THE REV. BRIAN K. MCGREEVY

I am honored to be standing before you today not only in my role as a priest of St. Philip's Church, but perhaps more importantly at this moment in my role as a friend of Preston Hipp. I've known Laura since we sang in choir together when we were five years old, and I've been trying to remember this week the first time I met Preston. Although we were both at Porter-Gaud together at the same time in the 1970s, he was two years younger, so we didn't run into each other that much then. I am pretty sure that the first time I actually talked to him was at Pete's Store on Meeting Street when he was 12 or 13.

Although I had known Preston for some time, we did not become truly close until Jane and I moved back to Charleston, a process in which Preston was intimately involved. The full story is too long to tell here, but suffice to say we believed that God was possibly calling us back to Charleston from my legal career in Atlanta, and we believed we were being led to come here and open a bed and breakfast.

It was a very confusing calling, because it seemed much more logical that if God were going to call us to something new, it would much more likely be something like mission work in Africa rather than a B&B in Charleston. We committed to pray about it, though, and we decided that the best way to clarify this situation was to find someone in commercial real estate in Charleston, and then if we learned it would cost $3 million to buy a bed and breakfast, we would be off the hook unless God were to send us a check for that amount in the mail. So, I called Jim Hampson at St. Philip's, whose children were good friends of ours in Atlanta, and explained our somewhat peculiar situation. He listened carefully and said he would think about it. I got a message the next day from Jim saying that I should expect a call from Preston Hipp, to whom Jim had explained our situation.

The Preston I knew in the 1970s did not seem a person likely to be recommended by a priest,

but then again neither was I in the 1970s, so I was interested to see what had happened in Preston's life. He called as planned and we chatted, mapping out the list of 14 criteria that Jane and I had come up with for a property and a price range, and he said he was happy to help but that frankly it was extremely unlikely we would be able to find something that would work, given our needs and constraints. That was actually a relief to hear, as it meant we might avoid the complete upheaval of our life in Atlanta.

However, God had other plans!

The next day, I got an excited phone call from Preston, saying I wasn't going to believe this, but he had just seen a new listing come across his desk that appeared to meet all our criteria. He sent me a fax of the listing, and we agreed that he and I should go look at the property on a business trip I already had scheduled to come to Charleston later that week. I was planning a best practices conference in Charleston for a group of around 50 CEOs of billion dollar plus financial services companies, so I arrived at Charleston Place in my limousine, and Preston was waiting for me and came up to my suite, which was one of the luxurious two-story ones at the top of the hotel.

Before we set out to look at the listing, Preston suggested we pray, and I will never forget his reaching out and grabbing my hand, and powerfully praying for the Holy Spirit to lead us. Within six months, I had quit my job and we had moved back to Charleston and we were running a bed and breakfast, a process through which Preston was by my side every step of the way.

That was the start of an amazing time of deep friendship with Preston that was centered and focused on encouraging one another in our walk with God and praying for one another. For the next nineteen years until a few weeks ago, Preston and I met to pray more or less every week. We completely shared every aspect of our lives together, sharing our journeys in our families, in our careers, in our relationships, in our ministries, in our church, and most importantly in our relationship with Jesus Christ. Often we would meet over a meal, most frequently at the Variety Store, and then we would sit in one of our cars outside and pray, often for quite some time.

Sometimes when we finished praying I would notice people looking askance at us, and we often joked that they probably thought we were in the car doing a drug deal. Preston was an amazing and faithful prayer warrior who loved Jesus with all his heart, mind, soul, and strength, and encouraged me to do the same.

Preston was instrumental in helping me discern calls from God to move back to Charleston, to enter ministry at Porter-Gaud, and to enter ordained ministry. It is hard to imagine how I would be standing here today as a priest without his influence and counsel on my faith journey. He was my main lay presenter at my ordination to the priesthood. Although not many people knew it, Preston was instrumental in the renewal of student ministry at Porter-Gaud, about which he was hugely enthusiastic.

He was my encourager-in-chief and prayer warrior without equal. He knew the names of all the student ministry leaders and would pray for them by name each week. He delighted in hearing about the work that God was doing in the lives of students at Porter-Gaud, and did everything in his power to help motivate and assist me in that ministry, praying for me every time I would speak or lead a retreat, and texting prayers for me every time I would preach at St. Philip's as well.

The following is a typical text he sent me early Saturday morning during our Jesus Weekend retreat earlier this year: "Father, Bless every person at Jesus Weekend with dreams of Your Kingdom. Greet them with Your Presence in the morning. Send Your Holy Spirit to fill their hearts. Bless Brian with strength and wisdom. Amen."

Preston loved his family and friends so deeply, and loved the beauty of God's creation in the Lowcountry, but

his truest and strongest passion was for Christ.

I was privileged to spend some time with Laura and the girls and some friends this afternoon at the Tradd Street house, reading an excerpt from the "Farewell to Shadowlands" chapter of C.S. Lewis's <u>The Last Battle</u>, a beautiful depiction of heaven that Preston and I had discussed many times.

> "It was the Unicorn who summed up what everyone was feeling. He stamped his right fore-hoof on the ground and neighed and then cried:
> "I have come home at last! This is my real country! I belong here. This is the land I have been looking for all my life, though I never knew it till now. The reason why we loved the old Narnia is that it sometimes looked a little like this. Bree-hee-hee! Come further up, come further in!"...
> Then Aslan turned to them and said:
> "You do not yet look so happy as I mean you to be."
> Lucy said, "We're so afraid of being sent away, Aslan. And you have sent us back into our own world so often."
> "No fear of that," said Aslan. "Have you not guessed?"
> Their hearts leaped and a wild hope rose within them.

"There was a real railway accident," said Aslan softly. "Your father and mother and all of you are—as you used to call it in the Shadowlands—dead. The term is over: the holidays have begun. The dream is ended: this is the morning."

And as He spoke He no longer looked to them like a lion; but the things that began to happen after that were so great and beautiful that I cannot write them. And for us this is the end of all the stories, and we can most truly say that they all lived happily ever after. But for them it was only the beginning of the real story. All their life in this world and all their adventures in Narnia had only been the cover and the title page: now at last they were beginning Chapter One of the Great Story, which no one on earth has read: which goes on for ever: in which every chapter is better than the one before."

Now Preston is home in his true country. May we who remain in the Shadowlands be inspired to go deeper in faith and in love by his magnificent example of a life well lived.

Brother-in-law Bunky drives the boat while Preston takes a seat; these two guys loved being out on the water.

By BUNKY WICHMANN

> "Heaven knows, but God decides just when to take the Prince
> of Tides." ~ Pat Conroy/Jimmy Buffett

It was the Tide which brought Preston to our family.

Rockville Regatta 1984
Preston was working at Charleston County Tax Assessors Office in the
appraisal department along with Joanna Drake
Preston put his boat in the Cherry Point landing and started down the
Bohicket towards Rockville. About halfway down the river, he cut the
engine off - unsure as to whether he should really enter the fray of the
revelers of the regatta as he wasn't convinced he had the discipline
not to stray from the straight and narrow. He said a little prayer and
prayed for strength. He almost turned around and went back the landing, but something inside him, or maybe something outside of him,
told him that he should go down the river and meet up with us.
When he pulled up alongside *Mobjack*, it was pretty much love at
first sight.
Preston's johnboat, *Oyster Catcher*, was every man's dream of a small
boat. We both marveled at each others boats.
Preston and Laura marveled at each other. I remember there was a
little competition for Preston, and I was seeing them ogling each other
and thinking - hey, he's *my* friend. Preston paid the ultimate sacrifice:
he married my sister so he could have me as a brother-in-law. As it
turned out -- Laura and I both won.
We sailed back to Charleston offshore later that day with about 20 people. As usual, it was an adventure, and we arrived at the James Island
Yacht Club late, late in the evening. Preston was asleep down below,
and everyone on the entire boat, including Laura, hopped off and
went home. Preston had fallen asleep in the cabin. When he awoke,
all he could see was my tail sticking out of the engine room.

Preston didn't abandon ship - he pitched right in with me and helped me fix whatever I was working on.

Then the two of us spent the rest of the dark night hours ferrying cars back and forth from Rockville and Bohicket. At 5 a.m. when we had finished our work, we both were wide awake and breathing in the fresh air of a friendship which we both knew would last for a lifetime.

```
This sums up how Preston approached
relationships - whether it be with
another person or God. He was always
there and always making you feel like
you were the most important thing in
his life - when really he was the most
important thing in ours.
```

Preston was immediately a part of our family through all of the ups and downs of his courtship with Laura - and later reinforced by marrying the love of his life.

Never did we, the Wichmanns, expect to have such a Prince of Tides as a member of our family. He was the brother I never had.

Quote from Prioleau Alexander:

"Every now and then, losing a great man is buffered by knowing-- for fact-- where he will be. I can only imagine the Preston-size smile when he hears the Creator of the universe say, "well done, good and faithful servant." Then Preston will greet a long line of people who are there because of his words, actions, and encouragement. Truth be known, I think Christ will be more apt to say, 'Hot damn, Dude. I've been waiting to meet you face to face-- Lotta people gonna be neighbors of yours, because you gave them directions to the neighborhood.'

Yes, every person matters, but Preston matters to an entire city. He is the best our little city could ever hope to produce. There is really no need to pray for Preston - he doesn't need my prayers: he secured his place in the front row of Paradise decades ago."

Preston is looking down on us. Praying for us all - as he always did. I see him in full strength out in the country, on the river, sailing to the islands with me…I would like to close by sharing a quote from a member of Preston's Friday morning Bible study group:

"I don't expect ever to meet a man closer to God than Preston Hipp." ~Shep Davis

HOMILY GIVEN BY RENNY SCOTT, FORMER RECTOR OF ST. PHILIP'S CHURCH

Right at the start, I want to express my deep gratitude to Preston and Laura for giving me the great honor of speaking today, and I want to thank Jeff Miller for allowing me the privilege.

Thirty-three years ago, Margaret and I moved to Charleston: 92 Church Street. A young Charleston Belle, who was just home from England, showed up at our door with a basket of goodies on her arm. Her name was Laura Wichmann. Margaret, the children and I loved her from the word go. She had been praying since ninth grade for The One she would one day marry. So we joined her in that prayer and prayed for Preston long before we met him.

When they were dating, Laura's romantic heart longed to hear Preston say wonderful things to her; instead he did wonderful things for her.

The newlyweds in 1988, Laura and Preston. Laura had prayed and waited so faithfully for God to send her "the One".

Her love language was words of affirmation; his was gifts of service. They loved each other, but didn't fully understand what the other was saying. But, fast forward to this season, Preston lavished Laura with words of love, and Laura has showered Preston with gifts of service – they had learned each other's love language, and it was a beautiful thing to behold.

My last moments with Preston were spread over a weekend, and they painted for me a picture of his heart.

On Friday night, Preston and Laura invited us to dinner with two other couples. We were all old friends. Most of us knew each other for more than thirty years and some of us for fifty years. As you can imagine, Laura was an amazing hostess. It was a dinner party in the elegant Charleston tradition. We shared the ups and downs of our spiritual journey with laughter, life, and love, and caught a glimpse of Christ through the window of each other's lives. That is what fellowship is: two fellows in the same ship. But, that ship has lifting power! If you are drowning, that ship can get your feet on solid ground.

<u>Preston lived life with the open arms of hospitality, because of the love of God in his heart.</u>

All of Saturday, Preston spent at a healing conference. In the evening, they opened it to the public, so we decided to go. It was a powerful time of worship, teaching, and prayer. Matt Pridgen, Lilly McGougin, Laura, Margaret, and I gathered around Preston.

Laura placed her hand on Preston's chest and prayed: *"Lord, this is The One. This is the one I prayed for. This is the one You gave me. This is the one I love. This is the one I want to spend my life with. This is the one I need You to heal."* When Laura finished praying, tears were running down our cheeks.

Matt Pridgen was on his knees and began to pray for Preston. The Bible tells us that sometimes, *"We don't know how to pray, but the spirit intercedes for us with groans that words cannot express."* Soon Matt was doubled over – all we could hear was loud groaning. Then, he would look up at Preston with a sheepish smile on his face. Then they both burst out laughing. All I could think of was Abraham, when he was one hundred years old and was told he was going to have a baby, he laughed. It was the laugh of faith.

But, how could Preston possibly laugh when his whole world was being wrecked by cancer? I think I figured it out. Preston knew two things that are absolutely vital.

When Preston was 24 years old, He met Christ and he discovered that God is in the restoration business. He can take our brokenness and turn it into a thing of beauty. II Corinthians 5:17 describes it this way: *"If anyone is in Christ, he is a new creation: the old has gone, behold, the new has come!"* As the Psalmist reminds us: "He restores my soul."

God is also in the resurrection business. We don't need to be afraid of death. We can serve in the middle of an epidemic, or stand where the earthquakes, or go where the bombs fall, because we are people of the resurrection. As Jesus said: *"This is the will of my Father, I shall lose none of all that He has given me and I will raise them up on the last day."* John 6:39

If God has our past, and God has our future, then we can rejoice in the present. No wonder, Preston laughed. He didn't know what the future held, but he knew the One who holds the future in His hands.

<u>Preston was a man of faith, who believed in the power of prayer</u>.

Sunday night, Laura invited us to a Bible study for young professionals that Preston was leading in their home, so we came. Present started by saying: This will end early tonight, because it is the last episode of Downton Abbey. I love that about Preston. He wasn't religious; he was real. He just loved Christ. Preston shared with that group what he called the four "D's" of answered prayer. When we ask God to do something, He does one of four things: 1. He does it; 2. He denies it; 3. He delays it; or 4. He just does it differently.

<u>Preston was a man of the Word, who wanted to pass it on to the next generation.</u>

So why is it important to know Preston from the perspective of his faith? I think all of us know that we are living in difficult days. The Bible describes it this way: *"Everything that can be shaken will be shaken."* The political world, the economy, cities and families. Charleston will need people like Preston, who live with the open arms of hospitality, because of the love of God in their heart, men and women of faith, who know the power of prayer, and people of the Word, who will pass it on to the next generation.

God did an amazing thing! He heard the cry of our heart and answered our prayers. He just did it differently. He didn't heal him for a brief moment of time, he healed him for all time. He wiped away his tears, he removed his pain, and has given him a new body and He has taken him home. One day, you and I will see Preston in that place that Jesus has prepared for all who know Him. *"Eye has not seen nor ear heard, nor entered into the heart of man what God has prepared for those who love him."*

If we knew what Preston now knows today about God and Heaven, we would clap our hands, and joy would flood our hearts. If Preston were here, he would pull each one of us aside, and look us in the eyes, and say in his quiet way: *"Follow Jesus. It is worth it!"*

Olivia, Delia, Victoria – I know you miss your dad. Grief is a funny thing; it comes in waves. It can blindside you with emotion. But, eventually, the pain will be replaced by beautiful memories of your dad that will encourage you all your life.

Laura, I know you can't imagine life without Preston, but I know that you know: *"If you draw near to God, He will draw near to you."*

Two Graveside Tributes

BY CLARK HANGER

Friday morning was a wake-up call for me. I was one of the people in the camp who hoped and tried to believe this day would never come. That Preston would be healed by a miracle or some medical earthly cure.

When I learned he had passed away, I frankly was in a state of disbelief. Preston never told me he was not going to make it. For years, he worked hard to revive his failing health, and I believed he would. I have been sad since Friday; frankly I am still mad that he is gone. So as you can see, I have some work to do. But helping me along the way, I know that Preston has conquered his battle and is in a much better place today. I believe this. I was with him Thursday afternoon, and the pain I witnessed is no way to live. Goodbye, sweet friend....

We have shared so much together. You have always been a sure and steady friend. Thank you Preston. Here I am sending you off in my own way with two things 1) some water I took from the Cooper River and 2) some sand from our Morris Island Bocci course. I put them here as a remembrance of our many great times together.

Bon Voyage, my friend

• • •

By George Kanellos

Yes, we will remember him. Preston was one of the exuberant lights of our lives. His faith and kindness, combined with confidence--and thrill seeking, gave us pleasure, self confidence, and hope.

Look around you. This is not a chance meeting at Magnolia Cemetery. We are a group of people who have been brought together by the life of one person. As we have no choice in the death of Preston, we are at liberty to mourn and grieve. We will have these feelings, by degree, all our lives. How sad it would be if we as humans did not feel pain in loosing someone we love. By being here now, we have a chance to grieve together, but also to feel a sense of gratefulness for Preston, who was happy, who loved us, and who made us glad to be a part of his group of friends, to belong.

Americans are famous for sitting around a table at Thanksgiving and saying what they are grateful for...but grateful to whom? To The Giver. Preston met Him in 1983, as did I, 33 years ago.
In a country of leaders, Preston stood out from a young age, being head and shoulders taller than the rest of us. But he became a follower of Jesus Christ, humbly surrendering his life to Jesus Christ. He committed his ways to Him. And thus began his acquaintance with The Giver of all good things.

In those early days, Preston and I both gave up secular radio, cursing, and drinking in order to know God better. Since that time, we reverted on some of those things, but it was those early attempts of following Jesus that gave us a Base for Living — and today we see — for dying.
If this is it, is all there is, then there would be real, inconsolable sadness, and our grief would be overwhelming.

But to know Preston was to get a glimpse of God — who delights in us and who takes pleasure in seeing us happy. And who likes to see us having fun. Preston could and did stand on the rail of the Morris Island Lighthouse, daring and brave and glorifying God in his coordination, the wind, and the height above the sea and sand; however, I do not recommend that particular risk taking, nor the igniting of an inferno of dried Christmas trees, decorated with propane tanks. Washington, D.C. on the Fourth of July cannot hold a torch, so to speak, to the show Preston delighted in putting on.

When one on one, Preston gave us his full attention and a heart that had compassion...both sharing our difficult situations as well as our joys. We will miss that presence and that wisdom that was Preston's to us individually, like Jesus to His disciples.

Last night I saw the three quarter moon, and this morning the stars Orion and the Dippers. I felt more comfort than sadness, as though they are the light of Preston now, with me.

As we go into the days ahead, I will look forward to when grief transitions to gladness, when we can remember Preston with a lighthearted spirit, and embrace the same Lord that Preston laid his life down to serve and worship. Belief in what Jesus accomplished on the cross for us allows us to come boldly before God with hope and assurance. Can any of us doubt where Preston is now?

May 23, 2016, Preston's 57th birthday, he and I spoke of the Resurrection of Jesus. When some days later, Jesus reappeared, it happened on the beach. The disciples were returning from a crummy fishing trip, tired, no fish, early one morning after an exhausting night. Following Jesus was over. He had been crucified. They went back to their old lives of fishing and were not successful there either.

When they least expected it, there was Jesus, on the beach, with a fire glowing. He was cooking fish — with a gleam in his eye. Preston and I said that on his next birthday, this scene would be reenacted. I had hoped here — I was mistaken.

But this is reality guys. Preston is not dead. His life continues in Heaven; his catheters and bags are gone, his body restored. He will be, as I can picture it, cooking fish for breakfast with Jesus, on the beach. *(Editor's note: Preston mentions John 21 and the narrative of Jesus cooking breakfast on the beach during a speech at church. See **Preston Gives His Testimony**.)*

Now, on to practical matters. Laura, I was thinking about Preston's old International truck. For those of you who do not know of The Green Machine, as it was affectionately called by Preston, it is a '50s model, stripped of everything except two seats and a steering wheel. May I have it? I was thinking if not, you could use it for your tours to add a real flair and an experience to remember. You'd be packing 'em in. Bad brakes, but you could learn how to down shift. No frills, no airbags, more "out of Africa" with panoramic views.

Stories:
As friendship with Preston was not exclusive, we can all share in the mirth. Preston loved the ludicrous. He howled at Gary Larson cartoons, especially ones that pointed out Preston's independent nature. "No man is an island....I am a continent." Laura got this one and pinned it up for years.

One day, years ago, Preston was a bit out of sorts but was carrying on, working on the side of their property on Tradd while standing on the tall brick wall. He was in a deep, dark, quiet mood that he could get into. My company did not particularly impact the time together to be more convivial. I had just finished eating a banana. For fun, I laid the peel on top of the wall and then pointed out a spot he had missed so that he would have to backtrack. Not wanting him to fall, at the last moment I pointed it out to him. Preston doubled over with laughter and laughed till he cried. The solemn spell was broken. (I liked when I could do that.)

Preston was honest. Once on the *Mobjack*, we were all feeling hungry for seafood. Preston pulled up a crab man's crab pot, emptied it in a tub, and then Preston calculated the cost. Following his father-in-law's example, he stuck an amount of cash in a plastic film container with a note of thanks, tied it to the pot, and threw it back in the water.

Preston was ingenious on building functional contraptions, applying the engineering skills inherit to the C.R. Hipp family. He built a box that fit on top of his car — sleekly designed to keep things in — of importance, you know. It was a box that would, for instance, deliver scratch/dried corn to be distributed to feed his pigs, the Wild Boars at his family land in the country at Bees Ferry that he ingeniously was trying to trap. They were on the loose, rooting up lawns to residents' doors. Yet another box was to keep his camera dry that took pictures of the hogs when they unsuspectingly dined at night. Then there was the Big Box in the back of the truck in which he kept Rope, chainsaw, knives, and guns — just in case.

As stars that are known to the night;
As stars that shall be bright
when we are dust,
moving in marshes upon the heavenly plain,
As stars that are starry in our darkness,
to the end,
to the end,
you remain.

Lastly, Preston was a wild man about the natural world.
Climbing trees.
Pruning limbs.
Exploring woods
or islands.
Swimming in the sea or a river.
Tearing through creeks at high speed in his boat, the Oyster Catcher,
picnics on board
of granny smith apples, peanut butter, and cheese.

The night world,
especially on the water, enchanted Preston.
He loved to share those experiences
under an explosion of stars
or under a bright, full moon.

Perhaps the most rare and magical of all
is when he would time an excursion on his boat
with the setting sun and the rising, big, orange moon.
The tide would be high, intensifying the experience all at the same
time.
It was Preston, the choreographer at work, the Prince of Tides in tune
with The Creator.

We will remember Preston and miss the life enriching experiences he
brought into our lives.

● ● ●

PRAYER WRITTEN BY LAURA WICHMANN HIPP FOR THE
FUNERAL SERVICE (to be read by The Rev. Marc Boutan)

Thank you, Lord, that Preston's light and momentary afflictions
have laid up for him an Eternal weight of Glory, that far outweighs

all his trials in the Refiner's Fire. We fix our eyes not on what is seen in the fragile body of Preston in his valiant fight, but on what is unseen, Preston restored to his sunshine smile, twinkle in his eyes, and zest for of life. "He who would valiant be" took up his cross " 'Gainst all disaster", trusting the Lord with his body entirely, never ceasing to believe that God is good, God is sovereign, and that God loves us. Preston's heart rejoiced in the blessed assurance that "Jesus paid it all, all to Him I owe. Sin hath left a crimson stain. He washed it white as snow."

Preston's hope was "built on nothing less than Jesus' blood and righteousness", and though Preston had the sweetest frame, his lifting high the cross taught us "wholly to lean on Jesus' name". For Preston, it was "on Christ the Solid Rock I stand. All other ground is sinking sand."

To know the heart of Preston was to know the heart of the Father. God does not see as man sees. Man looketh on the outward appearance, but Preston taught us through the Candle Light of Christ within him, shining purely and humbly, that the Lord looks on the heart. As much as we loved Preston's features and manly, angelic bearing, it was his pure heart after God that made us all fall in love with him along with Laura. She is the blessed one to have been asked to be his wife, for which she thanked him daily throughout their 28 year honeymoon.

Preston showed us how to <u>live life abundantly</u>, that You, Lord Jesus, came to earth that we might have that life. Equally, Preston showed us how to share in Your sufferings. Preston's life revealed that "a good name is better than precious riches, that the day of one's death is better than the day of one's birth, for truly it is better to go to the house of mourning than to go to the house of feasting, for death is the end of all men, and the living will lay it to heart. A man's wisdom makes his face to shine", and oh how Preston's face glowed with Your Glory.

Take our hearts of stone, and give us hearts of flesh, as you did Preston, that we might be wholly devoted to you. Cause us to know the way wherein we should walk, for we lift up our souls unto Thee. "So teach us to number our days that we may apply our hearts to wisdom," like Preston. From his home perch view across the green pastures, to the porpoises and sunlight dancing on the water, he focused on the cross he planted in the marsh across the Ashley River. Up in his prayer room office, Preston spent his early mornings in daily Quiet Times studying Your Word, leafing through the leaves of the Bible that are for the healing of the nations with such relish as in eating honey and ice cream. There the heart of Preston was that drew the strength to be to us the tall, strong man of God.

Thank you that Preston taught us that real men can love each other deeply.

`Thank you that Preston never lost his sense of play, with his male friends, and especially with his three daughters, nieces, nephews, Godchildren, great nieces and great nephews, and with Bentley and Chesterfield, his wholly devoted English Springer Spaniels.`

Thank you for broadening Preston's borders to include each one of us, who love the pilgrim soul in him. You heard the persistent heart cry of Laura for "the one" she would marry to have a heart after God, a heart after her, and if You would be so kind, good looks, too. With the birth of their three daughters, Olivia, Delia, and Victoria, you showered Preston with Daddy's girls, the love of many women. His girls are as plants grown up in their youth. Oh, that their daughters may be as cornerstones of Thy temple, polished after the similitude of a palace, each with a heart after God fashioned from their home family devotions, in Celebration retreats with Mike Allen, in St. Philips youth group with David Gilbert, and in Capers Cross's Canterbury choir.

May You give them each a man with a heart after God such as their father, though none can compare. May the Hipp girls not despair in their loss and grief but rejoice in having been so privileged to have as their father a man after God's own heart, and one so widely loved. May You be so kind as to have none but godly men come along beside them. May they feel and see the loving presence of each of us who love Preston, transferred to them, though none can take the place of their daddy.

Preston was in tune with your Spirit's flow along with the currents of the Ashley & Cooper Rivers. He was the Prince of Tides, who knew when it was high or low at any point of the day, his understanding like one who plays music by ear. Thank you, that he is bathing in that pure River of the water of Life, clear as crystal, proceeding out of the Throne of God and of the Lamb, washing away the dust and baggage of this world with which he was so encumbered. We do not understand from our point of view but trust You, Abba Father, who has THE View. We only see the loose threads of the underside of the tapestry of life, but You see it right side up.

Blessed is the one who perseveres under trial. Having stood the test, he receives the crown of life that you have promised to those who love You.

Preston has done all such good works as Thou hast prepared for him to walk in. We who have been loved and known by Preston consider ourselves his best life's work. We are his crown. Teach us to so number our days that we may apply our hearts to wisdom as did your servant Preston. He lifted high the cross, and like the

Gentleman that you, Lord Jesus are, allowed us to draw our own conclusions, living by example life set apart for your Glory, that others might want to taste and see that the Lord is good. Happy are the people whose God is the Lord.

Family & Friends Share Stories

While dating Laura, Preston expressed his ardor by putting his chainsaw to work to remove a hackberry tree in her little yard on Legare Street. Fall 1987. That Christmas, Preston proposed.

Memories from Family

BY OLIVIA HIPP

My dad was a man who carved out sanctuaries for himself. He was many things at once with an astounding ease - strong and meek, gregarious and pensive, daring and measured. As Walt Whitman writes, "I am large, I contain multitudes".

But seeking out time to reflect in the quiet of the natural world was a constant in his life. A self-proclaimed extroverted-introvert, he was a skilled escape artist. His office at our house was one of those sanctuaries, and I can hardly walk past the door without expecting to see his hand quietly turning the pages of his Bible or find him glued to a pair of binoculars watching the birds on the water. Sitting at my dad's desk, looking out over the wind whipped water with the flags at the Coast Guard Station blowing straight back, I find my own sanctuary. All of Dad's little keepsakes he liked to meditate on during his quiet time are still there, right where he left them. Flipping through the old photos piled high in shoe boxes, I was flooded with old memories.

Toward the end of my parents' courtship --- four years of breaking up and making up, my dad and his trusty chainsaw took down a huge hackberry tree that was looming out over my mom's little carriage house on Legare. One of my favorite photos shows him after this endeavor, sitting on the end of a carved up tree trunk looking straight into the

241

camera, resting his chin on the end of his chainsaw, surrounded by hewn limbs, coils of rope, and a ladder in the background leaning up against the stucco wall of the house.

Evidently, he often had a camera and tripod with him that he would set up to immortalize private moments like this. Mom marks this day as the moment Dad realized he had to marry her saying, "You don't understand the significance of what I have just done for you."

A natural born communicator, Mom was flabbergasted and started trying to sing his praises, even offering to pay him for his work, but he cut her off: "It's not just this tree. It's that I can think of a dozen more things I want to do for you, and I don't know when it would ever stop." Though I knew my dad as an older man, that quiet look was one I knew well -- equal parts cool and humble, daredevil and discerner, servant and leader.

At his desk I came across another photo, this one taken on my first birthday at the Legare carriage house. I've always laughed at my blind curiosity in this photo -- a round cheeked baby in a ruffled smocked dress reaching out, eyes closed shut, to grab the candle's flame on my birthday cake. But as I looked at it again, the scene took on a whole new meaning. Both my parents' hands are extended toward me, as if in a reenactment of Michelangelo's *Creation of Adam*, reaching out to protect me, this spark of life they created. You can see my mother's profile, nestled down beside my chair, but all you can see of my dad is his hand extended down from beyond the frame and already touching mine to pull me back from danger.

I would know my dad's hand anywhere - it was so recognizable, even in the end. I know how much he wanted to spare my sisters and me from the pain of a fallen world, and I cannot put into words how much I wish God had let this cup pass away from him. When someone has cancer, people are quick to give you advice: don't take this time for granted, think about what you'll regret more, live life to the fullest.

But no one tells you how impossible it will seem for the sun to still rise and set once they are gone. The moon will wax and wane; the tide will rise and fall; the world will move on with her festivities, and your eyes will still ache. No one told me how hard it would be to keep going without him. But we shouldn't shy away from talking about the dead in the present tense.

I can still see his hand in my life and the life of anyone who even just met him, even now that he is gone. How lucky am I to have had a guardian angel from year one there to protect me even when I couldn't see him? All I know is, death is bad, but God is good. And I am the luckiest girl in the world to have had the dad I have.

● ● ●

By Laura Wichmann Hipp (written on Nov. 17, 2015)

Preston, born May 23, 1959, grew up in the dirt roads of the Country Club playing in the crib with neighbor Barre Butler, both moving downtown when about 9, both going to Porter Gaud together all the way through. To have Barre with us for each of Preston's chemo sessions is a rare constant in life.

Preston tells of riding their bikes way farther than allowed before to upper King to buy a record, "Angel Aquarium", only the shop clerk had the discretion not to laugh but to figure out, "The Age of Aquarius". Barre's hard earned money and wallet were lost out of his back pocket and he cried like a baby riding up and down King Street looking for it.

Preston played tight end football for Porter Gaud with guys he is still friends with now, Barre, Winn Tutterow, Jack Sinclaire, Jody Bishop. Porter Gaud friend Malcolm Rhodes brings by his famous gourmet grilled meats. Jerry Poore and Preston burst into smiles and hugs when together after too long apart, with Jerry lamenting that he works too hard at his landscape business. Richard Hollowell comes over from his job and new life in China to see his old friend. The Hollowell family of countless boys was like a second family to Preston in the country at the old Pinckney home of Snee Farm.

Preston was a late surprise to his parents, a fourth child and second son when they thought they were finished. I often think how God was answering my girlhood prayers for my husband in bringing Preston, unplanned and unexpected, into his parents' lives. Bonney was his closest sibling by 6 years, Dee by 10 yrs, and Charley by 12. When Preston went to first grade at PG, Charley went off to Clemson and was soon a married man with daughter, Shea, followed by Charles Rucker Hipp III. Preston and Charles are much alike in mannerisms and humor. Preston is like a big brother to Shea and Charles as well as being Charles's godfather. Charles has always looked up to Preston.

Preston did not become a committed Christian until after college. He never spoke in tongues, so it is ironic that his testimony begins with this gift. He was dating a very sweet girl named Sheila with whom he went to Florida. They stayed with a married couple. Preston stayed up late talking to the Christian man who ended the conversation asking if he could pray for Preston. Preston said the moment this man with a slow Southern drawl started praying in tongues, the vacuum of his heart exploded with the reality of God; he knew it was not something this man could have made up as it was in sharp contrast to the way he spoke in English. "Tongues shall be a sign to unbelievers" was the case for Preston. He gave Preston a copy of *The Late Great Planet Earth*, by Hal Lindsey.

Preston read it and believed, but like the seed that sprouts up on the rocky soil immediately and then shrivels for lack of depth and water, Preston returned to his worldly lifestyle. He regretted the years he squandered during and immediately after college that could have been spent in fellowship and Bible study. Yet the seed had been planted.

After graduating with a degree in business at USC in the early 1980s, Preston had his first coat and tie job working for the Charleston County Tax Assessor's office. He worked alongside a man named Jim Hatcher. Jim Hatcher and his son-in-law Corky put an index card on the bulletin board simply saying Bible study at Corky's apartment on Ashley Ave.

One day Preston found himself asking Corky for directions, while at the same time saying to himself, "What are you saying?" He then drove to the Bible study again asking himself, "What are you doing?" (Editor's note: see the chapter, Preston Gives His Testimony, for more.)

Forever after to Preston, Jim Hatcher was Pastor Hatcher of Grace Bible Church. They memorized scripture in the Bible study, and Pastor Hatcher did expository teaching verse by verse, for a small group of adults of varying ages. Preston took to it like a fish to water. Eventually he went to their Sunday morning church as well. He said it was like drinking water from a fire hydrant.

When Corky and his wife moved, Preston got the apartment in the big Victorian house on Ashely Avenue, and the Bible studies continued in his apartment. While living there, Preston bought his first investment property directly across the street at 204 Ashley Avenue, the same year, the same month, that I bought my house at 57 and one-half Legare St. We both knew it was time to take a big step forward in our lives.

Preston gave up drinking upon his born again season of life. When his fellow co-worker Joanna Drake (Macmurphy) asked him to join us at Rockville on my father's boat, *Mobjack*, anchored off the Sea Island Yacht Club, he hesitated. He did not want to be tempted by the party scene. She reassured him he would meet a fellow Christian girl who took her faith seriously, which he did not think existed outside his small church.

Preston came by johnboat to ours and had a watermelon. Out of respect for our boat, he invited us down the side into his little johnboat to eat watermelon so as not to get seeds and drips on *Mobjack*. Our opening conversation was about the second coming of Christ and the book *The Late, Great Planet Earth* (by Carla C. Carlson and Hal Lindsey).

Our faith and bond to our churches kept us in lively discussions, dating and debating, for four years. To my surprise, he asked me to marry him Christmas morning 1987. I was afraid to blink for fear of the diamond disappearing, but afraid to wear it without Preston having asked my father for my hand. He knew my father and I are too close, and it would not be a surprise if he asked him first. When I told him I'd have to think about it, he was flabbergasted. "What have you been thinking about for four years? Don't tell me you haven't been thinking about it!"

April 9, 1988 we were married in St. Philip's Church, with a reception at the Carolina Yacht Club, after which we sailed away on the *Mobjack*, literally into the sunset!

Across the years and the birth of three daughters, humor and a daily Quiet Time in deep study of the Bible keep Preston and me focused on what lasts. Slow walks with our English Springer Spaniel, Chester, keep Preston refreshed as well as Bocci on Morris Island. Cancer in the bones is a nightmare, bad words I never imagined hearing. But the anchor holds. The veil gets thinner between us and the Glories of the Throne of God in Heaven. We are all on the same journey. It is going to be worth it all! He is worthy! A lump of coal is just a lump of coal unless under pressure. Then it becomes a diamond reflecting His Diadem of clear colors unimaginable in Eternity. It is a privilege to be married to the man of my dreams. I am blessed to still be in love with my husband, despite all the health issues. God gives us grace for each day, and each day is a gift!

After a festive wedding reception at the Carolina Yacht Club, Preston and Laura sailed away on *Mobjack*, April 9, 1988.

By Delia Hipp

One of my favorite stories about my dad and his unconditional love is when I got a 24 hour stomach bug when I was in high school. I remember lying on the floor of my bathroom switching between throwing up in the toilet and trying to sleep. It was not a pretty sight. I remember my dad picked me up and carried me to my room. He got me a blanket, ginger ale, and a trash can. He changed and washed my sheets for me and cleaned up the bathroom. He stayed home from work the next day and spent the entire day bringing me ginger ale and crackers. It was one of the sweetest things anyone has ever done for me. He ended up catching the stomach virus and was sick the next 24 hours but he never complained and he never showed any resentment towards me for getting him sick.

Another great thing about my dad is that he would randomly surprise all of us with little (or big) gifts or acts of service. He built us a tree house when we were kids and then bought a trampoline when we were too old for the tree house. He built us a rack to hold our bikes and built Victoria a basketball hoop attached to the trampoline so she could work on her skills. I came home from school one day and he walked into my room with an iPad. He told me it was for Victoria and me to share. He was so good about getting us wonderful gifts for no reason. Another time I came home to see that my dad had bought a new HD TV, a wii, a blue-ray player, and a skateboard for himself. He was such a kid sometimes. He ended up getting some serious road burn from falling off his skateboard later that week.

By Victoria Hipp

A few years ago I had full back surgery for scoliosis in the summer. It was scheduled for July 21. So when the 20th rolled around, I knew that was my last day of summer. I hadn't done much that day, but around 4:00 or so my dad asked me if I wanted to go on the boat. Automatically I said, "YES!"

We headed to the Yacht Club, just him, Chester and me. I was so excited I was finally going to do something. We get on the boat and I'm sitting in the front so I can ride the waves, and as always Chester is pacing back and forth. Dad is steering us towards Castle Pinckney, where Dad put up the white cross. The island is full of oyster shells, so you better wear shoes. Dad throws the ball for Chester, and I tell him I'm going to walk over to the castle. It's so beautiful with the sun shining down, and a port ship is heading out into the ocean right next to me. I finally arrive at the castle, but I see all these dead birds and it smells gross so I turn back. Dad just laughs and says that's too bad, and then we set off again.

**Delia with her Dad on the beach; another happy family day spent boating
and swimming in the Lowcountry waters.**

We head to the back side of Folly Beach, where all the trees have fallen. We play bocci, drip some drip castles, and balance on the fallen trees. The sun is starting to set and we see the tide went out. Our boat is now a ways out. Originally I had told him I didn't want to swim because I had just showered, but we both knew that wasn't going to happen. So we swam over to the boat and started jumping off. We jumped off the bow, and some of the seats. We played with Chester and Dad would play shark. Shark is where he would go down and swim towards me and try and scare me, and I would try and swim away. Sometimes I would be really good at it and whenever he grew close to me, I would swim over.

Overall it was an awesome day. No one can ever give me a better last day of summer. After my surgery I felt a lot closer to Dad. I wasn't going through his struggles, but I had my own now. We could relate to each other more through the shared pain. Dad was my rock through it all.

By F.C. "Bunky" Wichmann, Jr. (brother-in-law)

It's another one of those sleepless nights and I couldn't stop thinking of Preston - what with that full moon shining in my face and making me think of all the times we had together and how we had planned to spend this full moon together - out at the beach…

Preston and I used to go shrimping back in the '90s. We were younger, stronger, and each of us had a small child at this point. Our families were happy and all were healthy. One of the most memorable of those times was when we went down to Bass Creek at the north end of Kiawah in his johnboat, *Oyster Catcher,* to see how full we could get a 48-quart cooler with shrimp.

Victoria sits in her father's lap to drive the boat, while Dad demonstrates his iconic laid-back demeanor.

It was one of those days where the sun was not far from setting, the marsh was that bright tree frog kind of green, like just after a rain. The sky was starting to be lit up by a fiery orange sunset to the west with a few long wisps of clouds reaching into the heavens as if they were pulling the rays of the sun with them.

As the sun sank into the western sky, the moon started its rise in the east. It was the September full moon coming up over the scrub oaks, the palmettos and the marsh, as if it was choreographed by some larger being. One orb rose while the other fell. The moon was almost blood red as the sky completed wrapping the horizon with its crimson mist.

The air was warm and heavy, and you could smell the Lowcountry in every breath.

We could faintly hear the surf on the other side of the narrow spit of land before the road went in, and it was that final untouched section of the island.

I cast the net into the brown green water of Bass Creek and brought in our first shrimp of the season. The net popped and jumped as I hauled in that first load of shrimp. They were nice red leg shrimp making their way to the sea. We took this first catch and placed one on top of our Coleman Lantern to cook it and sample what God had offered to us. Preston said a prayer over it and we divided the morsel into two. We sat silently and smiled.

It was a perfect night --- as if we were in a John Carroll Doyle painting. That evening is frozen in time for me: a night that was just the two of us with God watching and rewarding us for our friendship. A time when we were young, strong --- and yes, healthy.

● ● ●

By Susan Owen (cousin)

To remember Preston is to remember the most fun parts of my life growing up, with my cousin, who was the absolute essence of LOVE. Love for life, love for people, love of God.

The first time Preston made an impression on me was on a family vacation. I was probably 8 years old, my sister would have been 3, and Preston was maybe 6 or 7. My family had gone to Charleston to visit our cousins, and the very first night, at the dinner table, Preston let out a huge burp. On purpose. I tried to hold in my laughter (it was terribly funny to me), and Preston got in trouble...all the while smiling with a little twinkle in his eye. The next morning at the breakfast table, there was that same twinkle. I started smiling, knowing something was about to happen, and sure enough; Preston burped the ABC's backwards and forwards. I laughed so hard I wet my pants, and Preston was grounded, but not for long.

From then on, throughout my life, I have loved being with Preston. He had such a joy for life, and he led a charmed one. He would lead us on bicycles, in and out of the deserted alley ways and through graveyards in Charleston. He could catch crabs, drive a boat (too fast), and jump off tall channel markers for fun. My sister and I could barely keep up. I wanted to be right beside him, soaking up all that love for life. He was irresistible that way. He loved people so much, and wanted them to have as much fun as he did. And did we ever! Preston was "Dennis the Menace" to adults, but for me he was an absolute blast. Climb a water tower at night? No problem. Sit on the very top? How cool. Shimmy back down? I thought I was going to die.

As a young adventurer, Preston lived briefly in the Colorado Rockies. January 1982.

Preston lived a large life....wild and free. He lived in the mountains of Colorado for a while and would write me letters of his experiences while there. Snowshoeing, snowmobiling, etc. Wonderful stuff. He drove all the way to Alaska on the Al-Can highway. I was so jealous, it sounded like such an adventure. (and not for the faint of heart). Preston really knew how to enjoy life to the fullest.

When Preston settled down, got married, and started raising a family, he wanted his dear family to know and learn the love he had...for life, for people, and for God. His wife and daughters were right there with him. Preston taught all of us so much; he knew all the answers about the water, the birds, the world of nature around the sea. He could fix a boat, fell a tree, build anything.

Preston also loved to just sit down and talk. Really talk with you. He always wanted to know how you were, what's going on in your life, what's important to you. I think I miss just talking with him the most of all.

Preston was genuine, a true gentleman, and the best cousin anyone could ever have.

Upon reading Cousin Susan's memory piece, Joyce Wichmann, Preston's mother-in-law, wrote this:

How I wish I could have grown up wild and free with Preston! He was unique alright and so comfortable in his skin. Everything seemed so easy and natural to him. I first started to realize this one day sitting on the patio when he caught a green anole lizard and nonchalantly made it hang off his ear like some far out hippy earring.

• • •

By Dee Hipp Pridgen (sister)

Preston was my baby brother and what a beautiful baby he was. He had blond curls and big blue eyes. I pushed him in his stroller and fed him baby food and he was a happy, easygoing little boy.

Of course we shared every family event — Christmas, Easter, Thanksgiving, birthdays and boating trips. However, a deep bond with Preston began when he was a young teen and our sister, Bonney, was killed in a tragic car accident. We grieved and mourned together as we had never experienced such sadness.

Soon afterwards Preston and I went on a trip to Pisgah National Forest for a few days. We hiked and camped out, and I discovered that we shared a joy in the great outdoors and the healing it can provide.

Preston and I also shared a love of snow skiing, and he visited me in Colorado when he was 23, and then he later spent an entire winter in Steamboat Springs.

Preston surprised our family when he became a devout, born-again Christian; this is when we developed a new bond in prayer. Preston would visit my husband, Bill, and me and our two young sons, Will and Matt. He loved to roughhouse with them and they would climb on him like a jungle gym and he would toss them high into the air. Then he would shower all of us with the most beautiful, heartfelt prayer.

Fast-forward almost thirty years and I was still enjoying every moment of being with Preston. He brought his daughter Victoria out to Colorado for spring break to ski and snowboard, and it was a wonderful week of adventure that happily also included my son Will. Preston had not skied in all those years and yet was able to ski beautifully.

A year later he and Laura and their middle child Delia visited me in the summer in Colorado, and we hiked and delighted in God's creation of wild flowers and magnificent mountains. It was God's timing to have Preston there then.

I once asked Preston how he learned to be a prayer warrior and he knew exactly the right thing to say for the person receiving his prayer.

"Well, Sis, you learn through practice," he replied.

I was fortunate to have such a brother as Preston.

• • •

By Matt Pridgen (nephew)

When I first met Jesus in 2005, I didn't have any Christian friends. I had been a self-proclaimed atheist for nearly three years, I used drugs every day and I hung around with people of like mind and lifestyle. When my Aunt Laura gave me a Christian music album for Christmas some years before, I scoffed at her faith and wrote her off as just another one of those religious nuts. Who cares about a man who lived two thousand years ago and a religion that seemed hell bent on killing my buzz?

Suddenly though, I found myself in an entirely new paradigm. I had encountered the power, the presence and most importantly the unconditional love and mercy of the God of the Universe, Jesus Christ. Although I had run from him, mocked him, spit on him, slandered him and rejected him in the worst way, he pursued me to the bitter end and ultimately prevailed in saving my soul from a watery grave and a fiery hell. Like the newly delivered Gerasene demoniac, I now sat at the very feet of Jesus, clothed and in my right mind, hanging on His every Word and ready to do anything in my power to serve Him and to advance His Kingdom on this earth.

In a moment's time, I went from having a music library full of tunes that spoke to my heart and warmed my soul to having one Christian music album that my Aunt Laura had given me years before. I went from having tons of like minded friends who wanted nothing to do with Jesus to having a couple of family members who followed Him with all of their heart. From that day on, my relationship with my Uncle Preston and Aunt Laura changed dramatically and became a relationship that would change me for eternity.

Uncle Preston was always cool. Although I did not connect with him spiritually in my youth, he would always wrestle with my brother and me and roll around on the floor with us from as far back as I can remember. Technically, he belonged to the generation ahead of me, but in my mind, he was my friend and most importantly, a human jungle gym. Needless to say though, Uncle Preston and Aunt Laura became a whole lot more to me the day I became a committed follower of Jesus Christ.

Instantly their home and their presence in my life became a beacon of Light that helped guide my way to the shores of Zion. Whenever I needed a pick-me-up, I would just stop by unannounced for fellowship and encouragement and what Preston and the girls called "rough games," where the tide turned and I became the human jungle gym for Olivia, Delia and Victoria. I remember standing in front of the house gazing at the warm light pouring out from the front windows and thinking, *this is home.*

Preston's Friday morning Bible study was the first Bible study I ever attended beyond my high school youth group days. His careful and heartfelt approach to rightly divining the scriptures provided spiritual nourishment for countless numbers of men week after week, year after year, decade after decade. His passion for God's word was contagious. So many men would show up at 7 a.m. on a Friday morning (which at the time, being a college student, seemed totally insane to me) that Preston was always debating about when and how to branch off a new group. Although he hated the idea because he did not want to miss being with any part of the flock, he knew that Jesus' call was to multiply and that was his primary allegiance.

As Preston's illness progressed, his passion for Jesus seemed to increase exponentially. This is difficult to say about a man who I considered my whole life through as being all-in for God, but something changed as he moved deeper and deeper into the Refiner's Fire. Just months before he went home to Glory, Preston shared a word with me that I will cherish for the rest of my life. He observed that many people just like us want to draw near to God and desire to enter into his presence more and more, but that there is one thing we don't take into account – the cost.

"God is a consuming fire," Preston told me with conviction in his voice and a deep passion in his eyes, "and the closer we get to Him, the more of us He burns up until there is nothing left of our old sin nature, but only His nature formed in us."

This was not a teaching but a living, sharp, and active Word. This was Preston's life of being crushed daily in the relentless crucible of God, bearing a weight that very few of us can imagine, enduring radiation and hormone therapy, procedures and hospital stays, poking and prodding and sleepless nights, tubes and bags and all sorts of mess that Preston never talked about because he was, well, Preston.

Yet in the midst of it all, rather than being bitter toward life and God and the lot he had been given, Preston never failed to recognize God's hand at work behind the scenes. He tapped into the greater storyline of his loving and perfect Father accomplishing a work that only the Sovereign Ruler of the universe could do under such bleak circumstances.

Please know that I am in no way saying that Preston's illness or any disease for that matter was sent by God. Jesus healed, not afflicted. Nor do I claim to understand why Preston was not miraculously healed during one of our countless prayer sessions, trusting in God's Word for the restoration of his body. As Preston would often note, "God knows every single one of the trillions of cells that make up our bodies."

For Jesus to heal Preston completely would be a cinch. Yet for reasons we may never know on this side of Eternity, the Lord allowed Preston's illness to persist even to the point of death.

Fortunately for all of us who believe on Jesus Christ for salvation, death is not the end of the story but only the beginning. God has a great way of using for good what Satan intends for evil. The enemy of Preston's soul heaped on him sickness after sickness and trial after trial, but rather than breaking down his faith and cooling the embers of his passionate love for Jesus, all of the pain and all of the struggle only served to strengthen an already mighty man of God's faith and love and conviction that Jesus Christ is every bit of who He says He is, the one and only Son of God who laid down His life for His beloved Preston and for all who believe in Him, who paid the ultimate price to save our souls, who tasted death so that we could taste life, who went to Hell so that we could spend Eternity in Heaven.

Satan pinned Jesus to a tree thinking that death would be the end of Him, but God turned the whole story around and used the greatest evil the world has ever seen to rob the perpetrator blind. Jesus rose from the grave with the keys to death and Hell in His possession, and this is a very good thing for you and for me and for Preston.

As Preston would always say, "Christianity is not a hope-so religion, it is a know-so religion."

Preston Hipp staked his entire life on the finished work of the cross of Jesus Christ. All the junk that Satan hurled his way to destroy him, God used to create a diamond of a man who will now eternally magnify the light of Christ for all of Heaven to see. I can't wait to get to Heaven and see the many crowns given to Preston through this trial and then to cast mine down with his at the feet of our beloved Jesus.

I miss Preston but it won't be long. I will see my friend and uncle and brother in Christ soon enough. Until then, I am determined to press into the consuming fire of God at all cost and to offer myself as a living sacrifice to God in the same way I saw Preston do it, through a life of love and service. And no matter what trials and temptations come my way, I will press into the heart of God more and more until there is nothing left of me, but only Him.

Preston was convinced that only a Revival of the Holy Spirit could bring about the changes we long to see in our city, state and nation. He was fully committed to being a vessel of that Revival, and so should every one of us who call ourselves by the name of Jesus Christ. Because in the end, it's not about Preston, and it's not about us. It's about the souls who God wants to reach through us. Are we ready to be fully surrendered as Preston was to Revival in Charleston? Are we ready to be used by God for any purpose at any cost? If so, let's commit to being all-in as Preston was for Revival and for Jesus. Then we will see a single seed that has fallen into the ground and died multiply and bear much fruit for the Kingdom of God.

As Renny Scott shared in conclusion at Preston's funeral, we all know what Preston would say to us if he were still here. He would pull each one of us aside individually and say, "Follow Jesus no matter what, because in the end, it will be worth it."

When we arrive in Glory and see Preston with all of the souls, the countless number of souls who are there because he gave it his all and because we gave it our all, then we will hear the same words that Preston heard, the sound that rings through the human soul like no other sound in all of creation, the sound that our loving, doting Heavenly Father longs to speak over each one of His precious children, "Well done, good and faithful servant. You have been faithful over a little; I will set you over much. Enter into the joy of your master."

Until then, dear Preston, until then.

● ● ●

By Will Pridgen (nephew)

As a young child, I absolutely adored my Uncle Preston. It's tough to put into words how cool I thought he was. He was smart, funny, tall, handsome and athletic -- and he would spend hours playing with my brother and me. He would swing us around in the air, climb in trees with us, give us tips on how to fish or throw a frisbee, and build towers out of blocks and let us knock them down. He was just the most fun uncle you could imagine.

I grew up during my early years in Myrtle Beach, which was a couple of hours away from Preston in Charleston, so that made seeing him even more special. One of my earliest and happiest memories is of Preston rolling around with us on the floor of my grandparents' house in Charleston and picking Matt and me up and pretending we were airplanes. We also loved to go to the house on Seabrook Island and play with Preston in the pool. He had a great time playing with a big green alligator float, and he prided himself on being able to make the biggest splash when jumping into the pool.

After I left for college, I always looked forward to seeing Preston when I visited Charleston or went to a family reunion. He always wanted to do something fun, something outdoors. He would take us on his boat and go as fast as possible, or we would go waterskiing, or we'd go out to the country and shoot skeet, or we'd play bocce on the beach. Whatever it was, Preston was really good at it.

A few years ago, my mom and I went skiing in Colorado with Preston and Victoria, and of course he was a natural even though he hadn't been skiing in many years.

Preston had a magnetic personality and a contagious smile and laugh. One Christmas Day, he collected some items from his house to give away during our extended family's "Chinese" gift exchange. Preston didn't realize that some of those items weren't his to give away -- they were the prized possessions of Daniel Massi, an old friend of Laura's, which were being stored temporarily in Laura and Preston's attic. At it happened, Daniel and his mother were also at the gift exchange and, when he noticed that his stuff was being given away, he started to object.

"Hey, that's mine! What's going on?!"

Preston realized what he had done and started laughing uncontrollably. He kept laughing and couldn't stop, and at least a dozen other people couldn't help themselves from busting out laughing with him. We laughed until we cried, especially Preston.

As I got older, I started to see that Preston wasn't just cool, smart, funny, tall, handsome and athletic. He was also incredibly faithful, holy, loving and devoted to his Lord and his family. He had a strong moral compass and a great character. I don't remember him ever speaking poorly about anyone. Everything he did, he did for Laura, Olivia, Delia and Victoria. He loved them so very much, and you could tell it every day by the way he looked at them, the way he treated them, and the way he spoke about them.

Preston's faith was at the center of his life, and he wasn't afraid to spread the Word. I was honored when he invited me to go with him to put up a giant cross in Charleston Harbor.

Through all of his trials and suffering, he showed his faithfulness and his hope. He regularly shared his experiences at the hospital through email updates as he persevered through various stages of cancer. You could tell how difficult and painful it was for him. He sometimes joked about those tough experiences, but he didn't complain. He always came back to one main point -- God has a master plan, and Jesus died for our salvation, so we don't have to worry. Preston remained ever optimistic, and his positive attitude and prayers for others gave so many people the strength to face their own challenges in life.

When I was five years old, I was the ring bearer at Laura and Preston's wedding. Twenty-seven years later, when my wedding in San Diego was right around the corner, Preston was in the hospital. We were worried that he might not be able to make it across the country, but Preston doesn't give up easily. It was nothing short of a miracle for him to be able to fly across the country so he could be there to celebrate our marriage with us.

I see Preston as a wonderful role model for myself, and it meant so much to me to have him at my wedding. My wife Ellen and I are expecting our firstborn in the next few weeks, and I hope I can be even half as good a dad to my son as Preston has been to his three amazing daughters.

When Ellen and I saw Preston at the Hipp cousin reunion at Pawley's Island in July, Ellen was six months pregnant, and Preston was so happy for us. As we were about to leave, we went into a bedroom where Preston was lying down. We wanted to say goodbye and say a prayer for him before we headed back to California. He struggled to speak, because he was physically weak and tired and his mouth was dry. But before we had a chance to say anything, Preston had mustered up the strength and he was praying for us and for our future son. That's how I will remember Preston.

●　●　●

By Louis Hipp (Cousin Lou)

When I think of Preston, these three words keep coming to mind.

Courage. Preston has always had the courage to be Preston. Pursuing, inquiring, exploring, sharing, connecting throughout his life, he was very comfortable being Preston. Whether sharing his faith, taking a risk, or pulling a prank, he showed courage throughout his life.

Patience. While Preston's faith was among the strongest (and clearest/easiest to understand), he was careful to share it in a way that was comfortable to those around him. He did not push; he did not insist. He encouraged others, but he waited until they were ready to take a step forward of their own motivation. His patience was one of his most beautiful traits.

Grace. Preston's ability to listen, to connect, to find and celebrate the best in others was amazing. He looked for opportunities to help or be of assistance or introduce someone to his faith, and he made sure that it was gracefully connected to that individual, not just something of Preston's that he wanted to foist on others.

I am ten years older than Preston, and have few memories of him in his early years. We lived in different towns, different states, and even when our families got together, I did not interact with him much. That all changed, at least in my memory, when I was about 20 (and he was 10) and my family came to Charleston to visit with the Hipp Cousins Reunions in James Island, I believe. I recall being outside in the yard when someone drove up in a muddy, beat-up Scout (Jeep-type vehicle, but cooler!). Well, who pops out of the driver's seat but Preston, all of age 10. This is my first memory of the man, who at age 10 seemed to have fished, hunted, and even driven (at least off-road) more than I had at age 20! At that moment I remember thinking, "This is a cousin I need to get know better!"

Lucky for me that my life allowed me to get to know my very special cousin better. Through our many visits to Charleston, our Cousins Reunions, and of course our family time in nearby Pawleys Island, I got to know Preston more and more, the life he had chosen, and his wonderful family!

I am grateful for every moment he shared with me, whether sitting on the porch, kayaking in Shem Creek, catching a wave, talking on the phone, or building sand castles.

Courage, patience, and grace. Preston made an indelible impact on my life and on my family, and we are all grateful for that.

We will miss him, and we will celebrate his touch on our lives every day!

• • •

By Joyce Wichmann (wife of Laura's father)

There are so many wonderful things about Preston that it's hard to know where to start. I admired him from the moment I met him, but I can't say there was instant rapport. Quite some years after I came into the family as his mother-in-law of sorts, I began to realize that he actually cared about ME. He picked up on happy events and on troubles in my life, and made a point to comment, praise, inquire, or offer help. Preston, who was way up there on my ladder of admiration, with all his wonderful qualities and his brim-full life, noticed and cared about ME. Even deep into HIS illness, he would call, text, or email to offer encouragement, and just as he did countless other people, made me feel special.

Another endearing quality was Preston's creative playfulness. He loved a good joke, even if it were on him. When my grandchildren came to visit, their first request was, "Can Uncle Preston come play?" He always made time to rough house, play hide and seek, or make a game out of anything.

Preston and his famous "Green Machine" around 1989.

Memories from Friends

BY MALCOLM RHODES, M.D.

It is very difficult to write about any one adventure enjoyed (survived?) with Preston from 50 plus years of Lowcountry jaunts. Midnight swamp walks to hear male alligators make mating bellows, all night flounder gigging trips, snipe hunts (yes, Wilson's snipe in rice fields), or shepherding a dozen girls on 60-foot sand mine mounds all rate high, but placing the first cross on Castle Pinckney gives some insight into Preston and his joy of the Lowcountry.

This adventure began solely in Preston's mind as he decided that all mariners in Charleston needed to be greeted with a waterside cross. Preston had procured the wood, manufactured the two pieces that would be joined at deployment, and painted the sections white. I was honored to be recruited for another mission so readily accepted, as did another friend, Ian Walker. My job was to purchase 6 more bags of concrete and pick Preston up at 7:30 a.m.

Did we have permission? No, but we could always ask forgiveness, was the answer.

The epic day was a Good Friday in March, during the early 1990s. We stopped by the St. Philip's Men's Bible Study to ask if anyone else wanted to embark on this adventure. No takers, a lot of quizzical faces but there must have been some powerful prayers.......

We arrived at the Carolina Yacht Club where the Green Machine held the cross pieces, a post hole digger, shovels and MORE concrete. Preston already had our transportation, his 16 foot customized johnboat powered by a 15 horse tiller steer engine, in the water. Realize this vessel would soon be filled with 500 pounds of concrete mix, tools, 3 adult men, AND the cross pieces, the 16-foot upright extending 4 feet beyond the bow to allow passengers.

Oh yes, I forgot to mention that this was NOT the Chamber of Commerce spring Friday but rather a gray, 40 degree morning with a wind blowing up the harbor creating whitecaps, that last vestige of winter.

Preston, the eternal optimist, was sure we could carry everything over in one trip so we loaded and loaded then loaded some more. Our captain cranked the engine, flashed his half-smile and we took off.

In the protected basin, everything was okay; we had at least 2 inches of freeboard. Then the crossing began with whitecaps coming right to the edge of the gunnels causing even Preston to have a moment of doubt, but we were halfway there and would get swamped if we tried to turn back, or if we encountered any vessel making a wake...

As you can imagine it was an extremely slow journey with the engine straining to push the load, waves lapping right to the top of the gunnels and no other boaters in sight if aid were needed. Somehow through prayers and the Grace of God, we bumped against the shell bank of Castle Pinckney. There have been few more joyous moments in Charleston Harbor as Preston began with shouts of praise, his patented, "I knew we could do it", and a dance of High 5's, this time with a full-on smile.

This is the epic Good Friday adventure, Preston, Malcolm, and Ian Walker raise a cross on Shutes Folly.

With the voyage over, the completion of the cross went smoothly. We came to realize that post hole diggers don't work well in a shell bank, but that shovels could slowly wallow an opening. We assembled the cross, stood it upright and poured 10 bags of concrete in the hole, which we then mixed in place using saltwater from the harbor.

In a perfect story, I would state that a sunbeam broke through the clouds illuminating the cross, a chorus of terns and gulls sang and porpoises did flips in the channel. Unfortunately, the weather just stayed grey and windy, but our hearts were light, the trip back was easy because there was about a foot of freeboard, the johnboat could cruise on a plane and.....the police or Coast Guard hadn't caught us in the act!

This was the first of several crosses placed by Preston. This cross did tumble after a big storm and was placed back upright. It was later totally uprooted and found miles away, but brought back to its locale. Eventually it was replaced. Preston placed another cross on the Ashley River side of the harbor where he could see it from his home.

● ● ●

Here nephew Matt Pridgen shares a memory of helping Uncle Preston erect a replacement harbor cross around 2005:

One of the very first things I ever did as a Christ follower was to travel with Preston on a little dingy boat across the harbor toting a giant wooden cross and bag upon bag of cement to Castle Pinckney. There were four of us in that boat, and the weight of us and the cross and all of our supplies caused the water to sit just inches from the top of the dingy.

My nerves stood in clear contrast with Preston's cool and calm. Just yards away from the island, the boat's motor died and we coasted into the oyster bank with graceful ease. After erecting the cross, we sat around reading Psalms until Uncle Charley arrived to rescue us. The whole time, all I could think about was the fact that if the motor had died just seconds before it did, we would have been floating around the harbor in a tiny boat with a fifteen-foot wooden cross.

This man had favor with God.

● ● ●

Prior to moving to a better life, Preston made yet another cross which was stored in a lot he owned. After Hurricane Matthew, Oct. 8, 2016, one month after his death, Castle Pinckney's cross was damaged beyond repair. A large group of men from Preston's Friday morning Bible study, along with Laura and Chester, made the trip. Here are two first-hand descriptions of that adventure:

From Laura:

That morning, the city and harbor were completely shrouded in fog, so much so that the captain of the hired boat asked which way we needed to go. Castle Pinckney was invisible, as was the city, the bridges, everything. Billy Barnwell answered: "Straight Ahead! You will hit it before you see it."

As the fog began to lift, only the tops of the church steeples, the top of a cruise ship, and tip tops of the Cooper River bridge became visible, while underneath remained in a white out. As the digging and cementing went on, the fog lifted, leaving a colorless bright, white rainbow connecting the city to Shutes Folly. We saw this as the cloud of His presence, combined with Preston's presence, among us. The men kept working, digging into those oyster shells to get that cross planted, pouring buckets of sea water to mix with the cement in the hole, while this surreal sign was going on right around them.

From Shep Davis:

It was a dead still morning, totally fogged in at the Carolina Yacht Club. Twenty friends of Preston had gathered to replace the magnificent cross he had erected years before on Castle Pinckney. We were a somber but joyous group, each one reflecting on the deep individual connection Preston had with him. We all know Preston *was* special to so many people, but let's never forget everyone *was* truly that special to Preston.

We loaded the beautiful new cross on a big flats boat and silently left the dock. As soon as we moved, the fog started to thin, imperceptibly at first but slowly rolling away from our path. As we reached the island a giant "cloud bow" formed north of us from shore to shore: I have never seen anything like this.

The sky above became clear blue and after a time, the tops of the bridge poked out. All became clear and glorious, not a cloud to be seen. And the water...the water was so pure and clear it was almost invisible to the eye.

We glided onto the oyster shells, unloaded our treasure, and set to work replacing the cross.

Small groups shared stories, some reveled in God's day, many were quiet. Some worked, some watched.
We closed with Matt Pridgen blessing the cross, and all joined in saying the Lord's Prayer.

As we swung the boat around the first thing I saw was St Philip's Church. It felt like a cord connected it with us and that cross as we silently motored to back to CYC. All were blessed.

A General Timeline of Preston's Harbor Crosses

"**G**ood Friday was always when he did this sort of thing," Laura said. "It was his Good Friday observance."

1) Good Friday, 1988 -- Preston and the Rev. Richard Dority, founder of the James Island Christian Church, put up the original cross at the Jetties at the entrance to the Charleston Harbor from the ocean.

2) The first cross on Shutes Folly/Castle Pinckney went up sometime in the early 1990s, erected by Preston, Malcolm Rhodes, and Ian Walker.

3) in 1998, Preston put up the cross in the James Island marsh in the Ashley River across from his family's new home beside the Coast Guard Station. The Hipps moved into 194 Tradd with the Ashley River water view in January, 1998.

4) Over time, salt water and storms damaged the crosses. Matt Pridgen and Herman Robinson helped Preston put up a replacement cross on Shutes Folly/Castle Pinckney -- Matt was born again in May 2005. He recalls that this adventure was that summer.

5) Preston put up a cross in the marsh near Porter-Gaud School in memory of Mitch Hollon, who was killed in July 2011 while riding a bike on the James Island connector. Laura says Preston

located this particular cross at the request of Patty Hollon, the widow. It just so happened that Preston's white cross can also be seen from the chapel of Porter-Gaud School. Preston was a member of the class of 1977 and remained close to many of his high school friends. He also prayed regularly with his friend Brian McGreevy, chaplain for 13 years, for the school's ministry to the students. The sight of the cross from the chapel was an unexpected benefit; "It was miraculous," Laura said.

6) Before Preston died, he had prepared a replacement cross for Shutes Folly/Castle Pinckney, but his health failed before he could finish the job. After Preston's death in September 2016, about 20 friends and members of his Friday Morning Men's Bible Study, along with Laura and Chester, put up Preston's final cross under a cloud of glory.

The original plan was to leave the older cross behind as flotsam and jetsam; however Belk Daughtridge decided to salvage the cross and haul it back that day to the mainland. With some effort, Belk found a carpenter who agreed to use the wood to build a beautiful bench. Under Belk's leadership and with the help of the Friday Morning Men's Bible Study, the project was completed with the bench being dedicated to Preston and set out on the upstairs porch of the Parish Hall at St. Philip's Church.

THE PRINCE
By Fraser Henderson, Jr.

The Holy City hath its prince
Spartan words he does not mince
Three daughters match three diamonds
On his maiden's hand

Morris Island tends his anchor
Where swift currents heed strict orders

Belk Daughtridge and Bruce Burris flank the cross as friends carry Preston's replacementcross out to Shutes Folly in Charleston Harbor. (Photo by Joe Nicholson)

There he floats in saline bliss
be-spanieled.

Its Batt'ry Wagner took many in
Their blood persists today
You can see it in the sand, taste it when you swim...
I know this, he told me.

These sanguine tides know his Father
They therefore fear the son
But his was not the glory for a cure
The IV poles were not to win

The eleventh hour progressed
to twelve.

Bells mourn, the people weep, lads drift –
But hear my secret – he still holds Court!
For when ye sip of Charleston harbor
ye sip with him!

● ● ●

by George Kanellos

How can I write adequately about Preston? How do I capture in a few
words all of the adventures on the *Oyster Catcher* (his johnboat) and so
many activities that centered around the water?

*(After hours of writing, rewriting, and tossing pages into the trashcan, George
eventually composed the following tribute to his beloved friend.)*
George Preston Hipp was christened at Second Presbyterian Church
where my grandparents, mother, and later I, were members. The

Hipps transferred their membership to First Scots, so I missed out on the opportunity of knowing Preston at an early age.

We met at a Bible study that was held at Preston's house on Ashley Avenue in 1984. We were both seeking to know God, to lead lives that were pleasing to Him, to study the Bible, to adopt the teachings of Jesus Christ into our own lives.

Edmund Hillary planted a flag to mark a spot many years ago; but it would be less than accurate to describe this era as the flag mark on Preston's timeline — rather it was the mark where, as he said, "I got it" — it made sense. Our friendship began easily and lasted a lifetime. We memorized Bible verses, went to and taught Bible studies, discussed *Pilgrim's Progress*: we loved the imagery of Christian on his journey, losing the heavy backpack/burden he carried, running ahead and calling: "Life!"

The Old Boy crossed the Finish Line last year — chest forward, senses keen, running for Life, right out of this world and into the next, into the arms of Jesus. Ba-Boom!!! (A Preston-ism)

I try not to think about Preston being dead. This is where earnest people say:

"Well, he is in a better place now."
"i'm just glad he's not suffering."
"We'll be together one day."

For me, I do not know what to say. I prayed to the last that God would heal him. I cannot fathom the mind of God, nor the depth of his loving kindness, nor the actions that happen in the world, specifically now. One thing that I feel strongly is overwhelming gratitude toward God for Preston Hipp in my life. I am not alone in my feelings.

And now, to share some stories:

I had the great fortune of owning an old log house in Chester County, S.C. My great grandfather, Sidney Alexander Rodman developed a little community that bore his name, Rodman. My mother, Hamilton Rodman Kanellos, said the population is about 25, but at one time it was double, if not triple, that amount!

I bought the house and a few acres at the center of a large beautiful farm of rolling hills, woods, fields, and stream owned by my cousin. I worked on that house, not a restoration but a fixer upper...it was built by one of my great grandfathers in about 1772. Preston went there with me some, and on one occasion, we removed a section of the house that had fallen into a state of disrepair (not that the rest of the place was much better).

We could have spent days taking down that motley add-on, but decided we would tie a series of ropes to it and pull 'er down. We attached the rope to the bumper of my old Chevrolet truck....one of us would drive, and the other pray. After the truck gained some low speed, the rope tightened quickly at that pace....we felt in our hearts that either the section would dislodge or the bumper would come loose. Luckily, the former occurred, and Preston was able to build a fire that satisfied his pyromania in a big way. The old house stood.

Another story from that place: there was a colony of bees living in the house that had, it appeared, been there a couple of years. I wanted them out, as they were a nuisance and prohibited me, or anyone for that matter, from fully enjoying the inside space. Preston was used to these things and had the proper equipment to get rid them. He said it would not take too much time, and it would be quick and humane. We would follow proper protocol to keep from killing the bees.

We arrived early one morning when everything was still. We had attired ourselves in full coveralls, armed with hand-held equipment that billowed smoke. The bees became docile, and we were able to cut out about 50 pounds of honey. We put the honey comb in tin tubs, but the bees somehow resented our invasion of their space and followed us to the truck; we had to leave on the bee suits, and we drove away with their honey in the back.

We stopped in Richburg to get gas and take off the coveralls and netted head coverings. We got plenty of stares from the people at the gas station...as though we were trying to look like space men.

Finally, as the years rolled on and Laura said she would marry Preston, they wanted to stay at the old log house on their honeymoon. Since there was no bed upstairs, I had to take off the siding of the gable to get a bed hoisted in the house....Other conveniences were an old ICE BOX (Preston had given it to me), a 1930's enameled cook stove powered by propane, oil lamps, and a hand pump out back. A P.S. here: I gave that house to my Aunt and Uncle, who restored the place to perfection.

Another locale of our friendship comes to mind: Folly was an Island that Preston liked....my grandfather had purchased a board and batten cottage during Word War II. My grandmother refused even to go there until my father and uncle, Navy and Army respectively, came home safely; they did, and we still have the cottage in our family.

Back in the day, Preston and I enjoyed spending time here. I brought out an old table that was under the house, covered with cracked linoleum which provided a great place to draw a map with lines, fissures and raised areas...this became a map of Israel and Judea for our Bible study on the porch. After a great swim, we traced the life of Jesus: this is where He was born....this is where the tax collectors lived, where the woman sat by the well, the sea where Jesus cooked fish for his disciples early one morning. This is the land where He died...and rose. The map allowed us to trace the steps....

Less worthy were the nights we spent in waders with blackened faces (the stuff athletes use under their eyes or that hunters use not to be seen). Armed with machetes, we would sneak into the canal behind our house at low tide when all was still....and hack away at the marsh grass. There was a reason for this. For sale was 13 acres of marsh, canal, two jutting peninsulas, and a very small island for $19K. In order to make the island accessible, some land would need to be filled in, but the Department of Natural Resources (DNR) does not allow that kind of portion to be filled, so if it was not there, a permit could be had — in theory.
That deal did not work out ...and the grass grew back two fold within weeks.

Stono Ferry was another playground for Preston. It was a fantastic Hipp family property: fields, woods, an island, and it was on the Intracoastal Waterway. Preston lived there for a time in a trailer in a state of utopia.

The last time I hunted deer was there with Preston. You might think that I was so sad after Preston died that I could not fathom hunting without him. Not so. Preston got so irritated with me talking, breaking twigs as we stepped through the forest, rustling leaves, and missing clear shots that I put down my gun and took up the brush. Now, I still go to opening Shoot at Sabin Hall, with my wife Molly's cousins, the first weekend in September. My son, Hill, and the others are blasting away, and I sit under a tree by the Rappahannock River and paint pictures of the birds. I cannot paint too well, but I paint better than I shoot. That is a good thing for everyone's quota as well as personal safety. Thank you, Old Boy.

Bees Ferry was another place Preston's family owned.....It is another great spot, and while it was not on the water, there were bogs and wet low areas. Preston was in heaven there. He built a barn/shed to hold his toys: a tractor, 4 wheeler, knobby tired golf cart (that could plough through water...usually) ...and of course, his Green Machine, an old International. It was fully equipped with things like doors and windows, but as it aged, the Green Machine was down to the bare bed with a seat, clutch, brake, and gas pedal and nothing else.

There was a large tree swing, and the barn was lit by solar power...a panel, about 4 inches square on the outside and on the inside, about two feet away, was a battery and two wires that went to a light bulb. A barrel collected rainwater at the back of the barn. There were lots of things to hunt: deer, squirrels, birds, and razor backs/swine/bore. Preston took Hill there sporting and shooting, and the two were in their element.

Preston told me, "This, George, is my country club."

• • •

By the Rev. Jay Fowler

Preston was one of the first people I met when I came to be the assistant pastor at St. Philip's Church in 1990. He and Laura took my wife, Janine, and me out on their sailboat along the Wappoo Cut and into the harbor. It was an amazing evening, especially for a guy from Kansas!

Not long after, Janine and I started a small group for young couples at the church who had been married for 5 years or less. Preston was a key leader in that group. We discussed many topics that couples deal with in their marriage. One topic was how to resolve conflict in a biblical way. Preston said, "When Laura and I get into a fight, I just leave and drive for a walk in the country. That gives me a chance to cool down and think things through."

I remember asking Laura how she felt about Preston's conflict resolution technique. Laura said, "I've always hated it when he does that!"

I asked, "Why?"

She said, "Because I am always wondering if he's going to come back!"

To that Preston replied, "Of course I'm going to come back. I'm just cooling down! I don't want to lose my temper and say something I'd regret."

They agreed that, when needed, it was okay for Preston to leave to cool down and think things through... but he had to tell Laura when he would be back! And when he returned, they would agree to sit down and work through the conflict in a biblical way.

One of my favorite memories of Preston was the time he took my son, Nate, and me out to the Morris Island Lighthouse on his small fishing boat. Nate was about seven years old, and I had always wanted to go to the top of the lighthouse. In those days the lighthouse was open, there were no barred doors or signs posted.

When we got to the lighthouse, Preston showed us the way to crawl up the concrete to get to the platform where the door was. He decided he would stay in the boat and fish, while we went to the top of the lighthouse.

I noticed after we crawled up the concrete side, that to get to the door required us to traverse a small ledge. In the water below there were metal spikes which were probably part of the foundation that had been washed away over many decades. It looked a little dangerous, but I really wanted to go up that lighthouse with my son. In spite of my concerns, getting my son and myself to the doorway wasn't as hard as I had thought it would be.

We scaled the rusty rod iron steps and braved the many bird droppings all the way to the top of the lighthouse. After looking around the harbor from that amazing viewpoint, we went back down the steps. Upon arriving at the doorway I looked down at the water and the metal spikes. We still needed to traverse the small ledge to get to a place that we could crawl down to the boat. For some reason, I just froze. I kept thinking, "Wow, if we fall on those spikes, it's going to hurt!" I couldn't figure out how to get my son, or myself, off of Morris Island!

Preston looked up from his fishing and noticed I was paralyzed. He came over, stood up in the boat and said, "Hand Nate to me, I've got him!" And he did! I was relieved. But now I had to figure out how I was going to get down. Fear still had me in its grip.

Preston noticed that I wasn't making any progress. I will never forget when he held up his strong arms, smiled at me and said, "Hey man, I can help you!" I felt like the seven-year-old child when I let Preston help me off the lighthouse platform and into his boat. I admit, I was embarrassed. But one of Preston's great traits was that he never made you feel stupid, inadequate, unmanly, or ashamed. Somehow he exuded an unconditional love and acceptance.

I believe that kind of love only comes from God. And that was a love I noticed in Preston throughout our entire 27 years of knowing each other. It's a love that I hope is apparent in my life as well.

• • •

By Apostle Herman Robinson, III

Preston and I were thrown together around 1990, when we were both working on the John Guest Series. At that time I was going through a spiritual battle with divorce in my life, and Preston encouraged me to go to a Presbyterian Cursillo. I spent that weekend with God's love being poured over me and into me; for me personally, it was a very difficult time. You might say, it was a time when one could think they were the black sheep of God's family. But we went through that weekend together, and God's love really made a difference in my life.

Afterwards Preston invited me to his men's Bible study group (at St. Philip's Church). We bonded in friendship and fellowship and started doing prison ministry together as well as community-type ministries such as men's prayer breakfasts. We were a part of that whole (harbor) cross thing together.

I got to thinking the other day about how much I miss him, as a brother in faith and a friend, because we always had those moments when we'd pray together, and encourage one another, and support one another. In growing up in downtown Charleston, Preston was that bridge to the other side of Charleston. I don't know how he managed to navigate himself through all those different groups, but he did. He had a real love for God's people.

When someone leaves an impression like that in life, it's hard to shake. The gravity of that relationship goes beyond friendship, brotherhood, comrades in the Gospel....Preston demonstrated the role of being a pilgrim, and he extended himself to others for the sake of God's love, whether you were up or down, whether you had all the answers, or you didn't.

I celebrate his life as a bridge builder, a conduit, a servant of the Lord, as one who would go wherever the Lord would lead him, strong and courageous, tall and yet gentle in his ways. Preston loved leading others to God and to Christ.

• • •

By David Gross

Preston knew who you were and really had a good idea of your essence. I like to believe that because he was a friend, that it meant that I was a good person and likable. Perhaps that is what makes a true friend.

Anyway what I really want to relate is the time he cured me. I had been quite ill for about 6 months, details not important except that no doctor of the many I visited knew what was the matter, why it was so difficult for me to walk up the stairs and why I had high fevers. During that time Preston visited me for lunch one day, in his work suit that to me never seemed to suit him, and kindly brought a Subway sandwich and soda in a cup with a straw. (I believe that was his go-to lunch, mine too.)

Preston made conversation but his reason for coming to visit was to pray and lay his hands on me, to help. He just mentioned that he would like to say a prayer and lay his hands on my shoulders as he was leaving. He did his thing as only he could do, without seeming pretentious and arrogant, and I started to heal the next day. He cared so much.

I got better in a few weeks. I attribute my cure to him and his power of belief, and I believe his belief in God was so powerful and true that it changed my life and everyone he knew.

• • •

By Clark Hanger

I knew Preston for only 25 years - the grown-up, adult Preston - with a wife and family. I am jealous of those here who have known Preston from his earliest years. Viewing photos and hearing tales from his good friends during those years, well, I missed those years and know he was a fabulous friend to have growing up.

Preston was not without his shortcomings however. Like the time in the Charleston Harbor after an intense Bocci tournament on No Name Island earlier. Preston called me to the side of the boat to view a pretty big school of tiny jellyfish. As I leaned over the gunnel for a closer look, Preston grabbed my feet and over I went. Scared of being eaten alive I quickly made for the ladder. As I approached the top of the ladder with maybe a few jellyfish on my legs, Preston unilaterally decided it was not my time to leave the water, so he blocked my passage and helped me back into the dark, infested Harbor water. For this action, my brother, I hereby FORGIVE you.

Another memorable occasion with my friend: once on a cold December evening out on Bees Ferry Road, we were preparing for anice campfire. Preston asked me to gather firewood for mini-big burn. When I returned he encouraged me to gather up close to keep warm and offered me a beer. What he really wanted was for me to feel the full force of at least one of the aerosol cans he had stacked in the fire.

BOOM - one can came barreling out of the fire in a big explosion and hit me right in the stomach. I thought I had been killed. It's a rare sight to see Preston laugh as much as he did that evening. I may still have the welt - I don't know. Nobody there felt sorry for me and Preston could only laugh out loud. You see - we shared a very similar sense of humor. He told me I deserved it, and we both knew he was right. I can only imagine how he was as a kid. LOTS of fun - and my kind of fun.

David's son, Hugo Hanham-Gross, was Preston's godson.

• • •

By Monti Hanger

We all miss you so much….. thank you, dear Preston. You are gone, but you have left us with richer lives because of our friendship and all the memories….

When we were just beginning our journey as new parents, Clark and I became close friends with David Gross and Victoria Hanham and their 2-year-old son, Hugo. Through them we met Laura and Preston. I will always remember never-reserved-Laura exuberantly declaring to me, "Why your Clark is the second most handsome man around!"   Whenever I thought of her observation, knowing how much she adored Preston, I was grateful that her opinion of my Clark ranked so high in our Holy City!

My story to share involves the evolution of the Big Burn. For many years we would celebrate the January birthdays of Clark, David and Bunky together with oyster roasts. When we acquired the property we called The Barony on Wadmalaw, the oyster roasts moved there. Since these gatherings were always early in the new year, the idea was born to gather from the streets of Charleston discarded Christmas trees to haul to the island for a bonfire.

You have to know that our beloved Preston was a man version of the fabled Mary Poppins. He was the-most-handsome-man-ever but inside was the kid who loved to have a good time. The assignment of gathering Christmas trees unleashed in Preston the joie de vivre of a boy given the most important mission in all the world. He hopped in his big ol' man-truck, hooked up his big trailer and enlisted every kid he could find to pile the flatbed high. Load after load of abandoned Christmas trees were piled high at Selkirk.

Year after year, this tradition grew to have a life of its own. Children would call to let Preston know they had been collecting trees for the Big Burn. Friends began eagerly to anticipate the scheduling of the Big Burn.

One cold afternoon, we were gathered at Selkirk preparing for the Burn. Some artful dad in the group- maybe Clark- decided to see what would happen if one of the Christmas trees were hauled to the base of a live tree and then lit. Naturally both trees caught fire. I was taken back, thinking this was not at all the right thing to do. Here we had all these perfectly dead trees and it made no sense to me to kill a living tree. Definitely this was not the message to teach our children. Now I had always had the utmost respect for Preston, and I knew he was so reasonable, responsible, and respected amongst the dads. He would see my point and put a stop to this nonsense. I expressed my dismay to him, and as I pled my case, I could see before my own eyes the twinkle in his eyes grow. He was having a vision, and he wasn't even listening to me anymore.

Well, Preston took that vision and ran with it. He picked out the perfect sacrificial tree and brought ladders, ropes and pulleys to Selkirk. Day after day he would single-handedly head out there, with Chester his buddy, to craft his tower of trees several stories tall. We women and mothers would gasp when we would see him atop this mound, which grew taller and more complex every year. We marveled at his engineering and courage, always prayerful when he climbed those ladders. I think he stayed up at night just thinking of what else he could add to his Tower of Trees.

In the end, Preston built a wooden box, filled it with thousands and thousands of firecrackers, and secured it to the top of the Mound. This he topped with the biggest wreath that had been gathered. Unbeknownst to any of us, he would stash several balloons filled with flammables within the trees. Then he carefully laid a continuous trail of firecrackers that extended out to the safety zones. This pathway would light the Tower. His final icing-on-the-cake was to distribute hundreds of Roman candles to the kids and adults in the crowd to initiate the lighting of the Big Burn. An increasingly brilliant Burn!

Needless to say, Preston did not agree with me. Every year he would map out that special sacrificial tree and begin planning. His massive towers of Christmas trees created memories for hundreds of us that we will never forget. It is such a blessing that through the goodness of this man's life and through the Grace of God that Preston's vision is now our vision. He will always be part of us.

Preston, I miss you so much…

with lots of love for you,
and for Laura, Olivia, Delia and Victoria

• • •

A Letter from Matt Miller, written 6 months after Preston's death
(*Editor's note: when Mr. Miller speaks of the Big Burn for Eternity, he is not referring to damnation but to an annual party, described in the preceding note by Monti Hanger. Also, when he refers to James and Philip, Mr. Miller is speaking of his old friends who are both deceased from cancer. He is hopeful that these dear friends have met Preston in Heaven and become his new buds.*)

Dear Preston:

The BIG BURN for Eternity……. How was the Big Burn this year? Did James and Philip help you? Where and how do you gather the trees? What are fireworks like in Heaven?

I am sitting at 'our' spot at Waterfront Park gazing out at "your" cross in the middle of the Harbor. I miss our walks each morning here and our talks about everything and anything. Friday Morning Men's Bible Study will never be the same without you. We have stalled to find our groove without our leader. I am struggling daily without my good friend and spiritual guide.

Ever since that first day I met you, standing at the front of the line in your sport coat, waiting to greet me at my first Wednesday's Men's Luncheon at St. Philip's. You were so gracious to invite me and wait patiently while everyone strolled past you and wanted you to join them at a table. From that moment and the Friday morning following that day in November of 2010, my life has been forever changed. You placed my hand on the doorknob to my relationship with GOD. Never did I know so little about myself and spirituality until I met you.

You have invited me and then my family into your home, your property, your BIG BURN event, your life and into your heart. I am forever blessed to have known you. Not a day goes by that I do not think of you, miss you and speak to you. Your gift to me of <u>Jesus Calling</u> is my constant communication with not only Jesus but with you. Your spirit for adventure, the outdoors, meeting people, helping strangers, listening and supporting others is only matched by your endless love and knowledge of all things spiritual.

You have made us all better people just by knowing you.

Whether for a lifetime, a few years or a brief moment, you allowed everyone to know your heart, mind and soul. A trait only a "chosen" few are blessed to have and share with others.

The LORD showed Himself to me with your arm around me and Rick Krass' right hand on my left shoulder. That Friday morning in

---

December of 2014, my knees were healed. GOD gave me the reminder that this is HIS world, HIS path for us all, HIS power, HIS control, and HIS confidence of life with us in Heaven. Why my knees are healed, and cancer has taken you and James away from us to be with HIM, are further evidence of HIS master plan.

The thing that keeps me from falling apart from the pain and raw emotion of missing you is the knowledge of HIS overwhelming LOVE which HE has for you in HIS kingdom. You gave me so much while here with us on earth. You continue to work inside of me through our 'new' relationship.

Your love for your family, shown in how you adore your wife, care for your daughters, prepare provision for them after you are gone, is the bar you have set very high for us all to reach with our own families. I asked you to send me a 'sign' from Heaven and yet I think I get one every day in so many forms. Thank you, my friend, for your love, laughter, and happier ever after.............Amen

Your brother in Peace...........Matt Miller

● ● ●

by Luke McBee

My wife Terry and I met Preston and Laura at St. Philips Church in the late 1980's. From that first meeting, we became close friends, which was brought about through our love for the Lord, as well as our worldly interests. The worldly interests included of course a lot of fishing, both inshore and offshore, with the occasional lighthouse to be climbed, the deer stand to be visited, and crosses to be raised around the harbor.

Throughout our adventures, Preston was full of life and love instilled in him through the indwelling of the Holy Spirit...he boiled over with enthusiasm for all things the Lord showed him or put before him. Nothing was physically or spiritually out of reach, and in his prayer warrior approach to life, he sought Jesus's blessing in all things.

There are many cherished memories, but I fear I might not be able to put them into words that would adequately capture a moment in time. But I will offer one memory that shows Preston's love for us all.

In the mid 1990's I began an e-commerce venture which promised to bring marketing efficiencies to the commodity beef, pork, and poultry industries. During the first two to three years of the startup I was able to raise some angel capital and actually had a small revenue stream going, which not many dot-coms of the day could claim!

But as with any startup, the challenges were great both monetarily and emotionally, especially when you are the first one to bring a new technology into an old line industry. "First movers" in the fledgling internet of the mid to late 1990s were like pioneers in early America: they got a lot of arrows in the back!

Throughout these most trying days, weeks, and years, Preston was there. As Barre Butler so eloquently stated during the funeral service about his childhood home burning, Preston was there to stand in the gap and provide needed brotherly love.

When it felt like my life was burning down around me, Preston was there. We would pray on Friday mornings after Bible study, then he would come to my office once a week with a sandwich for lunch. We would share our prayer needs and then bring them before the Lord.

In the end the business failed, but because of Preston's spiritual support and Christ-like love throughout those difficult days, I was able to survive and wait on God's almighty hand to move in miraculous ways going forward.

Preston's love for the Lord flowed abundantly into every aspect of his life. He truly was the hands and feet of Jesus on this earth, and I know he has a twinkle in his eye, a smile on his face, and continues to have a prayer in his heart for all of us!...Preston was the ultimate Prayer Warrior!

• • •

by Sarah Eppes

We met Preston and Laura in the pews of St. Phillips almost 30 years ago. They were the first couple to welcome us when we married and moved to Charleston. Laura- elegant, friendly, and often jubilant- wearing a hat every week. Preston- steady, kind, and always with a smile. Steadfast and caring friends. Over and over they have opened their home to us and our children, loved us, shared our burdens and our joys, and given us a feast of food, friendship, fellowship, and prayer.

Preston was both the life of the party, and someone who would sit quietly and listen to others, especially whoever was a stranger in the crowd. But it is in Preston's final years that I saw his heart shining out in a brilliance that was otherworldly. Always thinking of others. Emptying himself. Giving of himself repeatedly. In hindsight, it is stunning to consider how he got to the end of every bit of physical strength and energy— and yet still gave of himself in every way possible. God has used Preston's daily offering of himself for His glory.

I. Preston's Gift of FRIENDSHIP

News came that Preston's cancer had returned. Laura told me I could drop by the hospital for a visit. I went with a few of the children, and we found Preston holding court in his hospital bed with his room crammed full of flowers. I think most of Charleston had come by for a visit. Preston and Laura glanced at each other. Preston smiled at his love. To me, their love and commitment had never been more evident. A small bed for Laura was made up by the window. Embroidered white pillows graced Preston's bed. Laura had brought them from home. Nothing but the best pillows for her prince.

I wanted to find out how Preston was, and to be a help. But he would have none of it. He quickly turned the topic to my husband, who had recently moved 3,000 miles away to work in Seattle. A family relocation to the Pacific Northwest was impossibly complicated, and we had entered a seemingly endless separation until God either moved us together, or moved John home.

Preston and I talked about the distance, about the impact on the kids, and on our lives. He asked me to grab a small package nestled among the row of flowers. He told me it was a book that a mutual friend had mistakenly given to him twice. Now that Preston had two copies, he said, "I think you and John need this. We're both going through Red Sea moments. This book has really helped me and I want you to have it."

Later, I climbed into my car and opened the package in the dim light of the parking garage. Inside lay, *The Red Sea Rules: 10 God-Given Strategies for Difficult Times.* A small book. It didn't take long before I gobbled up the words and its wisdom. These words stood out, "…even when we are most anxious and distressed, God will make a way when there seems to be no way…… God works in ways we cannot see…[and] the same God who led you *in* will lead you *out*.…And as He does, don't forget to praise Him." Preston lived these words. He and Laura trusted God every step of the way. And they never forgot to praise God.

II. Preston's Gift of FELLOWSHIP
Not too long after Preston left the hospital, the kids and I were downtown for an evening at the Dock Street Theatre. We didn't have much time to make it to the theatre, and Sullivan (then 7) insisted on wearing a bow tie, "Like Daddy would wear." My attempts at tying it were ridiculous. We were running out of time, and I was feeling desperate. I started trying to convince Sullivan to just do without the tie. That's when he shouted out, "Mommy, why don't we get Uncle Preston to do it?!" In the twilight, we knocked on the Hipp's door. Within minutes, Preston was sitting on a dining room chair, fixing Sullivan's tie. I cried for the beauty of a god father in Sullivan's life to not only pray for him, but to also teach him to dress up and tie a bow tie.

Several months after the night of the bow tie, I had a crazy Saturday. I was still a geographically-single mom, and as the lone driver, I was taking kids to activities all over Charleston, and then hustling to Summerville for a wedding shower for my daughter-in-law to be. I dropped by Tradd Street to pick up Laura for the shower, and Preston offered to keep Sullivan and Rhys so they didn't have to spend the day at the wedding shower. Those little boys had the best afternoon ever with Uncle Preston.

Preston took them out on his boat with Chester. They went to an isolated stretch of beach where they had all the space in the world to run and dig and play in the waves. They collected shells in their hands and sand in their hair. When I picked them up they were sun kissed and happy. The shells spilled out of their backpack as they told me that the highlight of the day was Chester. They had gotten to throw the tennis ball for him all afternoon. Their one frustration was that every time, no matter who threw the ball, Chester ALWAYS took it back to Preston. "It was the BEST DAY EVER on the boat!!! Chester sure loves Uncle Preston......Mom, some day I want a dog just like Chester! Only he'll bring the ball to ME and not to Uncle Preston!"

Preston probably had a million things he could have done that day, but he chose to help me, and give the little boys a day on a boat. Something they hadn't done in a very long time. Tall, smiling Preston stepped into the daddy-starved lives of our little boys and gave time, himself, and an afternoon of fun. They have never forgotten it.

III. Preston's Gift of SERVICE

Over a year and a half later, John finally came home from Seattle. The day that he landed the rains started for the historic 1,000 year flood that inundated South Carolina. Mercifully, John was home when the waters filled the first floor of our house. Three weeks later, our downstairs was inundated with a fast growing mold, and we had to move to a new house. Laura texted. She and Preston were coming out to Summerville to help us move.

Laura, Annabel, and I set to work in the new house unpacking boxes while John, Preston, and the rest of our older kids moved furniture out of the old house, and into the new one. All of this was done in a steady rain. They worked so hard. It was exhausting. Through it all, Preston worked steadily without complaint, and encouraging everyone around him.

At 5:00pm, Preston walked into the new house and called Laura to go. We all gathered in the front hallway as rain continued to fall.

Preston asked if he could pray for our new home and our family. We stood in a circle, held hands, and listened as Preston poured out his heart for our family, his gratefulness at John being home in perfect timing before the flood, and thankfulness for our friendship. He asked for our home to be a blessing to all who entered. We had a mass of wet hugs, and he and Laura left to go home to teach their young people's Bible Study. Still serving others after a long day of moving our family. Blessing upon blessing for us. Blessing upon blessing for others.

Not long after that, we received an email from Preston. HIs cancer had returned. Through tears, I read the email over again. I looked at the dates and did the math. I called John and asked him if Preston had said anything about his health while they were moving. I felt literally sick as I realized that Preston had the news of the return of his cancer right before he helped us move. I could hardly believe it. How could he have done so much? Lifted so many boxes and pieces of furniture? How could he have done all that with the cancer back- and now in his bones?

The next time I saw Preston, I hugged him and thanked him again. I grabbed the moment to ask if my hunch was right- that he knew about the cancer before he moved us. He looked down, and gently demurred. He refused to let me make a big deal of it. He said, "I was glad to do it. It made me feel better to be doing something to help. And such a great occasion with John coming home!" That was classic Preston. Always finding a way to help, and refusing to take the praise for it. He gave his praise to Someone Else.

IV. Preston's Gift of PRAYER
Preston and Laura have prayed with us and for us for years. Our lives have been touched by their faithfulness. Perhaps the most touching

prayer came when Preston was in the most pain I have ever seen him in. It was about 8 months after our move, and I was downtown with Annabel, who had recently had an accident and surgery for a crushed pelvis. She's a competitive climber, and was finally back climbing at the local bouldering gym. When she was finished, we called Laura and asked if it was a good time to visit. Laura said yes, and directed us to come in and walk upstairs since she was lying down with Preston.

When we crept down the hall into Laura and Preston's room. Preston was curled up, and lying very still. He looked so weak, and in such pain that I felt like I was intruding. I didn't want to be in the way. Annabel and I talked briefly to Laura, asking what we could do to help. I ran down to the kitchen for some water for them, and then we were about to leave when Preston asked to pray for Annabel. He reached out and grabbed her hand. Laura and I joined the circle of hands while Preston prayed the most empowering prayer for Annabel. He lifted her up, prayed for her healing, and gave her talents and abilities to the Lord. He prayed that she would never forget Whose she was, and asked that the story of her accident, survival, surgery, and healing would become a story that shines forth His glory in her life. He prayed that she would always use her climbing to glorify God and bring others to Him. And he prayed all of this in an unwavering voice- in the Name of Jesus.

When Preston prayed it was like his pain dissipated. His voice was strong. He was calm and seemed lifted by the Spirit. It was a moment of light in that room. And it was beautiful. His prayer came straight from a man who knew that when there is no hope, there is prayer, and God is always near. Preston lived the words from *The Red Sea Rules*, "When you face impossible odds, pray urgently, unfeignedly, unitedly. And trust the great prayer-answering God who grants mercy and imparts grace to help in time of need."

In Preston's life, he gave and gave and gave. After he went to live with the Lord, it came to me. Preston got to the end of himself physically. He may have been weak, but the Joy of the Lord was his strength (Nehemiah 8:10). As his body was coping with the ravages of cancer. Preston's emotions and his spiritual life were rock solid. To the last day that we saw him, Preston served others. Prayed for others. Loved others. And when he could no longer use his body to serve, Preston gave smiles, hugs, love, and words of wisdom and encouragement. He lived out the wisdom of *The Red Sea Rules* where it says, "So, take a deep breath and recall this deeper secret of the Christian life: *when you are in a difficult place, realize that the Lord either placed you there or allowed you to be there, for reason perhaps known for now only to Himself."*

Preston gave many gifts to those around him. His final gift to me is the glorious truth that when I feel at the end of all my resources and strength and ability, there is GOD, Who gives everything we need to do all that He places before us. Preston personally lived this out and his shining witness is an enduring example for us all.

● ● ●

By Anne Badgley

I so clearly remember the day Preston walked into my office at the Lowcountry Crisis Pregnancy Center with a bag full of change he had collected for over a year. This was way back, in the early days, when every month was a struggle to survive. Our bookkeeper, Jim Terry, would ask which bills to pay and which to put off. And we were not in a high rent district! So, the modest donation was greatly appreciated! But, what meant much more was that Preston even knew I was there. He, a handsome young South of Broad Charlestonian, a pillar of The Mother Church, St. Philip's (then Episcopal), cared. I must have known him through dear Tracey Graudin, who served faithfully on our Steering Committee to help found the ministry in the mid-1980s.

Later, Preston asked me to be on his board, the Charleston Leadership Foundation, and much later I asked him to be on mine when I founded Heritage Community Services. I founded Heritage to try to reach young people *before* they were in crisis because of an untimely pregnancy.

Some years ago, when the Post and Courier brutally attacked me and my family with a Sunday morning headline (that we've yet to recover from emotionally), he wrote them a letter. I guess I was among some of the first of conservative Christian women to be denigrated by the liberal media! He stood up for me. He told them how well-run our agency is and about the good we are doing with the next generation. He was respected by their leadership and I guess they must have paid attention. While they never apologized, in spite of the fact that we had done nothing wrong (other than challenging the sex education status quo), they didn't come after us again.

Preston was our Chairman of the Board until he passed away recently. I told Laura that I had pleaded with the Lord, like so many others that so needed Preston, to let him stay with us. We wanted him, of all the people we've known, to be healed. We thought he would be healed, up until the very last moment, didn't we?! It's hard to stop praying for him to live, but here we are, without him. As Laura said, we didn't want our brother, the one so unlike himself in his last days, to continue to suffer. It was the vibrant, lovely, and unusually strong Christ-loving man that meant so much to us all that we hoped would rise from his sick bed. It was not to be. He was unique.

I feel lost without his support. I understand it is through our Lord that his loveliness was formed! I really do. But, Preston was that embodiment we so rarely experience here on earth! Of course, we'll be forever grateful to have been in his life.

I am so grateful for meetings held just a few times a year -- when I knew, without a doubt, that he trusted me and believed in me and had my back and would never, ever hurt me.

I will miss you, Preston, and I appreciate so much, Laura, that you and his girls shared your husband and father with us! I seriously doubt many of his friends even knew that he made that trek across town all those years to provide that much-needed encouragement to me! Thank you, Lord, for Preston's life. Thank you that he lives on through his family, his church, and yes, our little agency, and a world of other endeavors he helped along. And thank you, Lord, for the hope of Eternal life. When I consider what he packed into his years here with us, I -- for one -- think Preston will get a mighty fine mansion! And I know he'd laugh at that!

● ● ●

By Susan Maguire

On a balmy August evening in 1984, a 52 foot ketch clipped along offshore under full sail, from Rockville to Charleston. It was a momentous time, shared by friends and family on board the Wichmann's *"Mobjack"*. The full moon chased Laura and Preston, who sat closely together on the starboard side in rapt conversation about the "Lord of Life", as quoted from Laura. This bond became the mainstay of their 28 years of marriage.

Preston was a faithful and playful family man to Laura and their three daughters, and a devoted friend to many. His faith and his appreciation of nature were inseparable, and he was always eager to share that connection with others. Boating was a favorite activity. As he would pull away from the dock, Preston would stall the engine and say a prayer for a safe and blessed outing. I keep a sea urchin found while the three of us, plus their dog, Chester, strolled on an island beach during the summer of 2015. It's a treasure to me that represents the beauty of nature, friendship, and faith.

Preston was generous with his faith, in a way that was calm and committed. One evening, he read from the devotional <u>Jesus Calling</u> before one of Laura's delicious meals. I liked it, so a bit later, he handed it to me as a gift with the inscription, "May this book improve your friendship with Jesus". The book continues to inspire me.

Preston was always a fine fellow, and he seemed to me to become increasingly kind and gentle during his later years, while experiencing the hardship with his health. He was consistently gracious and would express heartfelt appreciation for small tasks done for him and his family. He seemed at peace in his faith even at our final visit, with a warm smile. He is an inspiration to me.

● ● ●

By Ann Kulze

I have many fond memories of my friend Preston, but would like to elaborate on one in particular as I think it perfectly illustrates the gift of his life and legacy.

Toward the end of His time on earth, Preston developed an infection that required a brief hospitalization. Laura kindly contacted me and asked if I could bring Preston some of my energy balls (eating was a challenge at this time). I enthusiastically accepted and stopped by the hospital to deliver them and visit briefly. Before leaving, Laura, Preston and I held hands and prayed out loud with reverence. In that moment I experienced something unforgettably sacred – a true jolt, an arresting jolt of profound peace and all-powerful love that was unquestionably direct from the Divine. The Lord's presence enveloped and filled the room - it was amazing! For me, it was a full-throttle transmission of God's grace, and something I will never forget. In fact, it instantaneously strengthened my faith in an ever-lasting manner.

Thank you, Preston, for your greatest gift – sharing and perpetuating God's infinite love and grace.

• • •

By the Rev. Dallas Wilson

Preston and I have a long history together that started in 1989! I served with him during the inaugural John Guest Series; we were co-chairs of the Pastoral Committee. During that same time, we also had the opportunity to serve together on the Habitat for Humanity's Board of Directors, which Preston chaired.

During that time, I not only fell in love with him, but his family as well. I loved his Father, Charley, Sr., his brother, Charley, Jr., and his precious wife, Laura, who is still with us, and his nephew and my parishioner, Matthew Pridgen.

"When wealth is lost, nothing is lost; when health is lost, something is lost; when character is lost, all is lost." Billy Graham

Preston's character and unwavering faith were always prevalent in his daily life. He portrayed genuineness and the ability to consistently project the "Fruit of the Spirit", e.g. his faithfulness, gentleness, and love. Preston was always sensitive to and concerned about those around him. Being an African American, I never sensed any guile or prejudice in or from him. Our fellowship was extraordinary.

Preston was as close to "immutability" as one can be in the flesh. His counsel to me was always godly, and what I found out during our time together was once he had committed to you or your ministry, his conversations always leaned toward our ability to "serve" together to enhance the "Kingdom of God" on the earth. I truly loved and still love my brother.

Revelation 12:11 (KJV) depicts the very nature of our brother's existence on this earth:
And they [Preston] overcame him (Satan) because of the blood of the Lamb and because of the word of their [his] testimony, and they [he] did not love their [his] life even when faced with death.

In addition, I see my brother in 2 Corinthians 3:2 (KJV):
Ye [Preston] are our epistle written in our hearts, known, and read of all men...

● ● ●

By Cathy Lawson

Laura and I have known each other since we were in high school. I lived on Logan Street, and she lived on Legare Street. I went to First Baptist, and she went to College Prep. We were introduced to each other through mutual friends during an amazing time of Christian revival in Charleston among high school students. It was something Charleston has known before – a type of "Great Awakening."

Laura and I were increasingly blessed to come together later in a Bible study group that would knit us even more closely as friends and sisters in Christ. We were all strengthened to have a wonderful Christian culture that surrounded us and was always available to us while we were students at the College of Charleston. We were protected and nurtured in this Body of Christ – which we knew was essential in order to participate in the world but be not of it. Especially as young Christian women, we were convinced that we should trust God completely with our futures, and we believed He knew our need for Godly men to come into our lives.

Laura in particular was certain God had men that He planned for us – what she called the "Number One Choice whom God has planned for us to marry." I would even say Laura was a cheerleader for me and other young women to "stay the course" and "stay true to God's promise" that we would only choose to have a relationship with a man who we felt would lead us spiritually, to know Christ, and who we could say we were "equally yoked" with in the church. Of course it is easier to maintain this enthusiasm about marrying a Christian man and seeking "that one" when you are young.

Before we knew it – we were past our mid-twenties and susceptible to discouragement about whether or not there was that number one man out there. But Laura was relentless in pressing into her prayers and exhortations to trust God. I don't know how many other women she encouraged to do this, but she encouraged me to write a prayer (as she had done) for my husband and to pray for him every day – that God would lead him and prepare him to be the spiritual leader in our marriage, home, and community, that he would be a man of respect and integrity in the business world, that he would let the Light of Christ shine in the secular arena.

I of course obediently wrote and prayed that prayer daily – as Laura had instructed. Laura also recorded her dreams in her journal, desperate for God to instruct her in the way which she should go. One dream involved being aboard her family sailboat, *Mobjack*, with friends coming and going. This dream renewed her summer family ritual of going to all the local regattas.

As time went on Laura and I both dated different men but there was always that bold admonishment from her to "be strong and hold out for that one God has planned for you." The day did unfold and I met "the one" that I knew God had planned for me. And about the same time, Laura met Preston – at the Rockville Regatta aboard *Mobjack,* and we ALL knew he was "the one" God had planned for Laura, though it took them four years to figure it out and marry. They created a synergy and compound of love and grace that was amazing and beautiful.

I know that God honored Laura and Preston because of their great love for Him above self, their waiting on God's best, and their commitment to purity despite their red blooded passions. Theirs was a real honeymoon, which lasted throughout their twenty eight year marriage, an icon of God's love and care for mankind.

And even in death – their love and life shouts the joy of the resurrection. Glory to God!

• • •

By Suzanne McCord

After seeing my son prayed for by individuals and the church as a whole and then seeing his healing from a TBI (traumatic brain injury) in 2010, I am convinced that prayer works, anointing with oil works, and listening to the promises of God for healing from the scripture works.

One Sunday in church the scripture was about the fact that God can use the prayers of ordinary people for great things. And I felt led to ask Laura and Preston if I could come by Monday morning before work to pray for them. Of course they said yes.

So I went with my Mahesh Chavda healing oil. I got there and they were just about to sit down to breakfast, so Laura invited me to join them. But Preston being more aware of the hour and the fact that I was on my way to work, graciously said, no, let's pray – that is why Suzanne has come. And so we went over to the living area and sat down. I shared the scripture and how I felt God had told me to come and that I did not feel worthy or gifted at all, but wanted to be obedient. They appreciated it and said that the scripture had spoken to them as well.

So I began to pray and then Laura prayed a prayer of agreement. And THEN Preston prayed... for me and Gerry. That I had not expected. But on the way to work I was thinking about how Job was healed after he prayed for friends. I felt the assurance that Preston would be healed as well.

One time when Laura texted how she couldn't sleep at night because her hidden anxieties would wake her as she was watching Preston waste away, I reminded her of the Louis Zamperini story in the book <u>Unbroken</u>. He was in that life raft and was nothing but skin and bones. He even looked up and saw angels singing over him and felt complete peace, but even then he survived enough to be imprisoned in the Japanese war camps. Laura and Preston had read it and were encouraged. Preston even texted: *no angelic singing yet but will keep an ear open to it. Thank you for all your prayers and support. Love, Preston*

Then early one Saturday (Sept 3), Laura texted and asked if I could come pray for Preston. I was heading to Statesboro, GA., to see my mother and sister, but I said I would come on my way out of town around 11:00. She wanted me to come then I think, so I got there just as fast as I could. Just as I was pulling up the Arnolds were pulling up too. We both went in to pray for Preston who was sitting up in the living room. We all sat down and Neal and Diane Arnold were sharing what the Lord had told them concerning revival beginning in Charleston and how Preston would be a part of it.

I did not have any word from God to share. I just wanted to anoint Preston's swollen legs and hurting hands. So I knelt down at his feet while they talked and poured out my oil on his legs and arms and hands. I felt a little like the woman anointing Jesus' feet, except I did not use expensive perfume or my hair. But I did believe that it could be possible for God to heal him. I know he was in pain and probably me rubbing the oil on him was uncomfortable, yet he let me finish. And he let Neal and his wife Diane finish. Then he asked for some pain killer. God can and does use both.

I have been blessed by Preston and Laura and their faith and patience with all.

• • •

By Cynthia Runge

"Scream, Cynthia, scream. Scream as loud as you want to," Preston said, putting his head on the bed next to my face as I was about to get my bones drilled. He grabbed my hand as the doctor asked,

"Are you ready?" As the drilling began, Preston was in the moment with me, a moment that I will never forget. I do not know anyone else who would be able to be there as intimately as he was. He knew. He knew what I was going to endure, I realized later. His empathy and compassion showed me the true kernel of whom Preston Hipp was.

He accompanied me to more doctor appointments. Also Preston gave me printed prayers, spoken prayers, and the book <u>Psalms Now</u>. He gave more than a prayer or the passing words,"I'm praying for you", which, while nice, is like saying, "How are you doing?" when the person really doesn't want to hear about it. Neither did I wish to tell about it. I had made up my mind not to talk about my illness or to name it and claim it. It was as if it didn't exist in me. I call it still, "That C word."

Preston understood; he knew what I was going through and what may be coming after the doctor had given me only two weeks to live and said it was likely that I would lose my leg. Literally, my first thought was, "Well, I will wear one high heeled shoe in my coffin. This little princess is going out in style."

Even from the beginning, members of the Hipp Family had been with me on the journey. This Good Friday it will be five years from when I was with Delia Hipp in the pew at St. Philip's Church. Her heart was moved to leave her family to sit with little ole me alone in my pew. Good Friday 2012, I had been to Zumba. I had been to the clueless doctor three different times about the pain in my leg. Then, racing to get ready for my son-in-law's birthday dinner, I slipped and broke my leg. I had been to the bank earlier that day, too, where I, who never met a stranger, struck up a conversation with a guy with a broken leg. He said if he had not stood on his leg after it broke, he would not have had so many problems. God has had angels there for me like this guy, and like Preston, *all along the way.* I refused to get up on my leg. The femur was broken as the ex-rays revealed Good Friday night, irreparable.

After having been given two weeks to live and no leg, now I am blessed. The doctors scratched their heads, bewildered and said, "NO TRACE!" (They can't find a trace of The C Word.) I now shout out loud in the hospital halls as Preston gave me permission to do, "To the Victor the crown! To the Victor the jewels!" I have my life; I have my hair; and I have the need to wear TWO high heals! I'm just so happy to be here to get to know my first grandchild, a boy, born last year 7/7 at 7pm after my daughter was married 7/7/07. Jesus had mercy on the weakest of his little lambs.

I now have time to reflect on the mystery of how my miracle of being alive came to be. Preston's presence was like the angel of the Lord, there for me, part of my alignment of many miracles, leaving me alive after chemo and isolation and getting over "the cure." Preston was a sweet, strong, spiritual presence in my life. He still is. I really thought he was going to make it, then that he was going to rise again, like Lazarus, who had been dead for four days.

For me, like Laura, Preston is ever present. He is in the presence of Jesus, and Jesus is with me. The same spirit that raised Jesus and Preston from the dead dwells in me. Old devil, you can't take that assurance away from me. Preston is having the best day of his life. I resolved what Laura has resolved, that Preston is living the life he wants to live. He is alive, and he is free. I still feel him here as well.

• • •

By Tanya Foret

I was visiting Laura from Texas for either her 50th birthday or our College Prep reunion, I don't remember exactly which it was, but I had the distinct pleasure of staying in her Charleston home for the weekend. Although Laura and I have known each other since elementary school, having moved to Texas as a young adult, I hadn't had the opportunity to get to know "her Preston." We were sitting down for breakfast before church on Sunday morning when one of their daughters joined the family at the table.

As she approached, Preston looked up from his tea and told her that she would need to change clothes. As a young teen, her dress was stylish, but quite short, showing her long, beautiful legs. She sat down and began to serve her plate, doing her best to convince her daddy that her dress was appropriate for St. Philip's. Of course, in the end, she did change clothes before we left Tradd Street for church.

What was so impressive to me was how gentle Preston was with her. I remember thinking as he spoke to her, "Should I slip out and let them have this conversation in private?" But Preston simply spoke directly and firmly to her. Having grown up for most of my childhood years without a father, even though my mother did remarry when I was 11, I was not accustomed to seeing such a display of gentle, fatherly guidance. The whole scene made such an impression on me, even as an adult.

• • •

By Debbie Compton

Sugah Cain "Plantation" on John's Island has been a place where the Comptons and the Hipps have gathered over the years to enjoy the slower side of Lowcountry life – breaking bread at the table, talking into the evening under the oaks, and games on the lawn. While Victoria was enrolled at Charleston Collegiate, Laura spent many a morning on prayer walks under the live oak canopy of Sugah Cain Lane. Our children launched themselves from the rope swing, flying through the air, and landing in a splash of giggles. Chesterfield chased tennis balls into the pond until the thrower tired on the game.

And Preston blessed many meals and prayed for God's protection over those who enjoyed this property.

The rope swing is a centerpiece among pond activities. At the edge of the pond, there is a high platform from which to jump. About 30 feet into the pond stand two tall telephone poles, with their highest point supporting a horizontal cable. A long rope with a round plastic seat at the base is suspended from the center of this cable, which is also fitted with a pulley system to enable those standing on the platform to retrieve the seat.

On occasion, this summertime entertainment is shut down because the retrieval rope jumped the track of the pulley system, rendering the whole thing useless. Fixing this situation is no easy feat, as it requires some fearless soul to access the midpoint of a cable suspended some 40 feet above the surface of the pond. Preston took the challenge, deciding on the most direct approach. From a canoe, Preston, who was in his early 50's and had been diagnosed with cancer, attempted to scale the rope like a child on a playground – anchoring the rope with his ankles, while using sheer upper body strength to inch his way up – hand over fist. He tried once to reach the height, only to lose strength and slide back down. Again he made an attempt. Same result. Determined, but realizing he had strength left for only one more try, he began his ascent. This time success! To David's enthusiastic cheers, Preston realigned the pulley and was the hero of the day.

Preston had a habit of ascending to heights, while we ground-loving mortals looked up in awe. It seems that Preston was always climbing heavenward, and as he did, he lifted our eyes in the same direction. On Sept 8th, 2016 Preston made his final ascent. But not without first inspiring a whole community of family and friends to look upward – "to seek ye first the Kingdom of God" and to know with more intimacy Jesus, who walked with him on the mountain tops and through the valleys.

• • •

By June McKnight

My thoughts of Preston

A Southern Gentleman
Love of God
Love of Family
Love of Country
Love of Manners

• • •

By Ann Hunley Harrington

I want to share with you what Preston wrote in a card to me. He had sent an email out awhile back, and it had Bible verses on it. I was in the middle of taking a study class on <u>Armor of God</u> by Priscilla Shirer, and the Bible verses sent by Preston touched me. I decided to make myself a prayer wall to where I would see the Bible verses each and every day. I emailed him and asked if I could pass on the email to my cousin and godmother in Charlotte, North Carolina. He didn't even know them but he had touched them with the Bible verses that he had sent and by what he wrote in the email.

This is the note that I received from Preston and I thought I would share it with you:

Dear Ann Hunley,
Thank you for all your letters of prayer and encouragement. It blesses me to know that the verses the Lord gave me have blessed you too, and even people in Charlotte. God is good. He always has a plan, and He

always has a final word on any issue. Your prayers do lift me up and give me strength I need for one more day.

Love in Christ,
Preston

• • •

By John McCrady Barnwell, II

One Sunday after Adult Sunday School in the parish hall Preston and I were walking together up Church St. to the church. I hadn't been attending services for very long after a long break with the church. I said to Preston that I felt like a hypocrite when I was trying to worship in St. Philip's.

He didn't hesitate. He said with all sincerity, "That's the devil." He didn't go into any lengthy explanation, but it gave me the confidence to continue on my path.

On another occasion he told me that he loved talking about the hunt or the football game, but what he really loved was talking about God and the Bible.

Then on another occasion Preston and Laura had me over for supper. After supper out came a book about Christianity that was popular at the time. We turned to a chapter about avarice and read out loud. Afterwards we talked about what we had read. When I left I couldn't help but think, "What a smart, healthy way to spend an evening together."

The last thing I'll mention: Preston and I were sharing some thoughts together in a church setting. We had both come to the conclusion that in all the Bible, the only thing you really needed to know with all certainty was that Jesus is Lord. Preston knew with all certainty that Jesus is Lord.

• • •

By Tony Saad

This is why I believe that Preston was so attractive. Christ lived in Preston.

When you love God, when you truly live by your faith (as Preston did), people will notice and ask what makes you different. Who inspires you to live the life you live? People will be attracted to you and your way of life. They will want what you have. Why? Because -- CHRIST IS ATTRACTIVE. Nothing is more attractive in a human than virtue. Wherever Christ went, people wanted to be with him. Whatever he was doing, they always wanted to be there.
When you live by faith, people will want to be with you. Why? Because it will no longer be you that lives but Christ in you.

• • •

By Nancy Blakeney

George Preston Hipp was a deeply spiritual man. He certainly achieved fame on this earth as man knows it, but he obtained greater recognition where it counts the most--in God's sight. Here was a man who lived his faith in God in quiet and humble ways which ultimately impacted this entire Charleston community. His funeral services were a testament to the impact he had on this community. The funeral visitation service ran for four hours to accommodate the throngs of people who came to pay their respects. These were people whose lives had been impacted in many ways by Preston's life, people who loved and respected the person he was, and by people who were changed forever because of his witness.

The burial service itself was like an old fashioned tent revival, attended by his best friend and companion, Chester, his loyal English Springer Spaniel. A nephew of Preston's gave a challenge to those in attendance to commit to continuing Preston's legacy, to come forward pledging to carry Preston's vision for the city of Charleston. Almost the entire crowd at the burial site stepped forward and participated in a moving group prayer. Preston's vision was to see our city overpowered by the presence of God and His son Jesus Christ. He longed to see a dramatic outpouring of love for God and to see a mighty move of God's Holy Spirit in our city. May his legacy come to be!

One of the highly visible legacies that Preston left was the placing of two 12 ft. tall white crosses in Charleston harbor, which was no small feat. He just felt they needed to be there. Two wreaths have been placed on the crosses to commemorate Preston's life. Preston: you are dearly missed by so many whose hearts you touched and whose lives were forever changed.

• • •

By Victoria Cox Buresch

In 1987, I was invited to play the piano for Preston and Laura's wedding reception at The Yacht Club in Charleston. My husband and I stayed in their charming home on Legare Street while they were on their honeymoon.

Later, Preston and Laura would stay in our Georgetown home in Washington, DC while we were on vacation abroad. They also visited us at our country cottage near Charlottesville, VA. The four of us had a wonderful rapport and so enjoyed the company of each other.

I believe we will all be reunited in Heaven, and that we will realize only then that this was the ultimate happiness of earthly life -- to be in the company of our best angels for brief periods of time so that we shall know immediately where we are when we reach Heaven.

By Kathryn Cox Hedgepath (Sister of Victoria Cox Buresch, above)

Two memories stand out: when I first saw Preston, and when I last saw him. The former was when my sister Victoria took me to Laura and Preston's home on Legare in the Summer of 1991, just before I set off for what was to be my exciting decade in Greenwich, CT (where Preston's aunt, uncle and cousins took me under their collective wing at my church and made me feel at home there from my very first day). In fact, I was technically homeless when I met them and they guided me to find my first room rental in an English manor house nearby.

In that first visit with Laura, she was telling me how pleased she was with Preston, as they had been married for a while and she had had time to reflect. She said that, before she met him, she had dated a fellow who was adept at making repairs of things like antiques or old properties. When they parted ways, she missed having someone "handy" around. Meanwhile, as she is telling me this out of Preston's earshot, we are watching him balance on the railing of their side porch with a well-equipped tool belt about his waist as he is defying gravity to make a repair. Yes, in addition to all of his other exceptional qualities, Preston was "handy."

That last time I saw him was perhaps the most precious because it was unwittingly my last. I had since married my own precious husband (who is also handy) and, for my 50th birthday, he gave me a ticket to Laura's extraordinary walking tour complete with an authentic Southern breakfast served in a mansion on The Battery and later tea in a gracious Charlestonian's home. My tour that day was unlike the others because I had Laura all to myself. She incorporated the the historical sites with places of my personal interest with priceless visits to family and friends along the way. It was a perfect gift.

After our outing, we were relaxing in her home when Preston walked in. He must have been having a particularly good day because his appearance defied the battle his body had been enduring for years. I dare say that he was more handsome in December 2015, than that day when he was wielding those tools on Legare.

I didn't know Preston and Laura early enough to be at their wedding, but they were at mine in 2004, and their daughters were in my wedding party. My sister as Matron of Honor was my only attendant, but in addition to our flower girl (a beloved neighbor of the groom), we had a flower court made up of the young daughters of my cherished friends and relatives that included Delia and Victoria. As Olivia was older, she was a flower court attendant. A group picture was taken of the church-full of guests outside under the oaks of Murrells Inlet, S.C.. Preston, Laura and the girls are easily spotted in the photo and will always be on display in our home. I love them all dearly and the expectation of spending the hereafter with them makes it all the more sweet.

● ● ●

By Ted Ray

My wife, Christy, and I have known the Hipps for years. Christy and Laura graduated from the College of Charleston together, and while they fell out of touch for several years, once contact was reestablished, Laura and Christy were in regular touch and we would always see them whenever we visited Charleston from our then-home in Richmond, Va.. The sporadic nature of my time with

Preston may have kept me from getting to know Preston as well as his many long-time Charleston friends, but there were qualities that were apparent to me early on, impressions that were only reinforced as I grew to know him better over time.

For instance, anyone who knew Preston at all knew he was a person of considerable faith. We learned early about Preston's illness. Over his years long battle with cancer, no matter how grim the news, I never saw him bitter; he was always upbeat and at peace with whatever the future held, certain that the Heaven of his faith awaited!

Preston was truly interested in other people. Earlier this year when I learned that a heart condition physicians had been watching for years would require that I have corrective open-heart surgery, despite being gravely ill, Preston took an immediate interest in my condition and pursuit of treatment. Up to the final days of his life, Preston still wanted to know how I was feeling and what decisions I had made regarding my surgery. We live in a time marked by intense self-involvement, egotism, and entitlement. Had Preston been a different person, he might have been a proud man; he had looks, smarts, class, a beautiful wife and family. But Preston was an exceptional person. He possessed the humility of a true Christian, and an interest in others that touched all the people he came in contact with. These qualities made Preston Hipp a wonderful husband, father, and friend.

I value the time I had with Preston; I regret there wasn't more.

• • •

By Linda Harper

We met on the streets of Jerusalem. A motorcycle was about to hit me when I jumped back just in time exclaiming, Psalm 91. My husband and I would recite this Psalm every morning and the Hipps heard me and asked about it. Laura had memorized it, too, in her 20s, at a low spot before meeting Preston. Going to Megiddo, the site of Armageddon, on highway 91, reciting Psalm 91 for the whole bus, was instigated by the Hipps. Blowing the shofar overlooking the plains of battle was something our guide said no tour had ever done. These are a few of the memories that bonded us. A love for the God of Israel, His homeland, and His Word drew us together out of the tour group of 48 people.

Preston and Laura were love birds, as if on a second honeymoon in January 2005. Actually, Laura was hoping to conceive in the Holy City of Jerusalem and give birth to her "Isaac" in the Holy City of Charleston. Our beloved Jewish guide was Isaac.

Our friendship blossomed. David, my husband, Preston always said, was an inspiration and an encouragement to him. David lost his leg and suffers from phantom pains with no cure in sight. Preston and Laura always encouraged us to make their home our home away from home when in Charleston for medical appointments. We watched their girls grow up, with David playing on the floor with them as Preston did when they were still little.

If not for the shared trip to Israel, we would not be friends. It had been Preston's idea for them to go to Israel in 2005. Laura felt he was asking her to jump off a high dive where they they might leave their children as orphans. But Laura would follow Preston anywhere! She said, "It was a trip of a lifetime." Laura was the only one who wrote down everything our guide said. When they got home, Laura exploded into research and study of her notes and questions, becoming a fount of knowledge and has shared it even on her tours, linking the two Holy Cities. I have gotten to go on many of these tours when in Charleston and love them.

October 2015 I wanted to blow the shofar over their house. I would blow it in each room, but this time Laura took me to the basement to blow the shofar over the new freezer full of muscadine grapes for Preston's smoothies. We left as the rains began that became the Flood of the Millennium. The freezer floated, was replaced, but the grapes stayed frozen, full of Resveratrol, the strongest source of antioxidants for fighting Preston's cancer. Praying and blowing the shofar with Preston and Laura was my first such declaration of faith carried out in a basement.

The blessings of Genesis 12:3 still live on in the Hipp household because of the spiritual leadership of Preston and his generous heart to go where the God of Israel was drawing him. He was a blesser of Israel. "I will bless them that bless thee, and curse them that curse thee, and in thee shall all families of the earth be blessed." Look what God accomplished in Preston's 57 years on earth. Going to Israel was a big part of what God wanted to give to Preston, more of Himself. The Lord showed me at his graveside after I blew the shofar over him for the last time that the generous blessings with which Preston blessed Israel were returning to bless Laura, the girls, and all of his beloved Holy City of Charleston gathered at St. Philip's where he was so loved and highly esteemed.

To me Preston was Mr. Charleston, a prince among us, with a wide smile, a man after God's own heart, with a persistent, generous prayer for Revival across our land. The Lord spoke to me at his burial, "SHOUT! The Lord has given us this city." God heard and answered the cry of Preston's heart. We must each carry his passion to be a people set apart for God's glory and purpose with a humble heart and a love for life like Preston. He was the best!

• • •

By Marnie Kerrison

I did not have the pleasure of being an acquaintance and friend of Preston Hipp and Laura's until he was already diagnosed with prostate cancer, so I feel I only knew a part of him. He was always so stately and grand in his quiet presence I often imagined him as being similar to King David. Like David, Preston had a heart for God and everyone knew it.

Preston quietly encouraged me to pursue a serious prayer life and to inject that life into our community. Even up to the end Preston was showing and teaching me about hearing from God. Preston's witness during his time of suffering taught me that we pray not to get what we want, but to align our hearts with God's, never giving up hope for the miracle, but allowing that God doesn't always choose miracles because he has a better plan. Hence, being in alignment with God, we are able to recognize God's goodness at work even when we cannot feel or see it.

Preston was praising His Lord Christ with his dying breath. What a privilege to have known such a man.

A Sample of Notes
Received by the Family

In Preston's memory: Olivia, Delia, Victoria and Laura (yes, and Chester too) pose in front of a wreathed harbor cross, September 2016.

Correspondence Received During the Final Days

From Bruce Wallace, June 2016

Dear Laura:

I woke this morning heartsick and with tears in my eyes. I was awakened by a dream that had me on a train that was carrying my love and me. Her stop was the next one, and she knew she must get off that train then, but she did not want to. I begged her, "Don't go," and held her close. I knew my stop was far down the line, but I told her I would be at the place on the hill where we were happiest together and would hold her in my heart forever.

Even now as I sit writing to you, my heart has such grief as I never imagined. If I were able to take your pain away, I gladly would carry it from you. Love and laugh and sing together now, hold hands and revel in your wonderful life as one. For Preston is not leaving. He lives in you, your children and grandchildren to come. You shall always see his joy in their eyes and smiles and in all that is around you; the cross in the harbor, and in the so many ways your amazing husband has loved you, and his life, and especially God. As Our Lord promised, so I am sure your Preston is as well: "I go to prepare a place for you. And if I go and prepare a place for you, I will come back and take you to be with me, that you may always be where I am."

Bruce Wallace

• • •

From Al Hitchcock, Aug. 17, 2016

Dear Preston,

I am sitting here in my office today being thankful for all the people I know and the opportunities I have had here in Charleston. I must tell you that your family made all of this possible for me……

You and your family have been a true blessing to me and my family and for that I am thankful. I fondly remember the rope swing out at the farm and the time you lived there and we visited. It was a special place and time.

I know I have never told you this, but because of your family and you, I am a better person and in a fortunate position. I live in a beautiful community and know nice people who care and give to each other. You are a great inspiration to others and through your life and actions have given so many people hope. Every time I see the crosses that you placed in our beautiful harbor, I think of you and Christ. Thank you for doing that; it means so much to all who see them. You see, Preston, you have touched people's lives in ways you never knew. You have been an example to many who will never tell you. I for one am thankful to know you and proud to call you friend.

Your friend,
Al Hitchcock
chairman, C.R. Hipp Construction, Inc.

• • •

The Hipp men, Christmas Day 2003. Back row: Preston, Will Pridgen, Matt Pridgen, Charley Hipp. Front row: Charles Hipp, Bill Pridgen, John Kuhn.

From Sarah & John Eppes, Sept. 7, 2016 (this one arrived the day prior to his passing)

Dear Laura and Preston,

I find myself myself almost unable to express our gratitude for you and all that you have done for our family. You've supported us with constant love and encouragement. Your prayers have carried us through countless times of stress and hardship. We will never forget your enthusiasm in helping us move last October after the flood. The driving rain didn't dampen your spirits. The echoes of your prayers in our new home still reverberate today.

One of the most lovely gifts you have shared with us has been your apartment on Ashley. That loving space made it possible for us to stay safely away from the stomach flu before Annabel competed at Nationals. Then you blessed us with it again when Annabel was in the hospital. It was a refuge from the storm in our lives. And the incredible and loving gifts of tea and croissants and bread and so many prayers and love - all while we were in the hospital - just helped carry us through in such a tangible, loving way. We especially loved the teapot and cups and saucers in the hospital.

You all live out your love in very real, heartfelt ways. Your friendship since 1989 has been a tremendous blessing. We love you all so much! Thank you for everything.
Sarah and John Eppes (and their 8 children)

• • •

Correspondence Received After the Death

By Bruce Freshley

Laura,

When grown men cry in your arms, they are only giving back to you what Preston shared with them...the pure, forgiving, and empowering love of Christ. It is a transforming love that all men hunger for but rarely do they find it in other men. They found that love in Preston.

That is why they weep.

At the end of our lives, I think that our glory in heaven is a reflection of our faith on earth. What was our walk? How many did we lead to walk with us? How many souls were changed in Christ Jesus? Did we build the Kingdom of God, or did we destroy it?

As you have seen, Laura, Preston led thousands, many (already) on their journey of faith, and some...saved for the very first time. It is my hope and the hope of his legions that we continue in Preston's walk...in the passionate and pure pursuit of a true life in our Lord Christ. Amen.

● ● ●

This is a letter that Mark Phillips wrote to his three children, Sept. 9, 2016

Dear Ashley, Louisa, and George,

As each if you now know, my truly beloved friend, Preston Hipp, died late last night. He was 57 years old.

Beach bocci buds Preston and Bruce Freshley.

Preston was so special to Mom and me, and was particularly important to me. He was very simply my spiritual mentor. He has helped me so much, particularly over the spring and summer of this year. His "small group" Bible study started over 25 years ago under Rev. Jay Fowler's direction, grew into four different Bible studies every Friday morning at St.Philip's, and now touches some 75 men who attend those studies.

Preston was a football star at Porter Gaud, particularly in the fall of 1976. This was a rather famous Porter Gaud team. We beat all the public schools and had a great time doing it. Preston really took me under his wing and looked after me once he saw that I was a formidable player, even as a 10th grader (his being a 12th grader then). That was the beginning of our deeper life-long friendship.

At some point after college, Preston became immersed in The Word through a local, small Bible church. He came to terrific faith while in his early twenties, and he found and fell in love with Laura Wichmann. He had read through the entire Bible many, many times. He knew, understood, and applied God's Word better than anyone else that I knew, lay or clergy. I had always had a pleasant relationship with Laura. Her brother, Bunky, was a year behind me in grade school. We went off to camp one summer.

As you know, Uncle Gator and I went to Mr. Hipp's Bible study for many, many years. It was truly amazing to watch people grow in faith, as Preston truly touched a number of lives.

This is not to say that Preston was anything but a ton of fun. He came up for Clemson games with the gang. He hunted with me, both at Oakland Club and at Cheeha Combahee. We went to the Bahamas together with other friends and had an absolute ball. He and Laura were on our "impromptu dinner party" list, and we were afforded similar privilege at their house. We were on each other's short lists.

I will miss Preston terribly. He is in a much better place. By way of providential fate, St.Philip's begins its new church year on Sunday, Sept.11. It might just be that our Almighty decided to take Preston home at this point, when St. Philip's Church is finally up and running on all cylinders.

Whatever the case, thanks be to God for my dear friend, Preston Hipp.

Love,
Dad

•   •   •

Liesel Eppes, Sept. 2016

Dear Aunt Laura:

It is the first Sunday without Uncle Preston in the world, and my heart feels so heavy with that in my mind.

He was one of the few people I have ever known who could talk to anyone and put them at ease instantly. He shone with God's love every day of his life.

The last thing he said to me was, "I love you", as Mom, Annabel, and I left. I think that speaks huge volumes about who he was. He always asked me how I was, even though sometimes it would have been very easy to talk about what he was going through. He truly had a servant's heart.

I will keep you in my prayers throughout the weeks to come.

"But the Lord has become my fortress, and my God, the rock in whom
I take refuge."
Psalm 94:22

My prayers are with you.

Love and blessings,
Liesel Eppes

• • •

Belk Daughtridge, Sept. 15, 2016

Laura:

There is nothing I can say that will make my pain subside.
There is no place for my sadness to run or hide.
I wish I could hold him, just for one more day,
But I know the good Lord took him away.
There is a void in my heart where all my tears have cried,
We are all lonely and empty without the Prince of Tides.

Love to you,
Belk Daughtridge

• • •

Tom Fisher, Sept. 26, 2016

Dear Laura,
It has taken me a long time to write you this letter. It would take a
thousand pages to share everything that is on my mind and in my

heart. I'm not sure what to say, but though I know the effort is futile, I will attempt to write coherently hereon.

Thank you for the blessing that you and Preston have been in my life. Your sincere kindness and friendship have meant more to me than I can say. Some of my most peaceful moments and fulfilling conversations have taken place around your dining room table or on Grandmumsie's sofa. Thinking of your warm hospitality brings a smile to my face though I write this with tears in my eyes.

Your strength, Laura, has been astounding. Everyone who knows you is better for it, and your beautiful girls are fortunate to have you as their example. If I can find a wife who possesses a fraction of your grace, I will be the luckiest man in the world. IF she and I can enjoy an ounce of the love, devotion, and sheer joy that you and Preston shared, we will be blessed beyond measure.

Andrew Thomas and Cooper Ray shared with me the news of Preston's death. Though we were all at a loss, endless stories about Preston were shared as we remembered what a remarkable man he was. "I can think of no man more deserving of Heaven's splendor, yet humble enough to eschew such praise as this": those were my first words in response to Preston's passing. They are so true.

I will miss having a male role model of Preston's stature. It is empowering for a young man to see someone of Preston's character, kindness, and faith wrapped into the body of a strong, masculine figure. I know he would roll his eyes at this flowery prose!

`Preston seemed to know the secrets of life. Maybe, in emulating him, I can discover them too.`

"Every man's life ends the same way. It is only the details of how he lived and how he died that distinguish one man from another." Ernest Hemingway

This may as well have been written about dear Preston. Preston lived with the tenacity and joy of a hundred men. He died with the courage and dignity of a thousand warriors. There are many things I will remember about Preston. The foremost, I think, is the way he lived as a walking, talking, breathing oxymoron. He was a gentle giant, a docile warrior, a rugged nobleman. He had the strength of a lion but the heart of a servant; boyish charms, but manly capabilities; mischievous tendencies, but virtuous deeds. Suffice it to say, Preston Hipp had it all, and he was one-of-a-kind.

The celebrations of Preston's life were the most powerful I have witnessed. I have never been so completely, steadfastly captivated by a religious service. Every word spoken, every praise song — it was all so evocative of Preston's spirit. I left St. Philip's and Magnolia Cemetery bursting with the love of God. Though broken, my heart was more full than it had been in quite some time.

It meant so much to spend time at your home after the burial. I do hope I didn't stay too long. I wanted so badly to do something for you, to show my love and appreciation through action. That day, this meant picking up plates and cups, wrapping up leftovers, and mopping the front porch. These were such insufficient gestures, but they were the best I knew how to do at the time. Please know that whatever you need, whenever you need it, I am always happy to help.

Take care of your whole heart and self. You and the girls are in my faithful prayers.

Always,

Tom Fisher

• • •

Barbara & Duke Hagerty, Sept. 2016

Dear Laura:

Please accept our condolences. Preston was the loveliest and finest of people.

He often took the girls to swim at the pool, and noticed that the back-yard palmetto trees looked very unkempt and in need of much TLC. One day he came to my parents' with a ladder, loppers, and a truck, and carted off tons of fronds. In the history of having the pool (since 1964), no guest or friend has ever gone to so much trouble or effort. Remarkable and memorable!

Sending much sympathy to you and you beautiful girls.

Barbara Hagerty

• • •

Jennings & Ross Cameron, September 2016

Our dearest Laura, Olivia, Delia and Victoria,

When talking about our favorite memories of Preston, Ross and I decided in one word: Bocci. We cannot explain how your family has for-ever altered the course of our lives. We mean that. Ross said he was like a father to him. He taught him a lot about life, marriage, and truly how to be a gentleman. We cannot imagine how a lifetime with him would have been, considering what an impact he had on us in just four years.

All our love, now and forever,
Jennings & Ross Cameron

Laura's note: Preston and I are forever linked to Jennings and Ross by being at their wedding, our last to attend together, on our last anniversary, April 9, 2016.

• • •

Capers Cross, October 1, 2016

Dear Laura:

You and your dear family have been much in my thoughts and prayers over the last several weeks. St. Philip's has lost a much loved and revered brother in Preston. The pain of his loss is felt by all who knew and loved him, from both near and afar. You have shown us how joy and grief can walk hand in hand, and in so doing you have enriched and strengthened our own faith.

Last year when my nephew died after a long battle with non-Hodgkin's lymphoma, Brad Wilson gave me a pamphlet of a prayer by John Donne, which became a source of great comfort to me. I have tried unsuccessfully to find it online, so I decided to type it out and share it with you. It is a bit lengthy, but full of the riches one expects from the pen and heart of John Donne.

May this prayer bring you solace and peace.

Your brother in Christ,

Capers Cross

"The Day"
An excerpt from the prayer before the sermon preached by John
Donne, Dean of St. Paul's, London, at the Commemoration of the gra-
cious Lady Magdalen Danvers, in the parish church of Chelsea, on 1
July 1627. *(Laura's note: Lady Danvers was the mother of the great poet George
Herbert; she was an educated, Godly, remarkable woman.)*

O eternal and most glorious God,
Who sometimes in thy justice
Dost give the dead bodies of the saints
To be meat unto the fowls of the heavens,
And the flesh of thy saints
Unto the beasts of the earth,
So that their blood is shed like water,
And there is none to bury them;

Who sometimes sell'st thy people for naught,
And dost not increase thy wealth by their price,
And yet never leav'st us without the knowledge
That precious in thy sight
Is the death of thy saints,

Enable us,
In life and death,
Seriously to consider the value,
The price of a soul.

It is precious, O Lord,
Because thine image is stamped and
Imprinted upon it;
Precious because the blood of thy Son
Was paid for it;
Precious because thy Blessed Spirit,

The Holy Ghost,
Works upon it and tries it by His diverse fires;
And precious because it is entered into thy revenue
And made a part of thy treasure.

Suffer us not, therefore, O Lord,
So to undervalue ourselves--
Nay, so to impoverish thee--
As to give away those souls,
Thy souls,
Thy dear and precious souls--
For nothing.
And all the world is nothing if the soul
Must be given for it.

We know, O Lord,
That our rent, due to thee, is our soul;
And the day of our death is the day,
And our death-bed the place,
Where that rent is to be paid.
And we know too that he that hath sold his soul before
For unjust gain,
Or given away his soul before
In the society of fellowship and sin,
Or lent his soul for a time
By lukewarmness and temporizing,
To the dishonor of thy name,
To the weakening of thy case,
To the discouraging of thy servants,
He comes to that day, and to that place,
His death and his death-bed,
Without any rent in his hand,
Without any soul to that purpose,

To surrender it unto thee.

Let therefore, O Lord, the same hand
Which is to receive them then,
Preserve those souls till then;
Let that mouth that breathed them into us, at first,
Breathe always upon them,
Whilst they are in us,
And suck them into itself,
When they depart from us.
Preserve our souls, O Lord,
Because they belong to thee;
And preserve our bodies,
Because they belong to those souls.

Thou alone doest steer our boat through all our voyage,
But has a more especial care of it,
A more watchful eye upon it,
When it comes to a narrow current,
Or to a dangerous fall of waters.
Thou hast a care of the preservation of those bodies;
In all the ways of our life;
But in the Straits of Death,
Open thine eyes wider,
And enlarge thy providence towards us so far,
That no fever in the body may shake the soul,
No apoplexy in the body damp or benumb the soul,
Nor any pain or agony of the body
Presage future torments to the soul.

But so make thou our bed in all our sickness,
That being used to thy hand,
We may be content with any bed of thy making,
Whether thou be pleased

To change our feathers into flocks*
By withdrawing the conveniences of this life,
Or change our flocks into dust,
Even the dust of the grave,
By withdrawing us out of this life.

*wool or hair

And though thou divide man and wife,
Mother and child,
Friend and friend,
By the hand of death,
Yet stay them that stay,
And send them away that go,
With this consolation:
That though we part at divers days
And by divers ways, here,
Yet we shall all meet at one place,
And at one day--
A day that no night shall determine:
The Day of the Glorious Resurrection.

(c) 1967 by the Episcopal Book Club

• • •

Margaret Scott, Oct. 4, 2016

Dear Laura,

I just love you so much! I am enjoying a quiet hour and have been rereading your beautiful letters of March, April, June, August, and the latest of September 22. I have notes in my journals from our phone conversations which encouraged my faith so greatly. I have mulled over

Edwin Smythe's visions and conversations with Preston. I imagined Preston's memorial service as I read every word of prayers, hymns, and scripture.

Your prayers are beautiful and faith inspiring. The emails and texts - Summer Lowcountry Boating, Waiting for God's #1, your seeing Preston in his glorious body making rounds at MUSC to let the staff know he is more than okay, the story and providence of Renny's first speaking on September 13, 1983, at the funeral of Stewart Walker at St.Philip's and then his last being 33 years later at Preston's service, on September 13, 2016. Oh, what a rich feast you have given me! I keep all the printed and handwritten treasures in a large envelope, so I can read them often.

My hope in Jesus soars whenever I read your writing. A man asked Renny yesterday how strong a Christian he [Renny] is. Renny's answer was so insightful. "I'm as strong as my dependence on Jesus".

I know this season has to be exhausting and full of emotion. I think of you and ponder Renny's answer. You are unashamedly devoted to Jesus, and leaning heavily on Him. Nothing is more beautiful in this world.

May Jesus keep the revelations, visions, insights, comfort, hope, strength, help, and love coming day and night. I love every one you share with me.

I love you dearly.
Margaret Scott

• • •

Edward Morrison, Oct. 10, 2016

Dearest Laura:

You and the girls have been consistently on my mind as I pray for you all. Reflecting recently upon Preston, I surmise that I probably knew him as long as anyone. We all played football, sports at East Bay Playground, starting probably around 1965 or 1966. Although Barre Butler and I pushed pushed Preston hard, he always remained calm, cool, and imperturbable.

Reflecting upon his life, his commitment to Christ and reading again his obituary, I realize how "far short of the mark" I am in my life.

"Well done, good and faithful servant; you have been faithful over a little; I will set you over much; enter into the joy of your Master." Matthew 25:3

In this parable, Jesus exclaims all that Preston embodied. He will remain always an example, a paragon for us -- especially Dads, fathers, etc. I admit, humbly, again how far short I have fallen in my life.

Preston has "entered into the joy of his Master". There can be no other reward, compliment to his life.

May God continue to bless you all. Let me know if I can help in any way.

Sincerely,

Edward

• • •

Norris Eppes, Dec. 20, 2016

Dear Auntie Laura, Olivia, Delia, and Victoria:

Preston Hipp was a man I always looked up to. This is of course because he was wonderful. But also, as memory snaps pictures at certain ages, I see him from about waist high looking up. He's collecting firewood or teaching me how to shuck an oyster. He had a great grin.

As a kid I looked up to him as an example of a strong Christian. How to act, how to behave. He was an expert at how to combine having fun with good manners. He always had a sense of humor and appreciation for the day, empathetic and caring. Some people make their laughs at the expense of others, but Preston's smiling at the world seemed different to me; kind, relaxed, thankful.

I almost worry to write, because words aren't objects we can hold, and I can only imagine that in a time like this they must lose meaning. Please know that I am thinking of you each these days.

With love,

Norris Eppes
(Laura's note: Norris is the first of eight children.)

Fleeting Glimpses

By Bunky Wichmann

We all continue to struggle with the loss of Preston. No one more than Laura and the girls. I have been blessed to have him come and visit every now and again to comfort me. He often comes and visits me in my dreams. He is never center stage in my dream, more like he is there in the background.

The first and most poignant dream was about three weeks after he died. I dreamt I was in a house with close friends, like a cocktail party or something. There was an adjoining room with a cased opening (large doorway) and then another room next to it with a cased opening. The details of the rooms were vivid: varnished pine floors, white cased openings, soft beige walls, no furniture other than the stuffed chair Preston was seated in and a soft afternoon light that Preston was looking toward. In that far room Preston sat comfortably in the big chair. He was his old healthy, strong self and he sat quietly, not wishing to really engage with the crowd, but content to sit peacefully on the periphery.

It was of incredible comfort knowing he was there; it was as if he wanted me to know that he was still with us, watching over and waiting for us all to be together again. How nice of him to come and visit and let me know that he is always there...

● ● ●

From Clark Hanger, quoting in memory of his departed friend:

"When he shall die, take him and cut him out into stars, and he shall make the face of heaven so fine that all the world will be in love with night and pay no worship to the garish sun."------- from William Shakespeare's *Romeo and Juliet*

● ● ●

PRESTON IS ALIVE
Laura's two dreams

"I am alive, and I am well,"
Preston has said to me twice.

In the first dream we were walking through the hospital, letting the staff see him in the halls. Everyone, especially Preston, was laughing with incredulity at him being alive. I asked him how he managed it, because we saw him breathe his last, and that we were "planning a funeral like you would not believe!"

Preston said,"I don't know. All I know is I AM ALIVE, and I AM WELL."

This dream motivated me to send a note telling the dream to MUSC E.R. and Hollings Cancer Center Infusion Lab along with Olivia's remembrance of Preston, as well as to sing Christmas carols at the E.R. on Christmas Eve. It is like Preston to be thinking of others who worked to prolong his quality of life, who could despair over the long term ineffectiveness of their job.

The second dream was of Preston driving the car, with me sitting next to him, like so many times before, as the wife in the passenger seat. All was as it should be, but it occurred to me and I said, "We had a funeral AND a burial! At what point did you realize that you were alive and well, because we saw you breath your last? Where were you? At Stuhr's?"

Preston said, «I don't have any memory of that.
All I know is that I AM ALIVE, AND I AM WELL."

I said, "I can see that you are alive and well, and I am SO GLAD!" I reached over while he was driving, and he reached over, too, to give each other a quick kiss. It was so satisfying; just a peck. We were back to life as it should be. It is what dream analysts call " a compensatory dream," compensating for reality. But it was Preston and me together, solid and business as usual.

The dream continued. "Now that you are alive and well, WHERE DO YOU WANT TO LIVE??? WE CAN SELL THE HOUSE, THE FURNITURE, THE SILVER, THE CHINA AND LIVE THE KIND OF LIFE YOU WANT TO LIVE!!!"

I am very much aware that Preston laid down his life for me. He said when contemplating marriage, he could be happy living out in the boondocks as a bridge tender, so that he could have contemplative time for reading and studying God's Word. (Our Victoria asked when hearing this story, "Where's the boondocks?") Preston shook his head and said, "This IS the life I was meant to live, with you." This was the conversation we were having in his last year and last days.

He pulled up to a green, historic house, with a flat roof, our destination. I did not want to get out of the car. "WHY when it's just the two of us and we are enjoying communicating do we have to break up the intimacy?" I asked with exasperation verging on a temper tantrum building within. He was patient but firm that it was time for me to go in.

Reluctantly I went in, not knowing where I was or why. I did not recognize the house. It turned out to be a shop. It was filled with beautiful stacks of linens, all Vintage, a lady's shop, elegant like Lois Daughtridge's, The Boutique. I said to myself, "Oh, oh, oh! This is MY kind of place!" The lady keeping shop was hoity-toity. She must not take me for a serious customer, I thought. I found a cloth of many colors and put in down on the counter firmly and deliberately saying, "I am GOING to buy this!" and then more timidly, "How much IS it?"

Laura and Preston's home beside the Ashely River and the Battery, 194 Tradd Street.

The shop lady unfolded it and found a large price tag that I did not need glasses to read. It was $6. I said, "That's a good price. I could use this as a picnic cloth on the ground at that price." The lady said, "Or to cover a bed."

This second dream ended here, but the images were so vivid that they kept me ruminating. I decided that the $6 represented my big 6-0 birthday that was fast approaching on Nov. 6, 2016. And I would be spending it without my beloved. Before he died, Preston had anticipated that I would be tearful without him that day, of all days.

Little did I know what would happen next.

On my birthday, I found a small box wrapped up by the front door with no tag. The shape, the orange silk ribbon, made me think, "That looks like a Croghan's box, but, (rueful laugh), my Croghan's days are over!" Preston was the only one who would ever shop for me at Croghan's. The gift lay unclaimed until the next morning when, after questioning the girls, I opened it.

It was a Gold Locket, VINTAGE, with an H in Old English engraved on one side, and a CROSS in tiny diamonds on the other, in that iconic blue velvet box from Croghan's Jewel Box! There is no one but Preston who would give this gift to me. I called Mariana Hay to ask if she knew who, what, how. Yes, she knew. She had delivered it. She said, "Preston wanted you to have this."

I thought of Preston's motto, "Prepare for the worst. Hope for the best." It was the kind of over-the-top, unexpected generosity that Preston would surprise me with, like on Christmas Day morning 1987, when he caught me off guard and gave me a diamond ring (from Croghan's) on bended knee. To think, Mrs. Ramsay knew before I did. He had put the engagement ring in a long narrow box wrapped in silver paper. The box said Sterling Silver Accessories.

I had prayed, "Lord, whatever is in this box, help me to appreciate it," anticipating a silver bracelet, and I don't wear silver. When I saw the diamond ring, I could not believe my eyes. I was afraid to blink for fear of the image changing. That is how I felt when I saw the Gold Locket. There must be some mistake. This gift must be meant for someone else. Mariana assured me, it was meant for me.

"Have you opened it?" I had not realized the locket did open, being flat. With effort, I got it open. Inside is a picture of Preston and me, our faces, from a black and white photo from when we were dating. "How did you get this photo?" I asked.

Mariana said her girls know how to do that kind of work. The other side was of Preston steering our beloved boat, focused, eyes straight ahead. Mariana said she wanted to be sure I knew that it was VINTAGE, engraved long ago with the H. The fact that it had an H as well as a cross, that it even exists, and then that it found its way to Croghan's and then to me is an alignment only God and Preston could put together through the kind hands of Mariana and her girls, Kathleen Hay Hagood and young Mariana Hay.

The dream of Preston taking me shopping for something Vintage foreshadowed the Vintage gift to top all, a gift from Preston in Eternity to remember that he is still with me, and is married to me as I walk into my sixties. People tell me, well meaning, that Jesus said we are not given in marriage in Heaven. I know. What he was saying is that we don't get married in Heaven, and are not necessarily married in Heaven. It depends on whether you have achieved a real marriage on earth. Love never fails. I know that what Preston and I had with the Lord's cross at the center will last into Eternity, forever and ever.

Preston and Laura, Valentines Forever, Feb. 14, 2015

Nostalgic Memories

Preston and Laura on a mountain trip with their young daughters, around 1999.

The Tug's Black Silhouette

Editor's Note: Preston wrote this account on June 20, 1982. It is reprinted with his capitalizations. This land described was Point Pleasant, what came to be called Stono Ferry. It was owned by Preston's father, C.R. Hipp. Preston and friends bush-hogged the land and lived on the water in the summer.

BY PRESTON HIPP

I went on a breathtaking "Titanic" cruise Sunday, just after Sunset, when the Light dies into a world of black and white, and of course, all hues in between. Fog shrouded the islets, marsh, and water to seem pre-historic and timeless. Tranquil, it sent shivers of Life down my spine, and I was so glad to be alive and free!

The trip had no function other than pleasure, and it was one, no traps to pull or set, no crabs to sort-cook-clean. My weekend in Raleigh, although VERY enjoyable, contrasted with my present environment, enhancing the beauty of the experience; the joy of newness made my perception all the more acute and full of emotion, as the Power of Life pumped strong in my heart.

Opening the refrigerator to calculate my dinner options, I noticed a pack of six chicken backs. Jerry (Poore) had told me there WAS NO crab bait. After a large salad, and a chicken pot pie, I was off to set the trap.

There was no moon, and the tide was unusually high, as high as I'd ever seen. The sun had set an hour ago, and my eyes adjusted to the dim light, mostly none. The old 4 horsepower Johnson fired after one pull from the start cord, a good sign from a usually temperamental motor. The leaks had all but subsided thanks to a recent caulk and paint job. The yacht was DRY except for an inch of water taken on from several practice maneuvers!

The loneliness of having Jerry and Richard (Hollowell) gone and Fox deciding not to go this time out, left me to conquer my fears of devil-ish ghoul-like creatures popping into existence to my immediate left, or right, or even of Lon Chaney splashing into the scene. (A silent film star of horror films such as The Wolf Man) I chided myself for my emotional fears and the disability to calm them immediately. I strained my eyes to the water to see where it transformed into min-iature forests of green marsh, grass tips signifying the existence of a marsh bank underneath, too close underneath.

An Angelic glow commanded my attention on the waterway south of me, a tug. The boat's huge spotlight illuminated a live oak with a bril-liant silver lining. I wanted to get as close as was reasonable to contrast the immense power of the Tug to "The Titanic", as small a johnboat as conceivable. The 4 horsepower Johnson was either running at its usual wide open "ramming" speed, or wheezing miserably, which I interpreted to be dead marsh grass adrift by the flood tide jamming the tiny propeller. After checking the prop a couple of times with no sign of weeds, I decided the motor was up to its old tricks again.

The Tug was passing my bow about 60 feet ahead. I shut the sick motor off to gain the full effect of the power of the Tug, the huge stacks bellowing out the purr of its giant diesel-gulping cat engines. The captain had yet to shine the spotlight in my direction, and I enjoyed the feeling of secre-tiveness, as if hiding in a small bush when a black rhinoceros thunders by.

The Tug's engines were suddenly pulled back idle. The dominating mass slowly lost its momentum and drifted to a semi-stop. The spotlight and forward running lights were cut off, leaving only the two stories of running lights on each flank of the Tug illuminated. It gave the Tug an evil, menacing appearance. I reached intuitively for the pull cord to be on my way. My original plan was to put the crab trap on a small creek on the other side of the waterway, but the moaning of the motor suggested otherwise. I patiently squeezed the pump bulb on the fuel line to send more gas to tiny pistons.

The Tug diesels roared, sending a wall of swirling, gurgling turbulence off its starboard side of the stern. I tried to believe the captain had just received orders to come get the barge I had seen him pushing earlier in the day from my view from the porch. I had never seen one turn around, and nervous vibrations were in the air. The Tug turned to the deeper, outside bank of the waterway, its stern to me.

Instinct and fear directed "The Titanic" to the protection of the old, shallow waterway. The johnboat was barely moving, but my eyes stayed focused on the Tug, not at correcting "The Titanic's" mechanical problems. My night vision was still terrible because the light from the Tug had prevented their adjustment. I sought the water covered marsh bank to put between the Tug and myself, just for insurance. A recent case of a tugboat running over and leaving a 40-foot yacht in New York made me increasingly paranoid.

To my amazement, the Tug continued its turn to 270 degrees, in other words, headed right for me! What the Hell!? I could hardly believe what was happening, but the splashing of the waves off the Tug's broad, flat, tall bow quickly focused reality for me. Holy----! Holy----! The gap between the Tug and "The Titanic" was closing in rapidly. Please motor, please run!

Adrenaline and terror controlled my body. The Tug's black silhouette grew in size and power as the Tug drew closer. The spotlight was cut on me, exploding a thick beam of light right on me. I felt like a World War II prison camp escapee. about to get machine gunned. "The Titanic" made little progress, its waning motor drowned out by the exhaust of the Tug. The splashing off the bow of the Tug became more vivid and threatening with each inch as it neared the low transom of "The Titanic".

"OH GOD! Please Help this motor!" The words must have been heard because just at that moment the second cylinder kicked in and the 4 hp had "The Titanic" sputtering at ramming speed, (=10 mph).

I quietly rejoiced when the tips of the marsh grass appeared ahead of my bow. It was reassuring knowing I, at least, wasn't going to be run over. My mind raced with the possible actions The Tug would take now that I was engulfed in the safety of the marsh bank. My paranoia increased when the spotlight was cut back off. The darkness gave me a sense of doom instead of one of camouflage. I crouched low in "The Titanic" as the Tug veered to the right, missing my bow by 50 feet, a distance which is totally relative to perspective.

I can only guess why the Tug reacted the way it did--drugs, fun, boredom? All I know is it was a pleasant sight to see it disappear behind the next bend in the river. A loud laugh erupted from my body. A forced laugh that is necessary to confront life's peculiarities. I threw out the trap and headed for home and a beer. Another day on The Farm had passed.

Laura's note: One August day 1984, two years after Preston wrote this account, a photographer, hired to promote the Hipp family Stono Ferry land for sale, took a picture of a sailing yacht going past. It was blown up and framed and put in the real estate office there. Preston saw it the next week. She was Mobjack, the Wichmann family's 50 ft ketch, on her way to the Rockville Regatta, where Preston would meet me for the first time the next day, aboard Mobjack.

Mobjack, **where Laura and Preston first met in 1984.**

NEWLYWED REPORTS FROM
MR. AND MRS. G. PRESTON HIPP
Written during Advent 1988

From the new bride, Laura:

When Preston told me he wanted to take me to an old log cabin without running water or electricity for part of our honeymoon, I was a little dubious. He said I'd love it, but I was not sure. When we got to the end of the dirt road in Chester, South Carolina, and he took off driving over the rolling hills, the questioning look on the faces of the cows we passed reflected my own as I tried to bite my tongue and be the submissive wife.

But he was right. I did love it -- so much so, we stayed an extra night. We were far removed from civilization and all its trappings and were able to feel at home in its simplistic lifestyle. There was a pump out back, a pitcher and bowl inside for washing and shaving, a porcelain chamber pot in place of a privy, kerosene lamps and candles for romantic light, and an old gas stove for gourmet meals of leftovers from our wedding feast. The biggest surprise of all was "the Bridal Chamber". Our friend George, whose cabin we were using, had said he would put a mattress on the floor for us.

As we climbed the staircase to the Bridal Chamber, I could see the sky and verdant spring countryside through the wide gaps in between the logs where the chinking had come out. The upstairs is one huge room with cathedral ceilings and glassless windows, the closest you can get to being outside while still being inside. The wind blows right through the upstairs so that you really feel you are inside a living, breathing house with a soul of its own.

To our surprise, towering above us in this pioneer setting, was a brand new heart of pine rice bed. George had gone to the extreme in preparing for the groom and his bride. We felt the love, good wishes, and prayers of our friend George, and of many friends and family who shared in the joy of our marriage. We knew at that moment we were blessed and loved.

St. Philip's Church, filled with smiling, joyful faces, and the angelic singing of the choir; the Godly wisdom of Richard Dority and Terrell Glenn who married us; the toasts the night before at the rehearsal dinner and my brother's toast in rhyme at the reception; the surprisingly large crowd waiting with joyful cheers to see us off in our horse and carriage, and then our dramatic getaway from the Carolina Yacht Club dock to my father's old wooden sailboat with, again, a cheering crowd, balloons and confetti, all combined to launch us into what is proving to be a thrilling life together. We feel tremendously blessed each day and are thankful for all our friends, family and loved ones who, in do many great and small ways contributed to our marriage getting off to a great start.

We are happily situated in a little carriage house on Legare Street, circa 1850, with a lovely little courtyard and garden, which we are buying. We certainly have our work cut out for us. However, Preston is proving to be more than I bargained for as a husband in that he has taken such an interest in the property and is so clever at getting things done that I would still be pondering over. We presently have the challenge of meshing our lives and possessions together in this small house, but even the boxes of his things that surround us serve as a joyful reminder of the reality that my forever friend is now my forever husband.

Mr. and Mrs. G. Preston Hipp march down the aisle at St. Philip's Church Charleston on April 9, 1988.

From the groom, Preston:

One Year Anniversary Report

One thing I can say after being married is that I certainly am more appreciative of weddings now that I know all the work and details behind them. I can also rejoice with the couple because I know what a great relief it is to be getting married rather than just mentally debating over the prospect of it or to be doing all the work leading up to it. I realize most single men are at least apprehensive about marriage and if they are like I was, they are terrified of it.

My fear did not pertain to Laura but to having such a long term and serious commitment to anyone, especially in lieu of the modern statistic that every other marriage ends in divorce.

I found the "to-be or not-to-be" marriage decision process very agonizing and was relieved to finally reach the decision of commitment. We wanted to get off on the right foot and went to not one but three different marriage counselors! All three were men of God who gave us new insight to the kind of relationship God intended for a husband and wife. We were greatly blessed by the blended wisdom of this counsel and highly recommend it to all who are contemplating marriage. A sure foundation is crucial for success.

One lesson God has shown me in this past year is that hate diminishes and love builds up. Those six words are so simple yet so vital to the life of the relationship.

One area that Laura has helped me is my recent career change. After appraising for the last five years, becoming a commercial broker for the Max Hill Company has been very exciting, filled with many highs and lows. It sure makes a difference to have a safe haven during the lows. On some days coming home to Laura is like an oasis in a desert. The mild winter and Laura's success with her business, The Charleston Tea Party Walking Tour, has also been a blessing.

Believe me, it is a humbling experience for a man to have the woman be the breadwinner. But Laura does not rub it in and the future looks promising for me in my new field.

Areas of common interests are important in marriages. One area of my life I am glad Laura enjoys is my ministry through Prison Fellowship out at Lieber Prison in Ridgeville, SC. Going into a medium/maximum security prison can be intimidating but Laura is a real trooper and enjoys sharing the Good News of Christ with the inmates. She agrees that true rehabilitation can only come through becoming a new creature in Christ.

Despite our cramped quarters in our carriage house, we have enjoyed establishing a home together. Laura always makes an effort to have fresh flowers and a decorative touch. It certainly has been a fast year and we have enjoyed bringing you this marriage update. One area we can particularly say we have been blessed is our family and friends. Thank you and God's blessings to you.

Sincerely,

Preston

• • •

Four love notes from Preston to Laura,
created by him on homemade paper hearts, now framed and hanging in their stairwell area:

1) April 9, 2015 (their 27th wedding anniversary)

Laura, my beloved one,
God knew you were the girl for me. What a blessed adventure we
have been on for 27 years! You have always been my eager companion, yearning to see what awaits us around the next bend of life's
twists and turns. 2014 was a hard year for me. Your love made it bear-
able. Whatever lies ahead, I know I can do it with you by my side.
With love and thanks,
Pres

Song of Solomon 2:10-13

10 My beloved spoke and said to me,
"Arise, my darling,
my beautiful one, come with me.
11 See! The winter is past;
the rains are over and gone.
12 Flowers appear on the earth;
the season of singing has come,
the cooing of doves
is heard in our land.
13 The fig tree forms its early fruit;
the blossoming vines spread their fragrance.
Arise, come, my darling;
my beautiful one, come with me."

2) Mother's Day, May 19, 2015

Proverbs 31:28-31

28 Her children arise and call her blessed;
her husband also, and he praises her:

29 "Many women do noble things,
but you surpass them all."
30 Charm is deceptive, and beauty is fleeting;
but a woman who fears the Lord is to be praised.
31 Honor her for all that her hands have done,
and let her works bring her praise at the city gate.

Underneath was penned: "To my favorite dreamer and schemer. Love always, Preston"

3) On another red heart, Preston quoted Proverbs 31:1-12:

10 [a]A wife of noble character who can find?
She is worth far more than rubies.
11 Her husband has full confidence in her
and lacks nothing of value.
12 She brings him good, not harm,
all the days of her life.

Laura says, "He called me his Proverbs 31 woman these last years: words of affirmation…The ultimate praise. It took the whole marriage to get to that point. To God be the Glory. I miss him SO!" (July 15, 2017)

4) Feb. 14, 2016

Laura, watching your JOY over the last two weeks, preparing for your Valentine's party while praising the Lord to Bethel music, has been a blessing to me. The Lord has brought me a long way over the past 32 years, and you are His primary agent of change in my life. Thank you for your persistent love and encouragement. I would not have come so far without you in my life. I am always thankful to the Lord for Rockville, 1984.

All my love,
Preston

A Devoted Wife's Closing Thoughts

Selected writings by
Laura Wichmann Hipp

Preston fooling around with a boa constrictor; years later, this photo would remind Laura of his fight against cancer.

Nov. 19, 2016

Being married to The Prince of Tides required a lesson borrowed from His Royal Highness The Prince of Wales. When he and Diana were first married, she had a row with him over not wanting him to go on the traditional Christmas Day fox hunt, leaving her alone with the rest of the Royal Family. I learned early on that if I kept Preston delayed for a moment from being with his family in order to walk into family gatherings with me, or denied him the pleasure of going to North Dakota for a pheasant shoot over my birthday weekend, or to the Bahamas on a stag sail with my brother, that I would pay, for he would feel like a caged animal.

When on the boat or a walk in the woods, or on a hunting, skiing or biking trip, Preston was refreshed by being in God's creation, re-energized to love me with a new zest and appreciation, lifting me up in his strong arms, swinging his little woman around the kitchen, and bestowing that wide smile and wet kiss on me. I never slept well without him, but it was worth the separation when he returned and I got to bathe in his love.

I had asked him whether he would come back from Heaven if the angel gave him the choice. Out of his love for me, he said he would try to return. Yet how could I have a claim on him once he could taste and see that the Lord is good in Heaven and exchange his cancer ridden body for a new one?

Preston kept a picture I didn't like. It was a boa constrictor wrapped around him. He said cancer is like a boa constrictor: it will squeeze every ounce of strength out of your body until there is nothing left. His rib cage mocked his free and vibrant spirit that was not one to be caged-in. He flashed one last smile at Joyce Wichmann, and at Clark Hanger that last day, September 8, 2016.

Clark and Hartley Watlington lifted him to a chair for his desired change of sheets on the hospital bed downstairs. That smile was as if to say *this body is not the real me; it is a mockery of the man that you and I know so well.* He also grimaced in such agony as only Jesus knows as he was being lifted so kindly into the chair and back to the bed.

Until then Preston had been able to walk the staircase from our upstairs bed. He had but *one night* sleeping in the hospital bed downstairs with me beside him in the reclining chair. I thought it was the end of one era and the beginning of the next, of our sleeping downstairs; however, Preston had warned me that a decline down the slippery slopes picks up momentum.

I said to him that last day a favorite but obscure verse I have had written on a card since my pre-Preston days of praying for my husband to be. "Gideon and the 300 men who were with him, reached the Jordan and crossed over, weary, yet pursuing." I then gave it one last valiant prayer and called on the 300 last strong fighting cells left in Preston's body to rise up and FIGHT! FIGHT! FIGHT! that cancer and TO LET PRESTON LIVE! That was the persistent prayer warrior he wanted in the room. He lifted his good left hand to give me the fist punch, unable then to speak.

The things that used to irritate him about me, my obsessing, as he called it, he came to appreciate in me. He said that once I latched hold to an idea or new found knowledge, I was like a pit bull; I was not going to let it go. You can imagine how I liked that comparison. But he came to see that trait was what was needed most in a wife when applied to fighting for his life with all the natural resources and physical presence I could muster. "It is such a Privilege," I said that last evening, "to be the one here for you, and not a room full of nurses, to lift up my hands in your name, and in His name in service to you. It is such an honor!"

He said repeatedly, "I don't know what I'd do without you."

"I couldn't make it without you."

"Thank you for your persistent, tenacious love."

He LOVED me more fully and deeply, like an ardent lover in the best romance, the harder it got to live! It was such a beautiful love story, more beautiful than I can convey with mere words.

All through the days of Preston's death and funeral, I would look up at the ceiling in our house. All I could see in my mind was the underside of the tapestry, the threads hanging down from the ceiling. It was a mess. But I knew in those days of Preston's death as I rejoice now to know: God is on the other side of the tapestry! This messy thread side is a chaotic point of view. The idea of the threads hanging from the ceiling has been a constant image for me down here. I am part of the mess. But I am also in the weave. I smile knowing that God has The Overall View from on top of the Tapestry of Life.

When Preston said that he would return if he could from Heaven, I asked, "Why?" He said, "Because you waited for me." He meant in waiting on "the one" for whom I had prayed to marry. A man with a heart after God. Him.

"It's not fair to you," he said."You don't deserve this."

I returned, "And the girls," to which he replied, "YOU would have been enough... If we had never had children, you would have been enough."

He had never said that before. I was stunned. We had tried for four years to have children, and I was already 31 when we married. He adored our children, putting other dads to shame, playing on the floor like a big kid with "Rough Games." But at this last stage of our lives, he was hoping he would live to see us be empty nesters together. His favorite days together were the simple ones dating in his little john-boat. Maybe he will be waiting for me in his old *Oyster Catcher* when my time comes to join him on the other side.

● ● ●

December 2016

I was getting ready Christmas Eve 2015, when it occurred to me I had not seen Preston in our dressing room. He must have gotten ready well ahead of time. I found him casually dressed on the couch downstairs in our library. "I'm not going," he said. "That's all right," I said. "You can go as you are," as my mind attempted to make the mental adjustment to the unthinkable. He repeated his first words adding the weighty truth that he was not physically up to it. He was on chemotherapy. "You and the girls go," he said.

The pendulum swung. The inner mind's defense: "It's Christmas Eve. Victoria, our teenage daughter, is singing in the choir. She has practiced for weeks. It's my favorite service of the year!" Then the pendulum swung the other way: "What if Preston has a momentary pang of loneliness? It's Christmas Eve. What if it's his last Christmas? I can't take that chance."

I vowed that I would not do anything else but lie on the couch with Preston and watch whatever he wanted to watch. I never sit and watch TV during Christmas. I'm too busy, making calamondin marmalade, etc, etc! (If you would like a jar, let me know!) Believe it or not, I had never ever watched,"It's a Wonderful Life." Last year, I did what every other American usually does Christmas Eve; I watched it on TV with Preston.

It was an intimate time of sharing the experience of a story that inspired us to reassess our own. Tête-à-tête, we talked in low voices, heads together with gentle kisses about what a wonderful life we have had together. God blessed us with being in love the whole marriage. Yes, there were rough spots, but the character of the whole, being in love, was never lost. I never stopped thanking Preston daily throughout our 28 years of marriage for the miracle of him loving me, for choosing me to be his bride when he could have had his pick of girls who were pining over him, as one tall, elegant lady told me she had been.

Preston said last Christmas Eve that if he were to die right then, he would have no regrets. We had had a rich life of so many blessings, more than most. God blessed us with three children. Delia, our miracle baby with three open heart surgeries had lived! Victoria had lived through full back surgery for scoliosis. We recalled our trip, just the two of us, to Antigua, Nevis, and Montserrat in the West Indies, when the Rhodes, Longs, and grandparents kept Olivia before Delia was born. She was actually conceived around the time we visited her Godfather, Daniel Massi, in foreign medical school in Montserrat. We recalled our trip to Costa Rica, a second honeymoon while our girls were at Camp Greystone. We recalled all our boating days, the life of daily, simple pleasures of living in the Lowcountry. Now was our time, for trials, to take up our cross, nor think til death to lay it down.

As I saw last night the film, "Jackie", and saw the long table set so beautifully at the White House with china and silver and flowers, I remembered Monti Hanger's toast last New Year's Eve, "Laura and Preston, you have brought us Camelot." For one brief moment.

This present Christmas Eve, 2016, I determined to go where Preston and I often went when he had a blood clot in his urine, the Emergency Room at MUSC. I walked from our house at the end of Tradd, passing by people coming out of Grace Church after the afternoon Christmas Eve service with their families. I was loudly singing Christmas carols. I always sing to push back the tears and to bolster my faith. No one looked at me; no eye contact; no greeting. The rush of Christmas, the compartmentalizing of the boxes in which we function, were apparent.

I passed by a weathered house in Harleston Village. I heard a bad word flung out to the world from a group of three men of our Gullah community as I passed by. I kept walking and then thought, "That house reminds me of the grubby stable where Jesus was born. It's just the kind of place a Pharisee like me would avoid. But Jesus wouldn't."

In response to my thought, I felt Him suggesting: "Take Me to them. Be My child in whom I delight. Let me make them three *wise* men."

I turned around and walked to the bare dirt backyard where the three men were drinking as they sat on stools, like a scene out of "Porgy and Bess". There was no one with me to tell me not to. I told them I had been sent to them, to deliver a Christmas carol.

"Wrong house, lady," one of them asserted.

"No, this is the one," I insisted.

"We don't want no carol, lady. We atheists. Leave!"

I reluctantly turned to go, but then defiance rose up as I wanted them to receive their Christmas blessing. I sang as I left with my back to them,

"O Come all ye Faithful, Joyful and Triumphant, O come ye, o come ye, to Bethlehem. Come and Adore Him, born the King of Angels..." I lifted my arms on the sidewalk in front of their abode, peaking back there to see if they had a gun pointed at me. When you long for Heaven, to be with your beloved, you have no fear.

Luckily, there was no gun, no threat, and I moved along. When I reached the ER, they let me in, asking if anyone else was with me. No. It's just me this time. The debutantes of Olivia's year had gone with me to sing in the halls of Intensive Care on a Christmas Eve when the late young Reid Patrick was there a few years ago. The staff had said no one had ever done that before. When the man leading me around the ER this year asked me to sing "Silent Night", I broke down. It took me back to Christmas Eve 1987, the night before Preston asked me to marry him.

This humble man guiding me through the ER, who had Christmas in his bashful eyes but was not used to singing, finished "Silent Night" for me. That was a Christ child moment.

After that, I walked back across town to join my girls and friends at my mother's old house at 103 King, now bought and restored by Delia's Godfather, Daniel Massi, where he had a delicious first attempt at Christmas Eve dinner. Again I walked, to save a pew for my girls and me at St. Philip's where Victoria was singing with the choir at the 7:30 service, remembering having missed it last year. When I miraculously secured our familiar pew, with room enough for my faithful brother, Bunky, and his lovely wife, Madeleine, I heard Preston say to me, "Look for me. I'm going to show up."

I replied to him, "I already know you are here. Marjorie Hanger said she saw you in a dream sitting with me, glowing, in our pew. She said, 'Preston, I know what you are doing. I can see you.' No one else could. You gave her proof of the Resurrection."

Preston said to me that he was going to show up in a bigger way that only he, Jesus, and I would know, but that I was going to want to stand up in the pew and exclaim it to the whole church. I had received this word earlier in the day. I had pulled out Preston's tuxedo for Jon Black, our daughter Olivia's boyfriend, to try on, not realizing how it would send back a flood of memories of the man filling the tux, of all the weddings, deb parties, and dances that we had been to together. I wrapped the arm of the tux around my waist and wept to remember the closeness of my man, and I felt Preston say, "You are going to find me at the Christmas Eve service tonight."

It might seem to you like a little thing, a coincidence, but to me what happened next was Preston and Jesus showing up to me personally, saying, "Nothing is wasted in the Kingdom of God. Nothing is forgotten when you do it for love." What happened was the Rev. Jeff Miller's first Christmas Eve sermon at St. Philip's Church.

He began, "In the Miller family, we have a Christmas tradition of watching every year, truth be told several times each year, a movie entitled, *It's a Wonderful Life*." I literally jumped off my seat. He then went on to tell the plot and then to transpose it to what if Jesus had never lived. This movie became the theme of a pointedly powerful Gospel message, complete with some of my tour quotes from America's Founding Fathers. He delivered the entire sermon without looking once at notes. It was worthy of Jonathan Edwards, George Whitfield, and Renny Scott! (Go to stphilipschurchsc.org to hear it yourself.)

Accompanying this full circle was Hamilton Freshley, 23, as the Archangel Gabriel up in the pulpit, his hair and robes gently blowing in the breeze. Preston had broken the female cast angel mold when he was Gabriel after Hurricane Hugo in 1989. His arms had stretched seemingly from column to column as Preston processed down the aisle in that nationally televised service. Hamp has been coming to our

Young Professionals Bible study faithfully on Sunday nights, taught first by Preston. We have known him since he was a boy. He is visibly realigning himself with Preston after a journey of questioning himself and the meaning of life.

To see Hamp there, taking his role as seriously as Preston did, was to connect the two as they truly are connected. Hamp was conscious of it, as well. Christmas Eve ended at the home of his parents, Martha and Bruce Freshley, for a cup of good cheer and fellowship, which our girls had enjoyed without us last year.

This first Christmas without Preston began with a sense of Preston's VOICE as BIG as the SEA caught up in the roar of Christmas. Charles Hipp's Christmas Boat Parade party, the glory of the blue sky, the Christmas lights and decorations, the setting sun beside us on the Ashley River all seemed to be Preston saying, "I am celebrating my first Christmas in Heaven! Everything is bigger and better up here. You're gonna love it! I am blowing Christmas Magic into your world!" My long time friend, Bonnie Gilbreth, confirmed this impression when she told me about a rare dream where Preston unrolled a scroll saying one word: ROAR!

As I step into 2017, it is not without tears as I say goodbye to the last year Preston and I and our family were together on this earth. I do not want time to go on without him, distancing us. But I am not alone. Preston walks beside me to cheer me on my way, my home stretch toward the finish line of this race set before me. It's just this last leg without him visible that I have to go. Pray for me, that I finish it in a manner worthy of Preston, for the sake of all he stands for, and for our girls, and for all our extended family, that I accomplish all such good works as Thou hast prepared for me to walk in.

• • •

January 2, 2017

At Deans Court, where I lived for a time with the Hanhams in Dorset, England, over a door it says, "Where Hearts Agree, There GOD Will Be." Our hearts are in agreement in loving Preston, in being blessed that we knew him, and in him hearing, "Well done, thou good and faithful servant. Enter into the joy prepared for you. You have been faithful in little. I will make you faithful over much." Preston is now past the book cover; he is into the best story of his life, where each page is better than the page before. He is pressing into our needs and joys with the Trinity, working for our good, as he is faithful over much.

Thank you for loving and cherishing the real man of Preston with me, and for mourning him with me, too.

Preston's sense of humor and playfulness brought mirth to simple moments; here he sports his wife's hat after church.

Pringle Franklin is the author of *Hope & Healing in Marriage, True Stories of Renewed Love.* She is also the editor of the blog *Living on Jesus Street,* where Preston's cancer journey was chronicled. Pringle and her family became friends with the Hipps through St. Philip's Church in Charleston, S.C., where Pringle has served for many years as a Bible study leader and Sunday school teacher. She is also a speaker in church settings, teaching on topics such as prayer, marriage, relationships, and forgiveness. In addition, Pringle teaches classes in the community on Centering Prayer, a method of cultivating closeness to God through silence and inner stillness. It is her hope that people reading about Preston will want what he had, a faith that fills them with hope and excitement, a faith that is anchored in a transformative love of Christ.